THE PRAISE
of PLEASURE

Philosophy, Education, and Communism in More's Utopia

By EDWARD SURTZ, S.J.

HARVARD UNIVERSITY PRESS

Cambridge, Massachusetts

1957

PREFACE

It is no accident that More's *Utopia* like Erasmus' *Moriae Encomium* is labeled on its title page: *libellus uere aureus, nec minus salutaris quam festiuus* — "a work not only . . . fruitful and profitable but also . . . pleasant and delectable" (Robinson). In a word, *Utopia* offers agreeable entertainment as well as wholesome advice. And it is the author's style and personality that have made *Utopia* a classic in two literatures: in Neo-Latin literature through the original text and in English literature through Robinson's translation.

The author of *The Praise of Pleasure* confesses that he is interested in *Utopia* primarily as a work of literature, that is, as an emotional, imaginative, artistic creation. Nevertheless, he is not concerned here specifically with its literary qualities: his purpose is rather to attempt the elucidation of certain obscure or controverted sections for the literary student or scholar. To this end he has had to enlist the aid of classicist, educationist, historian, political scientist, sociologist, philosopher, and theologian. Each of the latter professionally might feel inclined to cavil at materials used or views expressed in the book. The author's only defense would be the restatement of his purpose: the clarification of the text and the employment of the means necessary to that literary end. His research disclosed ever-broadening horizons, the exploration of which would have occasioned unconscionable delay and ultimately defeated his immediate practical purpose. His hope was — and is — that the devotee of literature, through the better understanding of the ideas and environment of *Utopia*, might thereby attain a deeper appreciation of its author's artistic ability and that the student of the social sciences might realize how much the literary expression modifies the theme and thought of the work.

There is another point on which the author has tried to effect a compromise. Just as he has wished to have literature and history help each other to their mutual benefit, so he has tried to bear in mind both students in the field and educated readers in general. The advantage accruing would be greater readability for all. Here his fundamental consideration was clarity and simplicity of style. For the same reason, spelling and punctuation of works before 1600 were modernized, and the annoying multitude of superior figures in the text was eliminated, or at least lessened, by grouping references in a single footnote at the end of each paragraph. Modernization of spelling gave rise to difficulties which were solved occasionally by retention of an archaic form, e.g., *other* for *either*, if given as a main or subordinate entry in *The Shorter Oxford English Dictionary on Historical Principles*.

Grateful acknowledgment must be made to editors for permission to embody in this book the studies which first appeared in their journals: Utopian Epicureanism, in *ELH: A Journal of English Literary History*; the defense of pleasure and the attitude toward Scholasticism, in *Studies in Philology*; the link between pleasure and communism, in *Modern Language Notes*; logic and Greek, in *Philological Quarterly*; and More's communism, in *Publications of the Modern Language Association*. Permission was granted graciously by the University of Chicago Press to quote from L. Bradner and C. A. Lynch's *The Latin Epigrams of Thomas More* and by the Harvard University Press to cite translations of Plato, Cicero, Seneca, Martial, and Diogenes Laertius in the Loeb Classical Library.

The Reverend Lothar L. Nurnberger, S.J., of the Department of Philosophy, Loyola University, was of invaluable assistance in the treatment of several knotty problems, textual and interpretative. The Reverend A. Homer Mattlin, S.J., University Librarian, was unfailingly patient and helpful. The author must not fail to express his thanks to the staffs of the Harvard University Library, Yale University Library, Newberry Library, Folger Shakespeare Library, J. Pierpont Morgan Library, Union Theological Seminary Library, Boston Public Library, New York Public Library, Vatican Library, Bibliothèque Nationale, and the British Museum.

The great generosity of the John Simon Guggenheim Memorial Foundation made possible the research and leisure requisite to bring *The Praise of Pleasure* to completion and rendered the aid necessary to ensure its publication. The courtesy, coöperation, and encouragement displayed at all times were unexceptionable.

E. S.

Chicago, Illinois

CONTENTS

I

PREMISES
FOR INTERPRETATION

Thomas More, through description by Raphael Hythloday, concludes his humanistic vision of Utopia in a temple with three solemn petitions: for the best and happiest system of government, for the truest and purest form of religion, and for the easiest and quickest passage through death to God. After this warm dream, he awakens to the cold earth of an England filled with discordant greed and injustice and closes his whole book in a minor key: "so must I needs confess and grant that many things be in the Utopian weal public which in our cities I may rather wish for than hope after" (*ita facile confiteor permulta esse in Vtopiensium republica, quae in nostris ciuitatibus optarim uerius quam sperarim*). Months earlier, Erasmus, the friend of More, had written to Antony of Bergen, Abbot of St. Bertin at St. Omer, on war and peace: "As for us, we can wish for the best, but wish only" (*Nos optare possumus optima, sed optare tantum*).[1]

Less than two years after the publication of *Utopia*, the whirlwind and tempest of the Protestant Reformation were to make More's sweet and reasonable fancy recede more and more into the distance and loom more and more remote on the horizon. Mounting the scaffold after twenty years of struggle for the truth, not in its refinements but in its basic principles, he might have wryly uttered, if he thought at all of his dream-like Utopia in the face of the real axe and death, the homespun words of the American poet: " . . . of all sad words of tongue or pen, / The saddest are these: 'It might have been!' " And what might have been ultimately was not the pagan Utopia painted in his Latin masterpiece but a Christian Holy City, apocalyptic yet existing on the face of this earth.[2]

The following chapters are based upon the humanistic interpretation of the *Utopia*. They presuppose certain premises. The term *premises* is chosen deliberately, rather than *postulates* or *presumptions*. The latter terms might imply that this interpretation is taken for granted in some way, either as axiomatically clear or as vaguely entitled to belief. *Premises*, however, supposes that proofs for the propositions have been offered elsewhere before. The repetition here of the arguments which have been marshaled in defense of the humanistic interpretation would prove otiose. It would not be useless, nevertheless, to outline in a simple and almost bald form the principal elements and features of the theory.[3]

First of all, the author of *Utopia* writes as a *Catholic* to Catholics. This premise rests not upon his later suffering and martyrdom but upon the evidence of his letters and works antecedent to and contemporaneous with the composition and publication of *Utopia* in 1515 and 1516. It is the eve of the Protestant Revolt, not its dawn. In spite of the survival and strength of the Waldenses, the Lollards, and the Hussites, the one world of western Europe is Roman Catholic in its length and breadth. For all classes and peoples there are still the same faith, the same sacraments, the same vicar of Christ. This one world has its weakness and its rottenness, but it has within itself also the means for the preservation of unity and the restoration of integrity. Ultimately the antagonistic and rival camps which it will spawn are to spring up as results of betrayal from within and violence from without.

Second, Thomas More appears in his *Utopia* and his early nonpolemical works as a zealous Catholic *reformer*. He is far from satisfied with the *status quo*. He is far from blind to the new need for Christian faith and Christian morality in every phase of European life. The *Utopia* contains, in a more or less disguised form, his ardent views on public and private morals, war and peace, economic suffering, social inequality, national politics, international intrigue, contemporary education, current philosophy, and formalistic religion.

Third, the future martyr and saint reveals himself in his reforming book, both in content and in style, as a *humanist*. In spite of Scholastic traits and traces, his humanism is not that of the Middle Ages but that of the northern Renaissance. He calls for a superb open-mindedness, equal to that of the Utopians, in the investigation and acceptance of the best wherever and however it is found. Explicitly the *Utopia* confines itself to a plea for the learning of Greek and includes a list of some "great books" to be studied in the original Greek. But implicit, as is clear from the letter to Dorp written at this very time, is an ardent plea for a return to the sources, especially to the Greek sources, both pagan and Christian, for all profane and sacred knowledge. Literature and history, philosophy and science, theology and the Scriptures, are to be studied in their pure, simple, and uncontaminated form. As a volume humanistic also in style, *Utopia* possesses dashes of wit, satire, and irony. These add zest to its perusal but make its interpretation intriguing and perplexing. Interpreters who see in the *Utopia* only a humanistic *jeu d'esprit* find marshaled against themselves the very mass of its patently serious passages and the unanimity of More's contemporaries and successors as to its grave purpose. Scholars who consider it to espouse Marxist class-struggle and communism or European colonialism and imperialism often seem unaware that it is a document of the sixteenth not the nineteenth century and that it is permeated by the spirit of Christian love, justice, and fraternity. Upholders of the *humanistic* interpretation can best describe it by use of the words of Sir Philip Sidney. *Utopia* is "a speaking picture, with this end, — to teach and delight," and Thomas More is a poet writing in prose because he is marked by "that feigning notable images of virtues, vices, or what else, with that delightful teaching, which must be the right describing note to know a poet by." Consequently, Richard Pace in his *Benefits of Learning* (1517) declares that he prefers Utopia to renowned and profitable Ceylon. Although the former lacks such spices as the Portuguese traffic in, nevertheless it is far more safely accessible and abounds in its own hitherto unexperienced delights. It is for a good reason that the old name of Utopia is said to be *Abraxa*, a heaven as it were. Basilides the Gnostic (d. *ca.* A.D. 140) had used the term *Abraxas* ('Αβραξας) as the symbol of his 365 heavens.[4]

Fourth, just as Sidney's poet converts the "brazen" world of nature into a "golden" world, so Thomas More by "making things either better than nature bringeth forth, or, quite anew, forms such as never were in nature," has painted for Europe an *ideal commonwealth*. All details in his republic are not ideal nor perfect. Ideal perfection would defeat his very plea for a spirit of receptiveness to better things and a spirit of emulation on the part of Europeans. Many Utopian laws and customs, More says, seem to him very absurd (*perquam absurde . . . instituta*), but there are very many, he declares finally, "which in our cities I may rather wish for than hope after" (*permulta . . . quae in nostris ciuitatibus optarim uerius quam sperarim*). But no matter how absurd or how desirable the institution, each and every description bears some relevancy to the European situation and conveys, in open or veiled form, More's view on some pressing European problem, either by way of destructive criticism or constructive reform. The precise nature of his view cannot be determined *a priori*, but the gravity or levity of each passage must be weighed in itself and in its context to discover if it attacks prevalent abuses or suggests practical reforms. It is safe to say, however, that the island of Utopia embodies, in some way or other, More's ideal state.[5]

Fifth, More's ideal state is based directly upon *reason alone*:

it is a *philosophical* city (*ciuitas philosophica*). According to the introductory hexastich, it stands as the rival of another philosophical city, the republic of Plato, and perhaps it may be even superior, since the latter uses only glowing words whereas More paints also with men and resources and laws of the highest type. But both Plato and More agree in employing only reason to arrive at fundamentals. Their principles are the most fundamental fathomable by reason: their ultimates are the most elevated conceivable by reason. This emphasis upon reason helps to reveal More's humanism. In a sense, it is true to say that *Utopia* constitutes a magnificent eulogy of human reason and that it pays Plato, the idol of innumerable humanists, the sincerest possible tribute — that of imitation and emulation. But this view would be far from expressing the complete truth. The praise of Plato and reason is but means to an end — a noble and divine end.[6]

Finally and most important, implicit in the depiction of More's ideal state is *the distinction between reason and faith.* The reasonable worlds of Plato and More differ *toto caelo.* Plato's world, in spite of its anticipations of Christianity, remains a pagan world. More's creation receives its peculiar cast from the fact of a Christian revelation. Even though, for special reasons, he restricts his humanistic vision by the self-imposed limits and capabilities of reason, More is speaking as a Christian to Christians. His is not the static world of Plato. His Utopian world is not his ultimate. It is to be surpassed, it *must* be surpassed, to the extent that divinely revealed Christianity is higher than any natural religion, to the extent that the order of grace is infinitely above the order of nature, to the extent that the Christian, fortified by revelation and grace in addition to being endowed with natural reason, is superior to the merely natural and reasoning man. As a matter of fact, present conditions in Christian Europe are worse, not better, than those in pagan Utopia. Awakened or shocked by the *Utopia* into the realization of his deplorable plight, the Christian will attempt now to live up to his glorious ideal and destiny and to reintroduce the spirit of pure Christianity into every phase of human activity — into public and private life, into national and international affairs, into intellectual and religious spheres. No department is to be exempt: Christian reform is to be general and sweeping.

This distinction between reason and faith is not introduced into the humanistic interpretation of the *Utopia* as a gratuitous assumption. Its basis and proof lie in the *Utopia* itself. To say nothing of the Utopians' prayers for divine guidance if their forms of government and religion be not the happiest, truest, and best, an explicit statement appears at the end of Hythloday's account of their opinion of virtue and pleasure. Here an express distinction is made between natural reason and revealed religion. Hythloday declares: "they believe that, unless *a religion sent down from heaven* should inspire in man a holier opinion, no truer one can be the object of inquisition by *human reason*" (*nisi sanctius aliquid inspiret homini caelitus immissa religio, nullam inuestigari credunt humana ratione ueriorem*). Robinson's failure to translate the word *religio* does not destroy the sense of the passage but certainly fails to give its full force and refinement: "they believe that by man's reason none can be found truer than this, unless any godlier be inspired into man from heaven." [7]

To sum up in a single proposition these six points. In the *Utopia*, written before the Protestant Revolution, Thomas More appears as a Catholic reformer, who draws a humanistic picture of an ideal commonwealth, actually founded upon reason alone but implicitly intended to shame the Christians of Europe into erecting a state whose every institution, activity, and thought would be permeated by the charity and justice, faith and grace, of Christ. His method of persuasion is *a fortiori*: if pagans with the aid of reason can create a noble nation where it is better to be a slave than elsewhere to be a free citizen, Christians with the additional help of God's revelation and Christ's grace can eliminate all injustice and hate and build a new Jerusalem in Europe's and "England's green and pleasant land." No matter what excellent institutions and moral characters the Utopians possess, the Christians ought to outstrip them in high morality, intellectual culture, and benevolent government.[8]

This over-all view, this humanistic interpretation, of the *Utopia* is based upon the spirit of the whole work and the evidence of its component parts. In addition, it is re-enforced by the study of the literary and epistolary labors of More and his friends, especially Erasmus, before and during the composition and publication of *Utopia*. Finally, it is confirmed by the subsequent comments of the humanists upon the "delightful teaching" demanded by them for any masterpiece. More is numbered among those poets who, in the words of Sidney, "imitate both to delight and teach, and delight to move men to take that goodness in hand, which without delight they would fly as from a stranger; and teach to make them know that goodness whereunto they are moved." It is little wonder that Sir Philip mentions Sir Thomas in the same breath with Xenophon and Vergil: "even in the most excellent determination of goodness, what philosopher's counsel can so readily direct a prince, as the feigned Cyrus in Xenophon? Or a virtuous man in all fortunes, as Aeneas in Virgil? Or a whole commonwealth, as the way of Sir Thomas More's Utopia?" [9]

The general principles for the humanistic interpretation of the *Utopia* in whole and in part may be said to have been established. But these general principles need to be applied to the particular passages which involve special problems. As it were, the science of casuistry, in the best sense of the term, is requisite here. Moral casuistry is the scientific application of the general principles of morality to definite and concrete cases of human activity for the purpose of determining what one ought or ought not to do. As far as *Utopia* is concerned, interpretative casuistry may be described as the science of applying general principles for the interpretation of *Utopia* to particular and difficult passages in *Utopia* in order to discover whether or not the general principles are there applicable and, if the answer is affirmative, to determine the extent to which the general principles are actually applicable. This method does not constitute a vicious circle because the major premises are based upon solid internal and external evidence. The procedure is not aprioristic because its purpose is to reveal *if* and *how* the general principles are valid in particular cases. Both rigorism and laxism must be eschewed, and at least a solid probabilism should be utilized in the interpretation of the most difficult, obscure, or controversial passages.

The present work concerns itself with, and confines itself to, problems of education and philosophy, together with the closely allied problem of communism, in More's *Utopia*. What arguments do the Utopians use to support their philosophy of pleasure? When are pleasures true and when false? Does a hierarchy of pleasures exist for the Utopians? What is the relation of Utopian education to Utopian philosophy? What is the reasonable attitude toward current Scholasticism? What is the role of Greek, both language and literature, in the intellectual life? What is the relation of the Utopians' communistic system to their hedonistic philosophy? What is More's real attitude toward communism? Since philosophy, education, and communism are fundamental and essential to the Utopian framework, the answers to the problems involved in them can help to the understanding and appreciation of the *Utopia* — as a Catholic humanist's cry of distress over the suffering poor and his call to reform in every department of human endeavor among Christians in England and in Europe.

II

THE PRAISE
OF PLEASURE

One of the greatest stumbling blocks to the acceptance of the humanistic interpretation of the *Utopia* has been the philosophy of pleasure espoused by the Utopians. They "seem almost too much given and inclined to the opinion of them which defend pleasure, wherein they determine other all or the chiefest part of man's felicity to rest." In spite of his minor qualification and disapproval, could More seriously wish the Christians of Europe to become Epicureans in philosophy? The answer must be that More is as serious in having his Utopians praise pleasure in the *Utopia* as Erasmus is in having Folly praise herself in *The Praise of Folly* (*Moriae Encomium*). Beneath the brilliant play of wit on the surface there are a serious criticism of contemporary life and a serious contribution to the solution of contemporary problems. Such a procedure is possible because of the nature of the literary genre in which they are working. Both the praise of folly by Erasmus and the praise of pleasure by More are declamations.[1]

Erasmus calls his *Praise of Folly* a declamation because it is a composition written for amusement and pleasure in order to exercise the author's native talent and to develop his literary power. For this purpose, the aspiring writer undertakes the ingenious defense and praise of such distasteful or disreputable things as poverty, exile, ingratitude, sickness, tyranny, scorn for studies, etc. He magnifies all the advantages of his subject and minimizes the benefits of its opposite. Since a declamation, by definition, is merely a literary exercise, it must not be treated as if it were a learned and sober tract. One must judge it, not by the objective truth of its assertions, but by the success of its style and form. In this respect, the declamation could be an extremely effective instrument for the proposal of unpopular innovations and an extremely dangerous weapon in the attack on the established order — as it actually was in the case of *The Praise of Folly*. Any serious purpose could be denied and disavowed. More's declamation on pleasure in the *Utopia* possesses no gravely subversive or radically revolutionary aims. But More did have a serious purpose in writing the section on pleasure in the *Utopia*. The nature of this purpose will become clear in the course of the discussion.[2]

At the outset, it is interesting to note that More, like Erasmus, does not defend pleasure directly and personally. Just as Erasmus had put the praise of folly into the mouth of Folly herself, so More commits the championship of pleasure to the Utopian philosophers. The device is a literary subterfuge which helps to forestall future attack and criticism.

More displays his rhetorical ability, above all, in his use of the term *pleasure* (*uoluptas*). Erasmus had earlier so manipulated the noun *folly* as to make it include the *folly* of Christianity and the cross. His friend More does much the same when he employs the word *uoluptas* to embrace even the "great and everlasting joy" of God's sight in the future life. It is this loose use of *pleasure* in its most generic sense which makes this section of the *Utopia* a literary triumph.[3]

Uoluptas, in the strict sense of the word, has always conveyed the idea or, at least, carried the connotation of gratification of the *body* or the *senses*. In *De Finibus*, Cicero admits that, speaking loosely, the "word 'pleasure' [*uoluptas*] can denote a mental as well as a bodily feeling," but insists that "pleasure [*uoluptas*] according to the usage of all who speak good Latin consists in the enjoyment of a delightful stimulation of one of the senses." He also observes that "joy" (*laetitia*) and "gladness" (*gaudium*) are not applied to bodily pleasure. Humanists, like Thomas More, were scrupulously careful about good Latinity in general and the distinction between synonyms in particular. Ficino may be cited as representative of the humanists: "When he divided the soul into two parts, namely, mind and sense, Plato attributed joy [*laetitia*] and gladness [*gaudium*] to the mind, and pleasure [*voluptas*] to the senses. . . . By pleasure [*voluptas*] Plato means a certain sweet motion in the senses, which results from the satisfaction of a need." [4]

As for the artful More, one must not fail to observe that he does not posit the Utopian definition of pleasure, as he logically should, at the very beginning of the debate on happiness, but almost at the end of the theoretical discourse. The reader, who had undoubtedly been startled — the author startled him designedly — by the contention of this ideal people that man's happiness rests in *uoluptas*, almost certainly had in mind gratification which was connected with the body or the senses. This false impression would continue throughout the Utopians' proofs for their view; and, not until important qualifications are made, does the reader begin to realize that the *uoluptas* championed is a very high type of pleasure. Only then does he come upon the definition of *uoluptas*: "every motion and state of the body or mind, wherein man hath naturally delectation" (*omnem corporis animiue motum statumque, in quo uersari natura duce delectet*). In spite of this clear enunciation, he will find difficulty in casting off his prepossession, for the Utopians, while conceding the primacy to pleasures of the soul, do lay stress upon bodily pleasures. The truth of this assertion is evident from the greater amount of space devoted to bodily pleasures in the whole discussion of happiness and from the numerous references to sensual pleasure, e.g., of eating, in the *Utopia* as a whole. [5]

More gains much of his effect by the use of synonyms for *uoluptas*. Thus, he explicitly identifies *uoluptas* with such general

and comprehensive words as *iucunditas* (*pleasantness*) and
delectatio (*delight*). Implicitly he makes *uoluptas* interchange-
able with *laetitia* (*joyfulness*), *suauitas* (*sweetness*), and even
commoda (*interests*).[6]

Thus, by the twofold procedure of making his *pleasure*
(*uoluptas*) embrace pleasures of body and soul, and of identify-
ing *pleasure* (*uoluptas*) with its synonyms indiscriminately, More
cunningly prejudices the argument and thus finds it much easier
to prove that pleasure is the essence of human happiness.

The Utopians belong to the tribe of philosophers who, as Erasmus states, are distinguished from all other mortals by their
profession of the good or happy life. The humanists usually recognize four great schools according to the opinions held on the
nature of the highest good: Platonists, Aristotelians, Stoics, and
Epicureans. The Utopians are Epicureans and consider the Stoics
their special adversaries. Aristotelians and Platonists are practically ignored. These four philosophic sects are all Greek in
origin; but, as Polydore Vergil observes in his *Originators of
Things*, most hold that philosophy came to the Greeks from the
Barbarians. The Magi among the Persians were accounted the
first famous wise men or philosophers. In view of the probable
Greek origin and the Persian-like language of the Utopians, their
depiction as philosophers is comprehensible.[7]

In his work entitled *The Four Sects of Philosophers*, Ficino
gives an admirable description of Stoicism and Epicureanism.
Zeno, the leader of the Stoics, regards what is virtuous as the
highest and the only good, and what is vicious as the greatest and
the only evil. The advantages of body and of fortune ought in
no way to be termed goods, for the reason that they come equally
to virtuous men and vicious men and do not necessarily make
good the men who possess them. In addition, all virtues are equal
and on a par, since all are perfect; for what is perfect does not
admit of greater or lesser. As far as the Epicureans are concerned,
Ficino does not share the uncritical popular view of their philosophy. In his eyes, Epicureans consider the highest good to be

pleasure, not indeed the pleasure which consists in physical motion or sensual sweetness, since such pleasure is mixed with pain
and unstable, but rather that which is experienced as arising from
an excellent condition of the body (which they call *indolentia,*
i.e., freedom from pain) and from undisturbed tranquillity of
soul.[8]

In his commentary on Psalm I, "Blessed Is the Man," published
for the first time in 1515 when More was working on the second
book of *Utopia,* Erasmus praises the zeal and perseverance of
pagan philosophers in investigating the nature and object of
that blessedness for which every mortal is created, after which
he aspires, and in which he longs to rest. But the absence of the
Spirit of Christ, Who is the sole teacher of true wisdom, caused
many to err and to embrace false shadows and empty appear-
ances as the true and highest good. Erasmus has pity for the
futile search of these pagans, but he has only amazement and
shame for the careless sloth of certain Christians who, immersed
in wealth or pleasure, or drunk with a violent desire of domination, make not even the slightest investigation into a matter of
such vital importance. In fact, Christians, in spite of Christ's
doctrine that God is man's highest good (John xvii. 3), are as
badly off as pagans in placing their happiness in things apart
from God. Using Aristotle's classic tripartite division of human
goods into external goods (or goods of fortune, such as wealth
and position), bodily goods (such as health and beauty), and
goods of the soul (such as knowledge and virtue), Erasmus'
Folly had earlier claimed that the vulgar crowd concede the
first place to riches, the second to favors of body, and the last
to the soul (if it even exists). The devout Christian, of course,
concentrates on God and the soul, to the neglect of the body and
the contempt of gold and silver. The Utopians "dispute the good
qualities of the soul, of the body, and of fortune; and whether
the name of goodness may be applied to all these or only to the
endowments and gifts of the soul." It is difficult not to make the
conjecture that More in depicting the Utopians as engrossed in

this problem wished to provoke Christians to some serious thought
about the nature and the object of human happiness.[9]

The constant teaching of Christian philosophers is that only
God can be the final object of man's *natural* beatitude, as of his
supernatural happiness. Under the leadership of Aquinas, for
example, St. Antoninus of Florence (1389–1459), rejects the following as the object of human felicity: riches, honors, glory or
fame, power, bodily pleasures, corporal health, operation of the
practical intellect, knowledge of the speculative sciences, and all
created goods. He concludes: "since every creature has partici-
pated goodness, and the universal good is not found in anything
created, but only in God, nothing therefore can quiet the will of
man but God alone Who is the universal good." Here is one point
on which the humanist cannot disagree with the Schoolman.
Ficino ends his *Discourse on the Highest Good* with the words:
"Therefore joy in the divine vision is the highest good of the
soul." The human soul, according to Erasmus, is so immense and
capacious that only God can fill it, even if, outside of God, one
supplies it with six hundred worlds. He writes: "The soul of man,
because it is divine and immortal, can find in this life nothing
in which it truly rests, unless it attains that for which it was
created. What is that, therefore, for which man was created?
That he, with both body and soul, may know, love, and glorify
God, his Creator, Redeemer, and Lord. . . . To know is to see,
and to see is to enjoy, and to enjoy is the ultimate term of beatitude." Here, of course, Erasmus is speaking of man's *supernatural*
happiness.[10]

The concept of God as the last objective end in which man
finally rests has been treated here because it is essential to an
understanding of the Utopians' idea of happiness. The object of
happiness for them is pleasure, but pleasure so defined and so
described that it rises from physical gratification in excretion and
copulation and from intellectual enjoyment in this life to eager
delight in the presence of God in the next. Hence, when an
Utopian is called by God through His messenger Death, he is

expected to run to Him gladly with a heart filled with hope of an eternal reward. Most revelatory of all is the solemn public prayer of every Utopian that "if it might stand with His Majesty's pleasure, he would be much gladder to die a painful death, and so to go to God, than by long living in worldly prosperity to be away from Him." The only conclusion one can draw from such statements is that for the Utopians man's highest good is God in Whom, above every created thing, man is to find his joy and gladness.[11]

Hythloday does not indicate whether this future happiness keenly anticipated by the Utopians is natural or supernatural beatitude. Man knows only from revelation that he has been raised to a supernatural order and destined to a supernatural happiness which exceeds all the exigencies of nature, namely, the vision of the invisible God face to face. Since the Utopians have only reason and not revelation to aid them, one may conclude that they have only a concept of a natural beatitude which answers to the needs and demands of man's nature. This natural beatitude consists in the intimate knowledge and deep love of God which arises from the contemplation of His perfections in His creatures and which satisfies all the intellectual and volitional desires of man. It is necessary to note, however, that at least once the bliss of the future life is referred to as the "great and everlasting joy" (*ingenti ac nunquam interituro gaudio*). *Gaudium*, however, is the consecrated theological term for the happiness of the beatific vision.[12]

The conclusion that More's Utopians find the ultimate object of happiness in God is strangely borne out in Ellis Heywood's Italian dialogue (1556) entitled simply *More* (*Il Moro*). As in the *Utopia*, the topic of discussion is happiness. Among the interlocutors, Carlo undertakes the defense of honor; Lorenzo, of riches; Piero, of love; and Alessandro, of knowledge. Thomas More, speaking toward the end of the dialogue, says that for him happiness can be nothing else than perfect contentment of soul. The only thing in the universe capable of being the highest and ultimate good is "that Being alone, from Whom proceeds and to Whom tends every other good, namely, the most high and only God, Who is everything in Himself, and in Whom is found perfect contentment, and outside Whom can exist neither contentment nor satisfaction of any kind." [13]

III

THE DEFENSE
OF PLEASURE

The Utopians, Hythloday observes, discuss virtue and pleasure, but the principal point of disputation is "in what thing, be it one or mo, the felicity of man consisteth." The Utopian presupposition is that man's final end is happiness or beatitude. The point at issue is: what is the *object* of this happiness or beatitude? It is worthy of note that the whole controversy is centered about, and is confined to, only two objects: virtue and pleasure. Hence, the protagonists of pleasure are at special pains to refute the defenders of virtue.[1]

In stating that the Utopians hold pleasure to be the object of happiness, Hythloday is careful to introduce a double modification of his statement. To state bluntly that the wisest of pagan peoples were outright hedonists would be too shocking. Hence, he asserts (1) that they "seem almost too much given and inclined" (*propensiores aequo uidentur*) to the defense of pleasure and (2) that they "determine other all or the chiefest part [*potissimam partem*] of man's felicity to rest" in pleasure. These qualifications entail a considerable weakening of the original proposition, and prepare the reader's mind for a more benevolent reception of the Utopian view.[2]

What reasons do the Utopians produce in support of their

opinion? First of all, they find in religion "the defense of this so
dainty and delicate an opinion." Religion affords them three
truths and only three: the immortality of the soul, the special
providence of God in ordaining man to happiness, and the reward of virtue and punishment of evil in the next life. But one
may read this passage in the *Utopia* several times without seeing
how the Utopians discover in religion the "defense" of their
theory of pleasure. The basis of their argumentation seems to be
the traditional view of the inseparability of religion and morality.
The exercise of religion, particularly love and reverence toward
God, is the psychological source and foundation of all moral
activity, which without religion generally cannot be genuine,
complete, constant, and persevering in the face of the difficult
temptations and perils of this life. The highest and most weighty
motives of moral action — such motives as are found in a God
Who is man's final end and object of beatitude and in a God Who
is the supreme legislator establishing a sanction in reward or
punishment to be encountered in the future life — are absent
without religion. Yet at this very time Pietro Pomponazzi (1462–
1525) was teaching: "Virtue is independent of the belief in immortality; it is most genuine when practised without reference
to reward or punishment." For the Utopians, however, the man
who denies the three basic truths mentioned above has no efficacious motive, especially the motive of a future reward, for pur-
suing good and virtue if the pursuit means the banishment of
sweetness from his whole life and even the voluntary toleration
of suffering. It is the thought of the sweet pleasures of a future
reward which sustains a man when assailed by the powers of
evil. The Utopians ask why man forgoes pleasure and suffers
pain in the practice of good. The answer expected is that he does
so in hope of the joys and delights of the future life of happiness
to which God has ordained his immortal soul in reward for his
virtue and good works. In a word, "grave, sharp, bitter, and rigor-
ous religion" itself thus affords the "defense" of pleasure as the
whole or the greatest part of man's happiness. [3]

But what is the relation between virtue and pleasure for the Utopians? Harsh as the response may seem, one must answer that, in the abstract, virtue is subordinate to pleasure: "all our actions, and in them the virtues themselves, be referred at the last to pleasure as their end and felicity." But this is not subordination in any gross sense. On the contrary, the "chief part" of pleasures of the mind "doth come of the exercise of virtue and conscience of good life." The Utopians practice virtue because they presume that pleasure is inextricably bound up with the performance of virtuous deeds and that a good conscience is a source of gratification. On the relation between the most just life and the most pleasant life, the Utopian thinks much the same as the Athenian in Plato's *Laws*: "So then the teaching which refuses to separate the pleasant from the just helps, if nothing else, to induce a man to live the holy and just life, so that any doctrine which denies this truth is, in the eyes of the lawgiver, most shameful and most hateful; for no one would voluntarily consent to be induced to commit an act, unless it involves in its consequence more pleasure than pain." [4]

The Utopian subordinates virtue to pleasure, or at least tends to identify the two. To the Stoic, on the other hand, virtue is supreme. The Epicurean says to the Stoic: "Your school dilates on the transcendental beauty of the virtues; but were they not productive of pleasure, who would deem them either praiseworthy or desirable?" Seneca answers that pleasure is but a necessary *concomitant* of virtue, in no way essential to it: "[I]n the first place, even though virtue is sure to bestow pleasure, it is not for this reason that virtue is sought; for it is not this, but something more than this that she bestows, nor does she labour for this, but her labour, while directed toward something else, achieves this also. . . . [P]leasure is neither the cause nor the reward of virtue, but its by-product, and we do not accept virtue because she delights us, but if we accept her, she also delights us." [5]

The second reason which the Utopians bring forward to sustain their position is that to pleasure, "as to perfect blessedness [*uelut*

ad summum bonum], our nature is allured and drawn even of
virtue [*ab ipsa uirtute*]." This is a sophistic *tour de force*: to make
virtue, in which alone their opponents place man's happiness,
serve to prove that pleasure is the highest good! The line of
argumentation is the following:

Virtue is life lived according to *nature*.
But life lived according to *nature* is the selection and
    rejection of things according to *reason*.
Therefore *virtue* is the selection and rejection of things
    according to *reason*.
But *reason* advises and incites us to lead a life as free
    from care and full of joy as possible, and to show
    ourselves helpful, in view of the fellowship arising
    from nature, in obtaining the same for all other
    human beings.
Therefore *virtue* advises and incites us to lead a life as
    free from care and full of joy as possible, etc.[6]

With respect to the *first major premise,* when "they define
virtue to be a life ordered according to nature" or "according to
the prescript of nature," the Utopians would find no objection
coming from the Stoics who in general held the same as Zeno.
The end of man, the latter says, is a life in agreement with and
according to nature; but this life is a life according to virtue,
for nature, to be sure, leads us to such a life. Stoic Seneca himself had admitted that Epicurus laid down the same rule for
pleasure that the Stoics had laid down for virtue, for "he bids
that it obey Nature." The *first minor,* too, would be granted by
the Stoics. For, as Cato the Stoic concludes in Cicero's *De Finibus,*
"The Chief Good consists in applying to the conduct of life a
knowledge of the working of natural causes, choosing what
is in accordance with nature and rejecting what is contrary to
it." Since the Stoics concede the first major and the first minor,
they must concede the *first conclusion.*[7]

The heart of the argument is really the *second minor,* and
therefore Hythloday is at some pains to give at length the Utopians' proof for it. The proof is basically a dilemma. A "joyful

life, that is to say, a pleasant life" (*uita iucunda, id est, uoluptaria*) is either good or evil. But it is not evil, because nature and humanity bid one to help men as much as possible to a joyful life by relieving their suffering and by restoring their joy. Therefore, a joyful life is good. But if it is good for all other men, it must be good for the individual personally, since nature "equally favoreth all that be comprehended under the communion of one shape, form, and fashion." Therefore, "even very nature (say they) prescribeth to us a joyful life, that is to say, pleasure as the end of all our operations." [8]

It is extremely interesting to observe that at a later period in his life More was to face the problem of joy and tribulation in a far more serious way in his *Dialogue of Comfort.* Vincent objects that "if it were . . . that perpetual prosperity were to the soul so perilous, and tribulation thereto so fruitful; then were . . . every man bounden of charity, not only to pray God send their neighbour sorrow, but also to help thereto themself." His uncle Antony answers: "I think in very deed tribulation so good and profitable, that I should haply doubt as you do wherefore a man might labour or pray to be delivered of it, saving that God which teacheth us the one, teacheth us also the other. And as he biddeth us take our pain patiently, and exhort our neighbours to do also the same: so biddeth he us also not let to do our devoir, to remove the pain from us both." More's final solution is the *natural* answer of the Utopians (insofar as God and nature teach that "thou . . . of duty art bound to procure it [a joyful life] to others . . . [and] to thyself") as supplemented and elevated by the *supernatural* and *Christian* view of faith, prayer, and suffering.[9]

In summary, one may say that the defense of pleasure as the ultimate end of human life is essentially a *declamatio.* Its purpose probably is to incite and provoke to serious thought careless Christians who are behaving as if wealth or glory, not God, were the end of life. More cunningly prejudices the whole question by using the word *pleasure* in its most loose and generic sense. In the best traditions of the *declamatio*, he astonishingly makes religion and virtue serve as two sources of arguments for the supremacy of pleasure. Careful analysis, however, reveals that the final object of Utopian happiness is delight in the presence of God in the next life.

IV

FORTUNES OF EPICURUS IN UTOPIA

The whole ethical system of More's Utopians revolves about pleasure. It is, therefore, only natural to ask what relation their doctrine bears to that of the great philosopher of hedonism, Epicurus.

Much has been inevitably said of the debt of More to Vespucci for the idea of making his Utopians the devotees of pleasure. In his *New World*, Vespucci had told how the Indians "live according to nature, and may be called Epicureans rather than Stoics." In his *Four Voyages*, he felt that he had to label as Epicurean the life of the Indians which was completely devoted to pleasure: *horum vitam (quae omnino voluptuosa est) Epycuream existimo.* The Indians and the Utopians, however, are poles apart in their degree of civilization. The Indians "live together without king, without government, and each is his own master." [1] The inhuman cruelty and the passionate lust of the savage Indians, which fill many a page of early accounts, are the antithesis of the humane kindness and reasonable conduct of the Utopians, to say nothing of the low stage of the cultural and social development of the America then known as compared with the complex organization of Utopia. The Utopians, on the whole, are humanistic in the best sense of the term. Consequently, if signs of their hedonism are found in the works of antiquity and the Renaissance,

humanistic documents, rather than explorative records, should
be considered as furnishing the basic material which More's
imagination transformed and utilized in the construction of his
literary masterpiece.

Epicurus, as always, was in general ill-repute at the time of
the composition of the *Utopia*. "There is no sect amongst them
all," observes Spudaeus in Erasmus' "Epicurean," "that is so much
condemned by a universal consent." Writing on the literary level,
Barclay had declared in one of his *Eclogues* through the mouth
of Cornix:

> Forsooth some wretches of manners vile and rude
> Have counted in lust most high beatitude,
> And namely the sect which follow Epicure,
> Which shameful sect doth to this day endure,
> Whom the philosophers and clerks nowadays
> Despise with words, yet follow they his ways.

In the section entitled "The objection of lust blaming virtue" in
Barclay's *Ship of Fools*, Lust says of the Epicureans:

> All their whole sect my quarrel doth defend
> For all their sect to this clause did assent
> That lust and pleasure was good most excellent.[2]

The attitude of Antoninus, an outstanding Thomist of the fifteenth century, may be offered as an example on the level of
Scholastic philosophy. In discussing pleasures (*delectationes*),
he refutes the Stoics, who claim all sensible pleasures are bad,
by maintaining that no one can live without some bodily pleasure
(*delectatio*). On the contrary, the Epicureans, he says, hold that
all pleasures are good. They err in failing to distinguish between
simple or unalloyed good (*simplex bonum*) and relative good
(*bonum secundum quid*). If the object in which man's desire
rests is in accordance with reason, it is simply good (*simpliciter
bonum*), and the pleasure received is simply good (*simpliciter
bona*). If the object, however, is only a relative good (*bonum
secundum quid*), for instance, congenial to sense but contrary
to reason, the pleasure will be only relatively good (*bona secun-*

dum quid); for, it will be good in relation to sense, but evil in itself (*mala simpliciter*), although appearing to be good. The example given is that of fornication.[3]

The judgment of many a humanist on Epicureanism is even more severe than that of the Schoolmen. In his *Oration on Happiness*, Philip Beroaldus (d. 1504 or 1505) takes the usual popular and pejorative view of Epicurus and his followers. Vives in his work *The Origins, Sects, and Praises of Philosophy* describes the fierce battle against the Stoics on the part of the followers of Epicurus. They reject the art of dialectic. In their struggle to place pleasure at the summit of creation, they cast down even virtue, the most excellent and most beautiful of all things, and foully command her, the queen of the universe, to serve as a handmaid to brutish exhilaration of the senses.[4]

But, in spite of such pronouncements by literary men, Scholastics, and humanists, the rehabilitation of Epicurus had already begun in the early decades of the fifteenth century. Diogenes Laertius by his excellent account of the life and doctrine of Epicurus undoubtedly played an important role in bringing the truer version of his philosophy of pleasure before the eyes of at least the more humanistic in Western Europe. It was no accident that Valla's momentous work *Pleasure and the True Good*, which is usually assigned to 1431, appeared after the completion of the most popular Latin translation of Diogenes Laertius by Ambrogio Traversari. From his reading of the *Lives of Eminent Philosophers*, Nicholas of Cusa (1401–1464) was able "to oppose Epicurus to the Epicureans and, in case of need, to combat immorality by the example of the moralist of pleasure himself." In his treatise, *The Highest Good*, Cristoforo Landino (1424–1492), after favorable comment on Epicurus, concludes: "Nay, if he had thought rightly of God, you would find nothing in his actions which could not justly be praised." In a prefatory message to his *Benefits of Learning* (1517), Pace tells the youth who would pursue pleasure at any cost: "In this very thing in which you think you are most sensible, you most act the madman, for you are ignorant of the true nature of either Epicurus or his pleasure." [5]

The great effect of Valla on the northern humanists may be gauged from a letter of Hegius to Agricola in which the former confesses: "I have been reading Valla's book on the True Good, and have become quite an Epicurean, estimating all things in pleasure." The presence of Valla's book in the circle of Dutch humanists allows one to infer that Erasmus read it early in his career. At any rate, he may have become familiar with Traversari's translation of Diogenes Laertius which had often been reprinted. This seems especially true in view of his statement that he composed *The Contempt of the World* as "a young man" and "at the age of barely twenty years." Thomas More may also have seen Traversari's translation, Valla's book, or favorable views of Epicurus in the works of various humanists. Erasmus also may have shown him *The Contempt of the World* and discussed with him the ideas which he was later to develop in the colloquy "The Epicurean." In the latter Erasmus defends the paradox that "none are greater Epicureans than those Christians that live a pious life." At any rate, the documents most akin in spirit to the section on pleasure in the *Utopia* are these compositions. To understand the theory of pleasure of the Utopians, therefore, it is necessary to become familiar with the more important passages on Epicurus and his philosophy in Diogenes Laertius' *Lives* and in Erasmus' two works: *The Contempt of the World* and "The Epicurean" in the *Colloquies*.[6]

The first and most important observation to be made on the relation of the hedonism of Epicurus to the ethics of the Utopians is that Epicurus would be among those in Utopia whom "they count not in the number of men, . . . much less in the number of their citizens"! For Epicurus denies the three fundamental truths which all good Utopians must believe: the immortality of the human soul, the providence of God over men, and retribution in the future life for good and evil. This denial is an inexorable conclusion from his premises. The happy life of pleasure which is the final end of man is impossible without the elimination of the most serious hindrances to human joy, namely, superstitious fears and the dread of death. To destroy the former, he does not annihilate the gods but makes them absolutely indifferent to human concerns. To abolish the latter, he proves that the soul is not immortal, and thus removes the fear of a shadowy, perhaps wretched, future existence. As Christian philosophers, neither Erasmus nor More could countenance the denial of these three truths. In fact, as is evident from their writings, they felt convinced that the source of highest pleasure lay precisely in the everlasting reward of one's good deeds by God. Independently of these truths, however, they could more or less subscribe, *mutatis mutandis*, to the principles of Epicurus. After all, even their Augustine had said in his *Confessions* that in his discussions on good and evil "Epicurus would certainly have won the palm in my judgment if I had not believed that after death there remained life for the soul and treatment according to its deserts, which Epicurus did not hold." [7]

One phase of Epicurus' thought which especially appealed to the humanists, however, was his unceasing war against religious imposture and superstition. Lucian, in particular, several of whose works were translated by More and Erasmus, stressed this aspect of Epicurean doctrine. His *Alexander or Pseudomantis*, translated by Erasmus, is rich in reference to Epicurus. Alexander the impostor hated bitterly Epicurus, "that is, the man who saw deep into the nature of things and who alone glimpsed what was true in them." He was well disposed to Plato, Chrysippus, or Pythagoras, and was on cordial terms of peace with them, but he hated "that intractable fellow, Epicurus" (as he used to call him); and his hate was well founded, for Epicurus considered all his tricks ridiculous and ludicrous. Alexander, therefore, solemnly burned the epitome of Epicurus in the middle of the forum. Lucian continues: "That impious character did not at all consider how great advantages that volume would bring to those who set themselves to reading it, and how great peace,

tranquillity, and liberty it would produce in them, for the reason
that it would release them from bondage to fears, specters, and
portents, and would take away vain hopes and unbridled desires,
and would implant a sane mind and the truth, and would thoroughly purify the soul . . . by right reason as well as freedom." [8]

Epicurus clearly teaches that man's highest good is pleasure
and its attainment by each individual: "health of body and tranquillity of mind . . . is the sum and end of a blessed life." Virtue
and knowledge have no absolute value, independent of their
relation to pleasure. In his letter to Menoeceus, Epicurus writes:
"Pleasure is our first and kindred good. It is the starting-point of
every choice and of every aversion; and to it we come back,
inasmuch as we make feeling the rule by which to judge of every
good thing." This fundamental truth was well understood by
Cicero, who causes Torquatus the Epicurean to speak in *De
Finibus* as follows:

This [the final and ultimate Good] Epicurus finds in pleasure; pleasure
he holds to be the Chief Good, pain the Chief Evil. This he sets out
to prove as follows: Every animal, as soon as it is born, seeks for
pleasure, and delights in it as the Chief Good, while it recoils from
pain as the Chief Evil, and so far as possible avoids it. This it does
as long as it remains unperverted, at the prompting of Nature's own
unbiased and honest verdict. Hence Epicurus refuses to admit any
necessity for argument or discussion to *prove* that pleasure is desirable
and pain to be avoided.[9]

These aspects of the philosophy of Epicurus were clearly apprehended also by Erasmus. In "The Epicurean," Hedonius
labels as "divine" the sentiment of Epicurus who "places the
happiness of man in pleasure, and judges that life to be most
blessed that has most pleasure and least pain." Pleasure, in fact,
is the only mistress who has all men so firmly devoted to her that
no evils can frighten and no arguments can tear them away from
her. "And Epicurus does not, perhaps, altogether absurdly make
the famous statement that mortals indeed make errors in their
judgments on pleasures, yet all of them with one mind desire and
seek them, some in one way, others in another." [10]

To Epicurus every pleasure is good and desirable, but not every pleasure should be indulged in, either because it can be ultimately the source of greater pain than pleasure or because it can be a hindrance to a greater pleasure. Hence, Epicurus was careful to enunciate to Menoeceus the following principle of selection:

[S]ince pleasure is our first and native good, for that reason we do not choose every pleasure whatsoever, but ofttimes pass over many pleasures when a greater annoyance ensues from them. And ofttimes we consider pains superior to pleasures when submission to the pains for a long time brings us as a consequence a greater pleasure. While therefore all pleasure because it is naturally akin to us is good, not all pleasure is choiceworthy, just as all pain is an evil and yet not all pain is to be shunned. It is, however, by measuring one against another, and by looking at the conveniences and inconveniences, that all these matters must be judged.

Hedonius in "The Epicurean" does not believe that "Epicurus himself would embrace a pleasure that has more pain in it, and of longer continuance than the pleasure itself." A very clear and important declaration of Epicurean principles of selection as applied to the advantages of the monastic life appears in *The Contempt of the World*:

Epicurus denies that one should admit those pleasures from which greater troubles result. As for us we do not commit fornication or adultery. We do not gorge ourselves or carouse after the fashion of profligates; sober we see the rising of the sun, sober we see the setting of the sun, both of which they deny they have seen. All these things never happen without bringing more distress than delight. We are neither capable nor desirous of becoming rich, or of being made illustrious by some official dignity; even in this we are not untrue to the teaching of Epicurus. For, since they are marked by little pleasure and much vexation, we wisely are unwilling to buy a very small convenience at the price of a very great disadvantage. In addition, he teaches that one must sometimes endure pains in order to escape greater pains, and likewise that one must forgo pleasures in order to achieve greater pleasures. What do we do? We suffer night-watches, fasts, loneliness, silence, and all the other hardships of this kind, lest we have to endure greater pains. . . . Did you believe that we had lost our pleasure? It was a matter, not of loss, but of exchange, and indeed of such an exchange that we received numerous intense pleasures for a few paltry ones.[11]

The similarity of these rules of selection to those of the Utopians is obvious. For "in all things this cautel [precaution] they use, that a less pleasure hinder not a bigger and that the pleasure be no cause of displeasure." In like manner, it is the hope of a future reward in the form of a greater pleasure which inspires the Utopians to follow hard virtue or to suffer pain and sacrifice for the good of their neighbor. The Utopians, it must be noted, add another rule of selection to the two already mentioned. It is the social principle that pleasure must "be gotten without wrong or injury" to one's fellow man. Epicurus himself, however, does not treat or emphasize this precaution in any way, except insofar as fear of detection of crime vitiates pleasure painfully.[12]

Even in his own lifetime, Epicurus realized that "ignorance, prejudice, or wilful misrepresentation" had painted him as the defender and high priest of sensual pleasures. "It is not an unbroken succession of drinking-bouts and of revelry," he insists, "not sexual love, not the enjoyment of the fish and other delicacies of a luxurious table, which produces a pleasant life; it is sober reasoning, searching out the grounds of every choice and avoidance, and banishing those beliefs through which the greatest tumults take possession of the soul." By pleasure he himself means "the absence of pain in the body and of trouble in the soul." This complete rest is the highest state of happiness that can be attained. In this respect Epicurus disagrees with the Cyrenaics. The latter will not admit a state of rest is a pleasure; they insist that pleasure must be accompanied by motion. Under the genus of pleasure, however, Epicurus embraces both pleasures coming from tranquillity and pleasures arising from motion. The latter, however, are inferior to the former since they imply the satisfaction of a want and are thus necessarily marred by discomfort, as, for example, eating by hunger. The Utopians, too, consider these pleasures, as "the basest pleasures of all, as unpure and unperfect," because "they never come but accompanied with their contrary griefs." [13]

Like the Utopians, Epicurus believes that pleasure and pain adequately divide all human experience. Torquatus the Epicurean in Cicero's *De Finibus* explains that his master asserts that "there is no such thing as a neutral state of feeling intermediate between pleasure and pain; for the state supposed by some thinkers to be neutral, being characterized as it is by entire absence of pain, is itself, he held, a pleasure, and, what is more, a pleasure of the highest order. A man who is conscious of his condition at all must necessarily feel either pleasure or pain." [14]

So far is Epicurus from being the philosopher of sensualism that he tenaciously holds, as Diogenes Laertius informs his readers, that mental pleasures are greater than corporal. The Utopians, too, account the pleasures of the mind to be "the chiefest and most principal of all." Erasmus, as might readily be surmised, feels that the man who should "lose the real enjoyments of the mind for the counterfeit pleasures of the body" is similar to the "foolish trader who should barter jewels for bits of glass." In *The Contempt of the World*, he exclaims:

Who is so blind that he does not see that the body is not even to be compared with the soul? As inferior, therefore, as the body is to the soul in dignity, just so far the pleasure [*voluptas*] of the soul is superior to the enticements [*illecebrae*] of the body. Mental pleasure, like the soul itself, is true, enduring, never cloying, genuine, virtuous, divine, and salutary. The enticements of the body, on the contrary, are false, passing, full of loathing, having more aloes than honey, foul, and death-dealing. It is impossible for the same person to enjoy both bodily and mental pleasure. One must be lacking. If his counsel were asked, what would Epicurus advise? Of course, that we should banish all those obscene enticements of the body lest they act as an impediment to the attainment of the more excellent and more sweet pleasures of the soul.

A special mental pleasure reserved for the learned is reading or thinking over the works of the most approved authors, among which are the Sacred Scriptures, the volumes of the Fathers of the Church, and even the lucubrations of such Schoolmen as Thomas

Aquinas and Albert the Great. "The writings of the pagan philosophers and poets are not to be eschewed by anyone who knows how to pick wholesome herbs among the poisonous ones." [15]

What, in the system of Epicurus, is the relation of pleasure to virtue? Prudence, the rational faculty by which man chooses and avoids pleasures and pains, is the greatest of the virtues. It is the source of "all the other virtues, for it teaches that we cannot lead a life of pleasure which is not also a life of prudence, honour, and justice; nor lead a life of prudence, honour, and justice, which is not also a life of pleasure. For the virtues have grown into one with a pleasant life, and a pleasant life is inseparable from them." On the one hand, Epicurus does not hesitate to proclaim that "we choose the virtues too on account of pleasure and not for their own sake, as we take medicine for the sake of health"; on the other hand, he stipulates that virtue is "the *sine qua non* of pleasure, *i.e.* the one thing without which pleasure cannot be, everything else, food, for instance, being separable, *i.e.* not indispensable to pleasure." After having thoroughly argued and weighed the question, the Utopians, like Epicurus, think "that all our actions, and in them the virtues themselves, be referred at the last to pleasure as their end and felicity," but, at the same time, hold that the greatest part of mental pleasure comes from "the exercise of virtue and conscience of good life." The sacrifice of a brief bodily pleasure in order to benefit one's neighbor is more than recompensed by a greater and triple reward: the approbation of one's own conscience, the remembrance of the gratitude of the recipient of the favor, and the firm hope of a future eternal reward. Epicurus holds somewhat the same view. In an essay translated by Erasmus, Plutarch writes: "Epicurus, who maintains that the chief end of man is a most deep tranquillity, which is like a quiet haven that is agitated by no waves and roars with no noise, says that it is not only more beautiful to confer a benefit than to receive one, but also more pleasurable, for nothing begets joy as much as beneficence." In fact, Epicurus stresses the pleasurable value of a good conscience. The man who has committed injustice, even if he succeeds in hiding his crime, is continually fearful that it should be discovered. In this way, the violation of justice cannot be reconciled with a life of pleasure.[16]

In "The Epicurean," Erasmus equates pleasure with piety, not virtue. He maintains that "nobody lives more pleasantly than they that live piously; and nobody more miserably and afflictedly than they that live wickedly." The basic assumption is that he who lives piously "enjoys true good," for it is "only piety that gains the favour of God, the fountain of the chiefest good, that makes a man happy." Then Erasmus, toward the end of the colloquy, proceeds to employ much the same *tour de force* which he had used in *The Praise of Folly* and to which many devout persons had objected. Just as he had made Christ the supreme example of foolishness, so here he makes Him the Epicurean *par excellence*:

. . . nobody more deserves the name of an Epicurean than that adorable Prince of Christian philosophers, for ἐπίκουρος in Greek signifies as much as an helper. Therefore, when the law of nature was almost erased by vice, and the law of Moses rather incited than cured lusts, when the tyrant Satan ruled without control in the world, He alone afforded present help to perishing mankind. So that they are mightily mistaken that foolishly represent Christ, as by nature, to be a rigid melancholic person, and that He invited us to an unpleasant life, when He alone shewed the way to the most comfortable life in the world, and fullest of pleasure. . .[17]

Erasmus in his *Paraclesis* recognizes the importance given to a good conscience by Epicurus: "Even Epicurus confesses that nothing in life can be sweet to man in the absence of a mind conscious to itself of no evil; from an innocent mind as from a fountain true pleasure [*voluptas*] gushes forth." In his *Contempt of the World*, in imitation of Epicurus, he names a good conscience as the foremost of the pleasures of the soul: "With Epicurus as our authority (lest we should depart from him), we maintain that freedom from the horrible torture of a guilt-laden conscience is even the greatest of pleasures; for he who has nothing to grieve him, has not a little what gladdens him." Hedo-

nius in "The Epicurean" insists upon the bitterness mingled with
false pleasure, above all, "the torment of conscience, enmity with
God himself, and the expectation of eternal torment." [18]

According to Seneca, it is the inseparability of virtue from
pleasure, espoused by Epicurus and misunderstood by voluptuar-
ies, which has drawn many debauchees to the profession of
philosophical Epicureanism, "and they do not consider how sober
and abstemious the 'pleasure' of Epicurus really is — for so, in
all truth, I think it." Seneca continues: "Personally I hold the
opinion . . . that the teachings of Epicurus are upright and holy
and, if you consider them closely, austere; for his famous doctrine
of pleasure is reduced to small and narrow proportions, and the
rule that we Stoics lay down for virtue, this same rule he lays
down for pleasure — he bids that it obey Nature. But it takes a
very little luxury to satisfy Nature!" It was statements like these
in Seneca (and Cicero, as has been seen) which undoubtedly
helped More to a greater understanding of the true position of
Epicurus and his philosophy.[19]

The student of the *Utopia* is now in a better position briefly
to evaluate the influences at work upon More when he pictures
his Utopians as the upholders of the philosophy of pleasure. The
observation of Vespucci on the Epicureanism of the barbarous
Indians, at best, could have been only a spark to set fire to the
rough material already lying stored in More's humanistic brain.
The Greek text and Latin translation of Diogenes Laertius made
possible a more correct appraisal of Epicurus after 1430. Valla,
in conjunction with the award of final victory to Christianity,
allowed an active defense of Epicureanism to form an integral
part of his opus, *De Voluptate ac de Vero Bono.* Erasmus in *The
Contempt of the World* (composed *ca.* 1490) boasts and proves
that the whole way of life of a true monk is Epicurean in its
nature. He employs the selective principles of Epicurus in a thoroughly Christian context. The most important change is to stress
the existence of God as man's greatest good and happiness and
the joys of reward in a future life, both of which Epicurus had

denied. It is to the advantage of Erasmus to say nothing of Epicurus' denial of the providence of God, the immortality of the soul, and future retribution. Later, in his colloquy "The Epicurean" (1533), he uses the same devices and applies the same tests to the life of pious laymen instead of devout monks. In a word, by interpreting him for the better (*in melius interpretando*), Erasmus christianizes Epicurus in a literary strain just as the writers of the Church had christianized Plato and Aristotle in their apologetical works. But Émile Telle is far too severe when he points out Erasmus' antimonasticism and compromises with the world and then labels his *philosophia Christi* as "nothing else than an Epicureanism allegedly Christian." [20]

The author of *Utopia* borrows from religion the fundamental truths which Erasmus had used to correct Epicurus, and then treats the whole question of happiness and pleasure, independently of revelation and Christianity, on the basis of pure reason. More is closer than Erasmus, who consistently emphasizes and extols mental and spiritual delights, to the true spirit of Epicurus, particularly in laying stress also upon bodily pleasures, including health. He dexterously combats the ill-repute in which Epicurus stands in the popular estimation by appealing to nature, virtue, and religion in defense of hedonism and by establishing for *true* pleasure criteria which insure the supremacy of ethical and intellectual pleasures.

In the last analysis, therefore, the theory of Utopian Epicureanism is perceived to be constructive and honorable, and its practice proves to be altruistic and fruitful. Appearing superficially low and degraded at first sight, Utopia's philosophy is gradually revealed as thoroughly wholesome and salutary — a triumphant tribute to More's powers of rhetoric.[21]

V

CRITERIA OF TRUE AND FALSE PLEASURE

The Utopians "determine other all or the chiefest part of man's felicity [*felicitas*] to rest" in pleasure [*uoluptas*]. But only the person who denies the immortality of the soul, the providence of God, and a future reward or punishment, would try, if he were thoroughly logical, to achieve pleasure "by right or wrong" (*per fas ac nefas*). The Utopians, conceding these three truths, do not hold that man's happiness lies in every sort of pleasure, but insist upon a certain kind of pleasure. Like Socrates, they deny that pleasures "are all alike and to be equally esteemed" and assert "that some pleasures arise from honourable and good desires, and others from those that are base, and that we ought to practise and esteem the one and control and subdue the other." The qualifications which they demand for the proper kind of pleasure are four in number, of which one is positive and three are negative.[1]

First of all, happiness resides "only in that pleasure that is good and honest" (*bona atque honesta*). The Utopians insist that true pleasures are "good and honest" by *nature*. This is the *positive* norm. "Pleasure they call every motion or state of the body or mind wherein man hath naturally [*natura duce*] delectation." There are many things which are considered pleasurable, yet "which of their own nature [*suapte natura*] contain no pleasantness," and which have "no natural pleasantness in them" (*natura nihil insit suaue*). Some people, for example, foolishly think that a gown of fine thread surpasses one of coarse thread "by nature, and not by their mistaking" (*natura non errore*). Every pleasure, therefore, is good or bad by *nature* and will remain so forever. "[N]o man's judgment, depraved and corrupt other by sickness or by custom, can change the nature of pleasure, more than it can do the nature of other things." It does not lie within the power of men "to change the things as they do the names of things." [2]

How is one to determine practically and concretely the *natural* goodness or badness of a particular pleasure? One can solve every problem by an application of the three negative norms. Only that object can be pleasurable by *nature* which does not involve (1) the loss of a greater pleasure, or (2) consequent pain and sorrow, or (3) injury to one's neighbor. These ill consequences "they think to follow of necessity, if the pleasure be unhonest" (*quod necessario sequi censent, si inhonesta sit*). Hence, they hold "no kind of pleasure forbidden whereof cometh no harm" (*ex quo nihil sequatur incommodi*). Of the three negative norms, the first two are of special importance and value to the individual; the third, to society. [3]

In Hythloday's account the first two negative norms are linked together on the three occasions when they are mentioned. For example, the Utopians use in all things this precaution "that a less pleasure hinder not a bigger and that the pleasure be no cause of displeasure" (*neu dolorem aliquando uoluptas pariat*). In this respect the Utopians follow the same principle as the man who disbelieves in the three fundamental truths and who, by a perfectly logical conclusion, would "do all his diligence and endeavor to obtain pleasure by right or wrong, only avoiding this inconvenience, that the less pleasure should not be a let or hindrance to the bigger, or that he labored not for that pleasure which would bring after it displeasure, grief, and sorrow" (*eam . . . quam inuicem retaliet dolor*). This latter statement accords with the assertion of Torquatus the Epicurean in Cicero's *De Finibus*: "The wise man . . . always holds . . . to the principle of selection: he rejects pleasures to secure other greater pleasures, or else he endures pains to avoid worse pains." Many years after the *Utopia* was published, More was to enunciate in his *Dialogue Concerning Heresies* a like principle of selection in speaking of the subordination of body to soul: "Wherein God would that we were learned rather to suffer our sensual parties plain and mourn than to follow their own hurt and ours too." [4]

The third negative norm is social in character. It is directed with special force against the masters of England and Europe: the "conspiracy of rich men, procuring their own commodities under the name and title of the commonwealth." The Utopians derive their argument from nature herself. Nature does not lavish special attention and devotion upon any particular individual as though he did not belong to the mass of humanity but stood above it as a superman: "no man is so far above the lot of man's state or condition that nature doth cark and care for him only." On the contrary, nature "equally [*ex aequo*] favoreth all that be comprehended under the communion of one shape, form, and fashion," that is, she treats with the same impartiality all the members of the same species, who share the same nature in common. Nature bids and moves one to help all one's fellow men, as well as one's self, to a life full of joy and free from care. The logical conclusion from this truth is that "verily she commandeth thee to use diligent circumspection that thou do not so seek for thine own commodities that thou procure others' incommodities." This, therefore, is always the condition for good and true pleasure: "so that it may be gotten without wrong or injury" (*ad quod neque per iniuriam tenditur*). For it is "open wrong" (*iniuria*) to "let another man of his pleasure whiles thou procurest thine own." [5]

This principle is the basis for the superb justice, both commutative and legal, of the Utopians. It is the basis, first of all, of commutative justice, by which a private person renders to another private person what is due to him by right. This kind of justice is exercised especially in contracts, whether gratuitous (such as promises or gifts) or onerous (such as purchases and sales, which, of course, can have no place, strictly speaking, among the communistic Utopians themselves, but only among their neighbors). Hence, the firm conviction of the Utopians is that "covenants and bargains made among private men ought to be well and faithfully fulfilled, observed, and kept." The same principle is the foundation for legal justice, by which citizens give to the community what is due to it in order to procure the common or social good. Legal justice is satisfied principally by the observance of good and just laws. These laws must be such as "other a good prince hath justly published or else the people, nother oppressed with tyranny, nother deceived by fraud and guile, hath by their common consent constitute[d] and ratified." This insistence upon justice is aimed against the rich in European countries who make laws out of the "means and crafts" by which they endeavor to safeguard their ill-gotten gains and further oppress the poor with impunity. The laws which in particular must be observed carefully and scrupulously are those which deal with "the partition of the commodities of life, that is to say, the matter of pleasure." Here Hythloday certainly has his eye upon the neglect and nonexecution of the acts to remedy the evils arising from the enclosure of the commons. From as early as the fourth year of the reign of Henry VII, 1488–89, to as late as the seventh year of the reign of Henry VIII, 1515, Parliament passed acts against the pulling down of country towns and houses. Hythloday seems to be echoing the very words of these acts when he insists: "make a law that they which plucked down farms and towns of husbandry shall build them up again." This law should have been carried out, since it dealt with the vital problem of "the partition of the commodities of life." Failure to observe the statute resulted in ever-increasing poverty and unemployment, thievery and robbery.[6]

Provided that just laws on the proper distribution of wealth and property are observed and are left inviolate, the Utopians consider it prudent sagacity to take care of one's own interests, and filial devotion to look to the public interests as well. But the deprivation of pleasure from one's fellow men as the price of securing one's own, is patent injustice. On the contrary, to deprive one's self of something in order to give it to another is the friendly service of humanity and kindness. This latter is always a greater gain than loss. The gain, in fact, is threefold: (1) compensation in the form of a return of favors, (2) greater pleasure (the consciousness of a deed well done and the remembrance of the love and good will of those benefited) coming to the soul than would have come to the body if one had not deprived oneself, and (3) the reward by God of "a short and small pleasure with great and everlasting joy." Epicurus himself, Plutarch tells his reader, says that "it is not only more beautiful to confer than to receive a benefit, but also more pleasurable, for nothing produces gladness as much as beneficence." [7]

Such, then, are the four qualifications which the Utopians require for pleasure, true and worthy of the name. The practical result is that the standards of morality set for these devotees of pleasure turn out to be as stringent and high as those established by the Stoic, or even Christian, defenders of virtue.

The Utopians have fixed with great exactness the nature and the attributes of true pleasure. They have not, however, done the same in regard to false pleasures. Four causes, however, are mentioned in the course of the treatment of false pleasure: bodily illness, base desires, false opinions, and, above all, perverted habits. (1) Sickness or disease, to be understood in its physical rather than moral sense, is once assigned as a cause of a corrupted judgment in regard to pleasure, but there seems to be no further discussion or mention of this cause. Thus, a sick or diseased man may like some things abhorred by a healthy person. (2) "The perverse and malicious flickering enticements of lewd and unhonest desires" (*peruersa improbarum cupiditatum illecebra*) cause many things which are unpleasant of themselves to be considered "not only for special and sovereign pleasures, but also be counted among the chief causes of life." These unrighteous desires have for their object, not only purely sensual pleasures as food and drink in immoderate quantities or of excessive delicacy, but also inordinate attachments to riches and honors. (3) Desires of a perverse and immoral nature, when yielded to without reserve, warp the mind with "a false opinion of pleasure." The result is that men who are deceived in this way choose from among false pleasures as if they surpassed other pleasures "by nature and not by their mistaking" (*natura non errore*). Intellectual error or wrong thinking, therefore, causes mortals to choose false pleasures. (4) Seduced into errors of judgment by alluring desires, men become victims of *corrupt habits or customs*. They look upon false pleasures as true pleasures since they do, as a matter of fact, derive gratification from them. Nevertheless, "not the nature of the thing but their perverse and lewd custom [*peruersa consuetudo*] is the cause hereof, which causeth them to accept bitter or sour things for sweet things, even as women with child, in their vitiate[d] and corrupt taste, think pitch and tallow sweeter than any honey." Driven by disease or incited by desire, they drive out nature with a "second nature," namely, habit, and judge false pleasures to be real pleasures. Whether the perverse habit or the erroneous judgment comes first is not clear. The quotation just given favors custom, since the next sentence speaks of a "man's judgment, depraved and corrupt . . . by custom." Nevertheless the judgment remains more important, since Hythloday is trying to explain why men set false values on deceitful and dishonest pleasures. The psychological sequence in most cases would be base desires impelling to perverse habits and perverse habits leading to erroneous judgments on the nature of pleasure.[8]

Six to eight years later (*ca.* 1522), More was to apply a similar statement to sin. The pleasure of sin, too, is painful, but "we cannot perceive [it] for bitter, for the corruption of our custom whereby sour seemeth us sweet." Here, too, he assigns error and

custom as the reason for our preference of bodily pleasure to
spiritual delight, using the very example he had employed in
Utopia:

> . . . like as a sick man feeleth no sweetness in sugar, and some women
> with child have such fond lust that they had liefer eat tar than
> treacle and rather pitch than marmalade, and some whole people love
> tallow better than butter, . . . so we gross carnal people, having our
> taste infected by the sickness of sin and filthy custom of fleshly lust,
> find so great liking in the foul and stinking delectation of fleshly delight
> that we list not once prove what manner of sweetness good and virtu-
> ous folk feel and perceive in spiritual pleasure.

He keeps insisting that it is "our blind custom" which makes us
persevere in "the gross and filthy pleasure of all fleshly delight"
and keeps us ignorant and "without care or cure" of "the sweetness of spiritual pleasure" — "as a sow content with draff, dirt,
and mire careth neither for better meat nor better bed." Erasmus
wrote truly in one of his adages that "no one is easily drawn
away from vices in which he has been born and reared; for,
things which in themselves are foul, seem beautiful and sweet because recommended by daily habit." [9]

The false pleasures picked out by the Utopians for special condemnation are the following: (1) the erroneous notion that the
better the clothes, the better men the wearers; (2) foolish pride
in useless honors, especially in poverty-stricken nobility; (3)
puerile delight in precious stones and gems, or in buried gold,
or in riches kept merely for contemplation; and (4) mad enthusiasm for diceplay, hawking, and hunting. It is essential to note
that, when Hythloday speaks of custom as the source of error in
respect to pleasure, he is referring, not only to the corrupt habits
of men as individuals, but also to the false estimates and vices of
social classes, even of contemporary society as a whole. For a
society furnishes the environment in which erroneous opinions
can spring up and grow; in fact, a society can, and does, insinuate
or foist its false notions on each generation as it rises. Thus, hunting can become a national false pleasure, as it did in the England
of the period; and honors and riches, an international false pleas-

ure, as in the Europe of the late Middle Ages and the Renaissance.[10]

False pleasures are countless (*innumera*). Individuals, classes, nations, and even the ordinary run of mortals, may mistake innumerable opinions and activities for pleasures. The Utopians remain undaunted by such formidable opposition because they realize that *by nature* such pursuits have no sweetness in them and that, therefore, they "have no affinity with true and right pleasure." Their opponents answer that their amusements must be true pleasures for the reason that they do flood the senses with sweetness — a function which belongs to pleasure. The response of the Utopians is that the cause of the sweetness is not the *nature* of the thing, but, as has been seen, bodily illness, inordinate desires, errors of judgment, and, above all, evil custom or habit. For example, honey by its very nature is sweet and delectable. The lovers of false pleasure can supplant original nature with a second nature, namely, custom or habit; they can come to like pitch and tallow better than honey. But this subjective preference of individuals or groups cannot change the objective character of a true pleasure. Honey will always remain sweeter and more pleasant than pitch and tallow — because it is so by nature. The taste of pitch cannot become a true pleasure because it is "against nature" (*praeter naturam*). Mortals can change the name, but not the nature, of pleasure. The nature of pleasure, as good or as bad, is immutable.[11]

VI

FALSE PLEASURES IN EUROPE

The whole doctrine of pleasure in the *Utopia* will become clearer after an investigation of the *reasons* for rejection of certain pleasures which the Utopians single out and label as false. The first of the sham pleasures detested by the Utopians and mentioned by Hythloday is love of fine apparel on the part of persons who, by reason of their presumedly better garment, consider themselves better men and consequently look for more signs of external respect from others. Herein lies a double mistake: first, that their garment is better and, second, that they are thereby better as men. The first is erroneous because, if one looks to the *practical* value of clothing (protection and modesty), fabric of fine thread is not superior to fabric of coarse thread; the second is erroneous because honor should be paid to personal merit, not to external appearance. The Utopians, to whom "the smallness or finesse [fineness] of the thread" is of no great value, have reached this conclusion by reason and common sense, for they wonder that "any man is so mad as to count himself the nobler for the smaller or finer thread of wool, which selfsame wool . . . did once a sheep wear, and yet was she all that time no other thing than a sheep." At the end of his life, More was again to enunciate the same truth, this time in the light of eternity, in his treatise on the passion:

How proud is many a man over his neighbor because the wool of his gown is finer. And yet, as fine as it is, a poor sheep wore it on her back before it came upon his, and all the while she wore it, were her wool never so fine, yet was she pardie but a sheep. And why should he be now better than she by that wool that, though it be his, is yet not so barely his as it was verily hers.[1]

Hythloday is hitting at a prominent abuse of his day when he declares that "not only gentlemen's servants but also handicraft men, yea, and almost the ploughmen of the country, with all sorts of people, use much strange and proud newfangleness in their apparel." Complaints on the score are found in contemporary poems, such as *The Ship of Fools* by Barclay and *The Manner of the World Nowadays*, attributed to Skelton. In an epigram written about 1513, More directed the shafts of his satire against an Englishman who affected the French language and fashions. Even Parliament at various times, e.g., in 1509–10 and 1514–15, had passed statutes in an effort to remedy the evil because "the great and costly array and apparel . . . hath be[en] the occasion of great impoverishing of divers of the king's subjects and provoked many of them to rob and to do extortion and other unlawful deeds to maintain thereby their costly array." In spite of the reward of half the forfeiture to the accuser, such acts remained dead-letter laws, as is attested by Master Fitzherbert's *Book of Husbandry* (1534) which still complains about "prodigality in outrageous and costly array" even in simple men and servants and the following statement of More's in his *Debellation of Salem and Bizance* (1533). From the sight of extravagant apparel arose the steadfast belief of many men that, in spite of some exceptions, "they that go now full fresh in their garded hosen and in their gay, golden, riven shirts and in their silken sleeves, that nought have to bear it out but gaming, will once, I warrant you, fall from gaming to stealing and start straight out of silk into hemp [i.e., the hangman's noose]."[2]

The reform of such abuses should be based on the function or purpose of clothing — as the Utopians say, on "the profitable use of the garment." Hythloday mentions in passing only pro-

tection against the cold as a practical use of clothing. But he
would undoubtedly agree with the Carthusian in Erasmus' colloquy: "Our garments are for two uses, to defend us from the
inclemency of the weather and to cover our nakedness." In accordance with this fundamental principle, More makes the clothes
of all the Utopians to be of the same cut, except that male and
female, single and married, are distinguished by differences in
dress. These clothes persist unchanged through all generations,
are not unsightly to the eye, and are adjusted for the free movement of the body. They are adapted to conditions of cold and
heat.[3]

Utopian working clothes, which last seven years, are made of
skin or leather. More may here have in mind the *baeta*, "good in
both summer and winter," which Erasmus describes in his *Adages*.
According to Suidas, the *baeta* is "a kind of skin garment which
seems suitable for both seasons, for in winter it repels the wind,
in summer the sun"; according to Julius Pollux, it is a leather
garment, "a very long tunic, covering the whole body." When
in public, the Utopians cover their simple working garments
with a chlamys of wool. The chlamys, which generally lasts two
years, has but one color: "the natural color of the wool" (*color
. . . natiuus*). In this respect, the Utopians are like Lycurgus,
who, as Erasmus tells in his *Apophthegms*, banished the art of
dyeing, "for, while the color deceitfully pleases the eye, the
nature of the thing is corrupted." Regard is had only for the
"cleanliness" of woolen cloth: no value is set upon "the smallness
or finesse of the thread." The same holds true for linen, which is
employed more than wool because it is made with less labor.[4]

Since the Utopians judge the value of all things according to
their nature, since clothes by their nature look only to the protection and modesty of the body, and since leather working
garments and woolen or linen chlamyses of undyed hue satisfy
the essential requirements, whatever is over and above is un-
natural. Therefore, the delight which prince and peasant take
in colorful garments of different fabrics is a false and unnatural

pleasure. What an indictment the lovers of true pleasure level against the Christian West where "four or five cloth gowns of divers colors and as many silk coats be not enough for one man. Yea, and if he be of the delicate and nice sort, ten be too few"! And it must be an indictment which comes from the heart of More himself who, according to Erasmus, "delights in simple attire, and does not employ silks or purple or golden chains, except when he is not fully free to lay them aside," for example, on official business or in public functions. Quite the opposite of the common sense of More and his Utopians is the more typical attitude of the Renaissance, well expressed by Pontano in his essay entitled *Splendor*. After praising the lavish use of purple and silk in dress and of gems and stones in personal adornment, household furnishings, and religious affairs, he admits that liberal and exalted personages like Dion of Syracuse had neglected all this pomp and ornament in order to appear modest to their citizens. But he concludes: "Even though we do not blame the stand of these men, nevertheless we consider it unworthy of the state for its prince to be niggardly in the midst of wealth and great power." [5]

Ignorant fools demand reverence and respect as their right (*suo iure*) "for their finer gown's sake." Such behavior is an example of the second kind of false pleasure: "a pride in vain and unprofitable honors." Honor may be defined as an external manifestation of esteem for another's worth, whether arising from his virtue or his authority. Silvester de Prierio in his *Digest of Digests* (*Summa Summarum*) draws an illuminating distinction. Postulating that honor is properly due only to virtue, he declares that a person may be honored on account of his own virtue, as in the case of personally virtuous men, or on account of another's virtue: "thus, princes and prelates are given honor even if they are wicked because they represent and bear the person of the virtuous God and of the community. . . . Likewise, wealthy men are honored, not because of their riches, for this would be acceptance of persons, but because they hold a higher

rank in the community." Pleasure which arises from the satisfaction of an *inordinate* desire for marks of respect, independently of these two titles to honor, is counterfeit, not "natural or
true" (*naturalis et uera*). Such honors are not natural and genuine
because they are fruitless and profitless (*nihil profuturi*). As
More satirically asks: will another man's genuflection heal your
aching knees, or will his bared head alleviate your deranged
mind? More himself, Erasmus told Hutten, was negligent of
the punctilious refinements of etiquette by which the vulgar
crowd measures the politeness of manners.[6]

Utopian strictures are directed only against the desire for "vain
and unprofitable honors." When is the pleasure from honor
"natural" and "true"? As far as respect for authority is concerned,
the Utopians pay their fatherly public officials free and willing
reverence, not forced and reluctant homage. But this aspect of
honor, its relation to authority, is merely mentioned in the *Utopia*.
Instead, stress is laid upon the connection of honor with personal
virtue. The views of the Utopians may be summed up in two
statements. First of all, honor is the *reward of virtue*. They "set
up in the market place the images of notable men and of such
as have been great and bountiful benefactors to the commonwealth for *the perpetual memory of their good acts*." Hence, they
"allure them [their people] to virtue with rewards of honor"
(*propositis . . . honoribus ad uirtutes inuitant*). Secondly, therefore, honor is an *incentive to virtue*. They erect the statues "also
that the glory and renown of the ancestors may stir and provoke
their posterity to virtue" (*calcar et incitamentum ad uirtutem*).[7]

The concept of honor as the reward of virtue is such a commonplace in the whole of philosophy and literature that illustrative
quotations would be useless. Nevertheless, it is interesting to note
that More makes a personal addition to his translation of the life
of Pico: learning and virtue are "the things which we may account for our own, of which every man is more properly to be
commended than of the nobleness of his ancestors, whose honor
maketh us not honorable . . . for honor is the reward of virtue."

Honor follows virtue "as a shadow followeth a body." A year after the publication of *Utopia*, Pace wrote in his *Benefits of Learning*: "That is true nobility which is the effect of virtue rather than a long and illustrious family line. . . . Honor accrues to nobility from virtue, not to virtue from nobility." Hence, Erasmus, writing to Faber in 1532, declares that Thomas More and his father merited the king's favors by their virtue, the parent of all true nobility. George Lily, too, points out that Thomas More was summoned to the most honorable offices of the state "only by the commendation of his virtue" (*sola virtutis commendatione*). If this is true, it is a tribute to the farsightedness of Henry VIII and his ministers. As for Germany, Geiler in his *Bark or Mirror of Fools* had complained some years before that the highest offices of church and state were filled by men chosen for blood and nobility, not for virtue, learning, and prudence. The result was the appointment of stupid, foolish, corrupt men.[8]

Honor, the Utopians realize, serves also a social function, that of a spur and incentive (*calcar et incitamentum*) for others. Virtue must be conceded to be its own reward; yet, as Philodoxus maintains in Erasmus' colloquy *The Lover of Glory*, virtue "delights to be known as the sun does to shine; for this very reason, that it may benefit a great many and draw them to an imitation of itself." Imitation and emulation of one's virtuous and noble forebears is a most efficacious means to the pursuit of virtue. In his life of Pico, More reasons that "the more worshipful that our ancestors were, the more vile and shameful be we, if we decline from the steps of their worshipful living." His friend, John Fisher, agrees with him in his "Month's Mind Sermon of Margaret" (1509): "If ought be good in the nobleness of blood, it is for that thereby the noble men and women should be ashamed to go out of kind from the virtuous manners of their ancestry before." Erasmus later (1523?) told Thomas More's son that "degeneration [from the perfect example set by your father] would be most disgraceful."[9]

In his *Praise of Folly*, Erasmus pillories persons who fail to

emulate the doughty deeds of their ancestors but who "flatter
themselves beyond measure with the empty title of nobility."
What good is it to boast of a genealogy extending back to Aeneas,
Brutus, and Arthur, when one is almost more without sense and
worth than the inanimate busts and portraits of one's ancestors?
A superficial glance at the *Utopia* might lead one to conclude
that More is attacking the same folly as Erasmus. But a careful
reading of the text reveals that More is poking fun, not at empty
titles of nobility, but at wealth — a fact which ties this section
more closely to a central problem of the *Utopia*, that of wealth
and poverty. The Utopian system of communism involves the
abolition of money, to which alone common opinion attributes,
as More ironically observes later, "the true ornaments and honors
. . . of a commonwealth," to wit, "all nobility, magnificence,
worship, honor, and majesty." In the section on pleasure, More
enunciates the principle that in contemporary England nobility
is nothing else than wealth. Whether a man bears a noble title
or not, in a sense, is inconsequential as far as More's purpose is
concerned: now wealth alone confers nobility. Nor is the wealthy
man content merely with gold and silver: he invests his money
in landed estates. Hence arises, in part, the evil of enclosure.
In order to "compass about and enclose many thousand acres of
ground together within one pale or hedge," he fraudulently or
violently forces the farmers to leave their fields and homes, sometimes without even a pittance of compensation. Yet this "covetous
and unsatiable cormorant and very plague of his native country"
demands for himself and his wealth a bended knee and an un-
covered head — those signs of honor which are properly due
to virtue alone. His descendants even more foolishly yield themselves to the sweet madness (*suauiter insaniunt*) of false delight
in vain and useless honors. They flatteringly congratulate themselves with the ascription of "nobility" because they chance to
be born of a long line of wealthy ancestors. Nor do they appear
in their own eyes a fraction the less "noble" if their fathers have
left them never an acre or if they themselves have squandered

everything. They still crave for and take joy in the outward signs of honor, now due them for neither their virtue nor their wealth! [10]

The discussion of happiness in Heywood's dialogue, *More*, is interesting because of its echoes from *Utopia* and its parallels with *Utopia*. Lorenzo argues for wealth as the object of happiness because it contains within itself honor and power. Carlo objects on the score that, not only is wealth distinct from honor and power as instrument from effect, but the making of the one is the unmaking of the others. On his part, Carlo defends honor as the object of happiness. Leonardo declares that there is too much uncertainty in regard to honor, some placing it in riches, others in noble blood, even though the descendants do nothing to live up to the virtuous and valorous deeds of their distinguished ancestors. Carlo replies by placing it in virtuous action of body or of soul, and especially in genius. As Piero had done earlier, so now Paolo gives the fundamental objection: honor has no real existence in the person honored; thus, honor cannot be said to exist in the dead. Happiness ought to be something within the soul of the man who wishes to be happy. More observes that man constantly deceives himself, whether by preferring the lesser delight to the greater or by acting solely for pleasure and thereby actually procuring the direct opposite, namely, pain. He mentions in particular "the sordidness of riches and the smoke of honor," with which man's eyes are so blinded that he cannot see "the bright fire which burns within." The point of departure for More, as for the Platonists, in the quest for happiness is the distinction between reason and appetite.[11]

Delight in honors which have no relation to virtue as reward or incentive is foolishness and madness. But people who take pleasure in mere formalities without substance are not alone in their insane folly. The Utopians maintain that two other classes are just as bad: (1) men who are so infatuated with gems that, if they lay their hands upon an extraordinary one, they deceive themselves with delusions of divinity (*dii quodammodo sibi*

uidentur facti), and (2) men who never use their golden riches
but keep them only to feast their eyes upon them or to bury them
in the ground. These persons are as foolish as the Anemolian
ambassadors who, by a preposterous display of gold and gems,
"determined in the gorgeousness of their apparel to represent
very gods" (*deos quosdam repraesentare*).[12]

The first class go to the extremes of buying, but after oaths
by the seller as to their genuineness, only unset stones which are
in fashion. The Utopians castigate these persons by declaring
that the man incapable of discerning the difference between a
counterfeit and a true gem should logically take as much pleasure
in one as in the other. In this regard, More could point to a prank
perpetrated by himself and perpetuated by Erasmus in the pages
of *The Praise of Folly*. With little expense, he increased his young
wife's love for him by presenting her with counterfeit gems: she
took as much delight in them as if they were genuine — to the
great amusement of her husband! Later, in his *Four Last Things*,
More lays to ignorance the folly of those who prefer bodily
pleasure to spiritual sweetness — "as those that lack insight of
precious stones hold themself as well content and satisfied with
a beryl of crystal all well counterfeited as with a right natural
diamond." At the very end of his life, More was still wondering
in his *Treatise on the Passion* at the foolish pride of men: "How
proud be many men of these glistering stones, of which the very
brightness, though he cost thee twenty pounds, shall never shine
half so bright nor show thee half so much light as shall a half-
penny candle." The Utopians, too, marvel that "any men be so
foolish as to have delight and pleasure in the glistering of a little
trifling stone, which may behold any of the stars or else the sun
itself." [13]

The second class, divided into two groups, keep their resources
out of use and circulation for either of two reasons. One group
gloats over possessions out of the sheer delight of gazing at them.
Since wealth is obviously and naturally directed toward use and
not contemplation, the Utopians do not even trouble to show the

folly of these men but merely put the rhetorical question: "Do they take true pleasure, or else be they deceived with false pleasure?" The second group bury their treasure and thereby commit, according to the Utopians, a double error: (1) they lose their precious store because its removal from use, whether their own or others', is a loss, and (2) they absurdly receive, for long years, an equal amount of pleasure and use, whether their treasure is left safely untouched or whether it is stolen and they die happy in ignorance of the theft.[14]

What is the basis of the Utopian views on gold and silver and, of course, on gems and stones? The norm, as always, is *nature*. Every Utopian values "precious" things no more "than the very nature of the thing deserveth" (*quam rerum ipsarum natura meretur*). For example, gold "of the own nature is a thing . . . unprofitable" (*suapte natura . . . inutile*). How do the Utopians argue to this conclusion? First of all, they maintain that nature (*natura*) has given to gold and silver no use without which man cannot easily survive. Such a metal as iron, however, is as essential to man as fire and water. Secondly, they feel that nature has placed all the best things (such as air, water, and soil) in the open, but has removed as far from sight as possible "vain and unprofitable things" (*uana ac nihil profutura*). The latter epithets are the very ones applied to empty honors — an indication that the principles for judgment of values remain the same throughout this section of *Utopia*.[15]

In his serious works almost twenty years later, More was to refer twice to the *natural* superiority of iron, on account of its *usefulness*, to gold and silver. In the *Dialogue of Comfort*, More in the person of Antony asks: "what great thing can you or I, yea, or any lord the greatest in this land, reckon himself to have by the possession of an heap of silver or gold, white and yellow metal, not so *profitable* of their own *nature* (save for a little glistering) as the rude rusty metal of iron?" And in his treatise on the passion he meditates on how foolish it is to take pride in one's personal endowments, as beauty or learning, and how even more foolish it is to take pleasure in external goods, for example, gold and silver: "How proud be men of gold and silver, no part of ourself, but of the earth, and of *nature* no better than is the poor copper or tin, nor to man's *use* so *profitable* as is the poor metal that maketh us the ploughshare and horseshoon and horse nails." Erasmus, too, in his *Enchiridion* realizes and expounds the stupidity and baseness of avarice. "Take away the error of men," he cries, "and what will gold and silver be but red and white earth?" Shall the man who is the disciple of the poor Christ and is called to far better possessions esteem what pagan philosophers contemn? The latter agree that among useful goods riches hold the last place; for example, Epictetus teaches that, outside virtue, all other things are external to man. Gold and gems, Erasmus argues, are useless. They cannot increase the mind's intelligence, prudence, or learning, nor the body's health, strength, comeliness, or youth. They can buy only fatal pleasures: they can attract only the false honor rendered by fools or knaves. "True honor," he concludes, "is the reward, not of riches, but of virtue." [16]

To show their philosophical contempt for precious metals, the Utopians use their gold and silver for "chamber pots" and all the "vessels that serve for most vile uses" (*matellas . . . ac sordissima quaeque uasa*). Where did More get this ingenious notion? His fertile imagination and whimsical humor of themselves could easily have conceived such a use. But he might have caught the germ or conceived the development of the idea from contemporary books of exploration and from classical sources. In both his *Four Voyages* and his *New World*, Amerigo Vespucci mentions the Indians' lack of esteem for precious things like gold. Pietro Martire d'Anghiera, in the First Decade (1511) of his *New World*, contrasts the Indians' contempt for gold with the Spaniards' lust for it, and in the Second Decade (1516) repeats the tale of a chief's son that "the cacique Tumanama, and all the mountaineers living on the other slope of the mountain, used kitchen and other common utensils made of gold; 'for gold,' he said, 'has no more value among them than iron among you.'" In classical antiquity, Plutarch relates how Lycurgus had eliminated from Sparta such crimes as stealing and bribery by substituting iron for gold and silver. Plato in his *Republic* had forbidden his guardians to have anything to do with gold and silver and in his *Laws* had restricted the possession of gold and silver by private persons to a few necessary coins. Neither in Plutarch nor in Plato, however, is there any suggestion of the lowliest use to which the Utopians put their gold and silver. A definite clue, however, is found in Erasmus' explanation of the proverbial phrase "To urinate into the pot" (*In matellam immeiere*). Martial, explains Erasmus, humorously censures a certain Bassus because he defecated into a golden vessel, but drank from a glass one: "Your bowels' load — and you are not ashamed — you receive in a golden vessel — unhappy urn! Bassus, you drink out of crystal; therefore your evacuations are the more costly." Because this epigram of Martial is the only source which explicitly mentions the use of gold for purposes of excretion, it is likely to have furnished the suggestion for More's *Utopia*, especially in view of the fact that it appears in Erasmus' *Adages*.[17]

No definite parallel has been suggested for the amusing episode of the Anemolian ambassadors except an incident in Lucian's *Nigrinus*, where the Athenians teach discipline and moderation to a vulgar millionaire who had expected to excite them to envy by his extravagant dress and jewelry. Plutarch also relates how Solon had depised the attempt of Croesus to awe him by decking himself with "everything in the way of precious stones, dyed raiment, and wrought gold." As for "the great chains of gold" of the Anemolians, Erasmus had earlier held them up to ridicule in his *Praise of Folly*, where he pillories all those courtiers of whom "each is the more pleased with himself the heavier chain he can carry about on his neck, as if he were showing off his strength rather than his wealth"![18]

The final example of "foolish pleasures" (*ineptae laetitiae*) is furnished by the devotees of dicing, hunting, and hawking. Hawking is not berated separately, but is undoubtedly subject

to the same strictures and refuted by the same arguments as
hunting.

Earlier in the *Utopia*, Hythloday had classified diceplay among
"foolish and pernicious games" (*ineptos ac perniciosos ludos*).
The sane Utopians, in fact, know the "madness" (*insaniam*) of
dicing only by hearsay, not by experience. Their fundamental
objection to the amusement is based upon the assumption that
constant repetition begets satiety and tedium. Now, in diceplay
there is an endless throwing of the cubes. Therefore, diceplay
must be a wearisome and pleasureless game. In their argumentation, the Utopians violate the axiom: "No line of argumentation
is valid in the face of a fact" (*contra factum non valet illatio*),
since zealous diceplayers, as a matter of fact, do find pleasure,
even if it is essentially false and unworthy pleasure, in their game.
It is noteworthy that More terms dicing a "madness" (*insaniam*).
Erasmus had earlier hesitated to admit gamblers with dice to his
College of Fools. Folly's reason is that, although dicing is ludicrous and foolish, "the game usually passes over into an angry
quarrel, so that it appertains to the Furies, not to me." In other
words, the madness of gambling is not always innocuous or
benevolent. But whether the madness was violent or harmless,
More himself, as Erasmus informed Hutten, was altogether
averse to dice, cards, and other games of chance by which distinguished society was wont to while away the tedious hours.[19]

Many contemporary references reveal that gambling, whether
by dice or by cards, was a serious evil of the time. A poem attributed to Skelton, "The Manner of the World Nowadays," has
the following lines:

> So many carders,
> Revellers and dicers,
> And so many ill-ticers,
> Saw I never.

No one, claims Barclay, is immune from the evil:

> There is almost no manner of degree —
> Man, child, woman, poor man, or estate,

Old or young — that of this game are free:
Not yet the clergy, both poor priest and prelate.

Barclay is no Puritan: he has no objection to cards and dice if played for recreation at the proper time, without betting or impatience. In this respect, he agrees with moral theologians such as Silvester de Prierio who approves the playing of dice, cards, etc., for recreational purposes and their manufacture and sale for the same reason. But he approves also of the divine and civil laws which prohibit dishonest gambling as the cause of strife, envy, and murder. In his *Book of Husbandry*, Master Fitzherbert laments an individual's loss in a single day or night of as much money as would supply food and drink to his whole household for a month, a quarter, or even longer. In that case, gambling is not a sport or pleasure but "a disport or a displeasure," which causes players often "to sell their lands, disherit the heirs, and mayfortune to fall to theft, robbery, or such other. . . ."[20]

Sir Thomas Elyot gives the viewpoint of an English humanist more or less contemporary with Thomas More. Elyot fiercely denounces "playing at dice," but concedes: "Playing at cards and tables is somewhat more tolerable, only for as much as therein wit is more used and less trust is in fortune, albeit therein is neither laudable study nor exercise." Nevertheless, lovers of virtue might easily invent games with cards and tables which could furnish at once good entertainment and educational profit. One example given is the invention of "contention between virtue and vice." How much this amusement would be in the tradition of the Renaissance is evident from the fact that even the Utopians play two chess-like games. Their "battle of numbers" (*numerorum pugna*), according to Lupton, "might answer to more than one still familiar game." As a matter of fact, the last five pages of a book of Jacques Lefèvre d'Étaples, e.g., in the second edition of 1514, are devoted to a "battle of numbers" (*Rithmimachie* [= *Rhythmomachiae*] *ludus qui et pugna numerorum appellatur*). The game is recommended to tired students for relaxation of mind so that they might refresh their spirits by useful and

honest leisure. More enters into greater detail in regard to the
game in which "vices fight with virtues, as it were in battle array
or a set field." Elyot recommends the game of chess above all,
especially if the players have studied "the moralization of the
chess," most probably, Caxton's *Game and Play of the Chess.*
His reason is that in chess is "right subtle engine, whereby the
wit is made more sharp and remembrance quickened." [21]

The Utopians couple hunting with dicing as an absurd form
of recreation. Their arguments against hunting, basically three
in number, vary in seriousness, importance, and strength. First,
the cacophonous barking and howling of dogs should normally
produce dislike and disgust, not sweetness and delight. Second,
hunting is fundamentally a race. If he enjoys racing, a man should
take as much pleasure in watching a dog pursue a dog as in
watching a dog pursue a hare, since there is racing in both cases.
The third argument is an appeal to humaneness. It must be "the
hope of slaughter and the expectation of tearing in pieces" (*caedis
spes, laniatus expectatio*), that is, the wild lust of beholding
violent death (*spectandae necis libido*), which constitutes the
essence of the pleasure of hunting. Any pleasure which essentially
depends upon cruelty cannot be natural and true (*naturalis et
uera*). On the contrary, mercy and pity should fill one's heart
"to see a seely innocent hare murdered of a dog: the weak of
the stronger, the fearful of the fierce, the innocent of the cruel
and unmerciful." The Utopians are convinced that the pleasure
which comes from the contemplation of the killing and mangling
of little animals may arise from a cruel disposition of soul in the
inhumane hunter no less than in the unreasoning dog. At any
rate, such pleasure finally terminates in habitual cruelty in both
dog and hunter, resulting from repeated acts of savage delight
in slaughter.[22]

Degeneration into beasts, Erasmus declares in his *Praise of
Folly,* is the logical fate of hunters for their pursuit and devouring
of wild game. Yet these foolish fellows declare they are the re-
cipients of unbelievable pleasure from the lowing of horns, the

howling of dogs, and the elaborate formalities connected with the dissection of game — which butchery is permitted only to a gentleman! A note by Lister points the satire especially against the British. But all humanists do not agree with More and Erasmus in their estimation of hunting. Elyot, for example, is enough of an English gentleman to see nothing cruel in hunting and hawking. In fact, they receive his commendation "if they be used with opportunity and in measure." [23]

Among the ancients, Greeks and Romans are divided on the value and decorum of hunting. The very fact that there is no debate on the liceity and propriety of hunting in Plato's *Republic* or *Laws* indicates the addiction of the Greeks to the sport. Plato's spokesman in the *Laws*, the Athenian, after having excluded various kinds of hunting, continues: "Accordingly, the only kind left for all, and the best kind, is the hunting of quadrupeds with horses and dogs and the hunter's own limbs, when men hunt in person, and subdue all the creatures by means of their own running, striking and shooting." In marked contrast with the Greeks, however, the early Romans display no affection for the hunt. The Utopians impose hunting as "the lowest, vilest, and most abject part [*infimam partem*] of butchery" upon their slaves. The Romans, too, left the destruction of wild game to professional huntsmen coming from the classes of slaves and freedmen. Polybius relates that Scipio the Younger (185–129 B.C.) was the first distinguished Roman to engage in the hunt as in all other Greek pursuits. But Scipio found few successors with any predilection for hunting, except among Romans residing in the provinces. In his work entitled *Youth*, James Wimpheling asks why a king or prince should spurn the most honorable exercises of mind and spirit and occupy himself exclusively with the art of hunting — if it deserves the name of art: "Even a churl of mean extraction, of no importance, of no wisdom, of no virtue, can both know and exercise the art as well as the prince himself." [24]

Whatever the attitude of the classical authors or contemporary

humanists might be, the author of the *Utopia*, according to Erasmus' letter to Hutten, found free and easy conversation with a
learned and sincere friend a greater pleasure than dice, chess,
hunting, and music ever were to their enthusiastic devotees.
Such a description, corroborated by numerous statements in his
life and letters, reveals that More was incapable of being delighted and seduced by the glittering tinsel of gold, gems, garments, honors, gambling, and hunting. To say nothing of help
received from revelation and grace, he set up nature and reason
as positive norms for his pleasures and employed harm and
injury to the individual or society as negative criteria to aid him
in the determination of true and natural pleasures.[25]

VII

TRUE PLEASURES IN UTOPIA

After having exposed the roots and specimens of false pleasures, Hythloday turns to true pleasures. This section appears to be the least well organized and logically sequent in the whole *Utopia*. After the initial classification into pleasures of the body and pleasures of the soul, the latter are briefly indicated in two sentences. Then follows a relatively long discussion of the two classes of bodily pleasures: (1) the delights of the senses, such as eating, drinking, etc., and (2) the blessing of health. After the arguments for health as the highest bodily pleasure despite the lack of pleasurable motion in it, one hears in a sentence that the Utopians chiefly prize pleasures of the soul, two of which are mentioned briefly. At this point, the preëminence of health among bodily pleasures is enunciated and its superiority to eating and drinking is established. Finally, contempt is not to be shown for bodily pleasures, for these take their rise in love lavished on men by mother nature. With this assertion the formal treatment of pleasures comes to an end. The arguments for pleasure as the essence of happiness are clinched by pointing to the happy results of the doctrine among the Utopians themselves. The section on the Greek classics follows immediately, not as a specific instance of pleasure, but as an example of Utopian indefatigability in scholarly pursuits.[1]

The apparently involved nature of the whole section and the

difficult character of the individual parts make it profitable to
rearrange and to analyze the basic thoughts in these pages of
the *Utopia*. To preserve the proportions of the work, a brief
enumeration of the pleasures of the soul first may suffice, for
in spite of the repeated emphasis laid upon these as the supreme
pleasures, they merit no systematic and detailed development as
do the pleasures of the body.

As the devotees of reason and common sense, the Utopians
logically fulfill one's expectation that they love and cherish
pleasures of the soul as "the chiefest and most principal of all"
(*uoluptates . . . primas omnium principesque*). Such pleasures
may be divided into three classes. The first class takes its origin
from the self-rewarding exercise of the virtues (*ab exercitio
uirtutum*). The second class constitutes, as it were, the rewards
of virtue: the serene consciousness of one's own moral excellence
at present, the sweet memory of one's virtuous conduct in the
past, and the unshakable hope of bliss in the future. These echo
an earlier passage (in the section on the criteria of pleasure) in
which the pleasurable rewards of an act of sacrifice are given:
the consciousness of the good deed, the remembrance of the
loving good will of those benefited, and the compensation in the
form of overflowing joy in eternity. In Erasmus' "Epicurean,"
Hedonius declares that "the remembrance of a life innocently
passed, and the hope of a better to come . . . are the two
crutches upon which old age is borne up." The third class of
pleasures of the soul is born of the contemplation of truth. Like
Plato's philosopher, the Utopian despises the false pleasures of
wealth and honor in comparison with "the delight of knowing
the truth and the reality." This is the ultimate reason why manual
labor has been reduced to an absolute minimum in Utopia. At
the end of the earlier chapter on work, it had received solemn
pronouncement: "in the institution of that weal public this end
is only and chiefly pretended and minded — that what time may
possibly be spared from the necessary occupations and affairs
of the commonwealth, all that the citizens should withdraw from

the bodily service to the free liberty of the mind and garnishing of the same. For herein they suppose the felicity of this life to consist." [2]

Do the Utopians establish a hierarchical arrangement of mental pleasures as they do for bodily pleasures? As health is preëminent among bodily pleasures, so the "chief part" of mental pleasures comes from "the exercise of virtue[s] and conscience of good life." This is the true liberty and culture of soul (*animi libertatem cultumque*), and therefore even intellectual pursuits are always to tend toward greater purity of conscience and acquisition of noble virtue. In the versified *Twelve Weapons* published five years before, More had written: "Thou shalt no pleasure comparable find / To th' inward gladness of a virtuous mind." Even earlier, Erasmus in his *Enchiridion* had exclaimed: "The true and only pleasure [*voluptas*] is gladness [*gaudium*] in a pure conscience." The emphasis on good conduct rather than on intellectual preoccupation as the source of pleasure for the soul is characteristic of the Utopian character and frame of mind. But, in his report of the Utopian views on pleasure as the end of man, Hythloday has few words to say on the delights of the soul.[3]

Just as the Utopians divide true pleasures into those of the soul and those of the body, so also pleasures of the body are of two kinds. The first permeates the senses with readily discernible sweetness: common examples are eating and drinking. The second consists in the untroubled and well-tempered disposition of the body, undisturbed by any pain or distress (*in quieto atque aequabili corporis statu . . . nullo interpellata malo sanitas*). This second, of course, is nothing else than physical health. That the "tempering of moist, cold, hot, and dry" results in excellent health is a commonplace, but what the Utopians insist upon in health is the absence of any attack or siege of pain. Health free from suffering is in itself a delight. In a word, it does not belong to the first kind of pleasure in which "delectation is sensibly felt and perceived" (*quae sensum perspicua suauitate perfundit*), for health is "not so plain and manifest to the sense [*sese minus effert, minusque offert sensui*], as the greedy lust of eating and drinking." [4]

Many Utopians maintain that health is "the greatest of pleasures" (*uoluptatum maxima*). Since no qualification or limitation is made of the word "pleasures," the reference must be to health as the greatest of all pleasures, whether of body or soul. That health is a *great* one (*magna*) is admitted by almost all the Utopians, who recognize in it the foundation and basis of all pleasures. Their reason is that, even alone and by itself, health can render existence peaceful and desirable, whereas upon the disappearance of health no room is left for any pleasure at all. As Erasmus echoing Plutarch says: "the body is incapable of experiencing pleasures, unless it is well-tempered." The absence of pain without the presence of health the Utopians term insensibility, not pleasure.[5]

The great value attached to health finds manifold expression in classical literature and philosophy. In the *Republic*, Plato places health among the kinds of goods which "we love both for its own sake and for its consequences." In the *Laws*, he declares: "Men say that the chief good is health," and confesses that "health ranks first" among human goods. In one adage, Erasmus cites Aristotle and Aristo of Sicyon. Aristotle's *Rhetoric* reports that everyone's conviction is: "Good health in a man is excellent." In a paean in praise of health, Aristo sings: "O Health, most ancient of the goddesses. . . . With thee all things bloom, and the spring of the graces smiles again. Without thee, in truth, no one is happy." [6]

At the present time the Utopians "agree almost all in this, that health is a most sovereign pleasure" (*sanitatem uel in primis uoluptati esse*). But the view that health holds the primacy among bodily pleasures had not always been triumphant among them. The question as to whether or not enduring and untroubled health was to be considered a pleasure at all had once been zealously argued among the Utopians. The negative opinion, however, had now been rejected for a long time. Its proponents

had argued that the quiet possession of health could not be perceived to be present unless on account of some counteraction or
contrary motion, an essential of pleasure which was nonexistent
in this case. Pleasure was felt in eating, for example, because of
the motion involved in the gradual displacement of hunger;
pleasure was felt in drinking because of the motion involved in
the gradual elimination of thirst. At present the Utopians are
upholding in reality the opinion of Epicurus against that of
Aristippus and the Cyrenaics. The latter also think that pleasure
is the end of man, but they maintain that it lies essentially in
the perception and enjoyment of motion. Diogenes Laertius informs his readers that Epicurus differs from the Cyrenaics on
this very point: "They do not include under the term the pleasure
which is a state of rest, but only that which consists in motion.
Epicurus admits both." The counterpart of this theory of motion
is found also in the doctrine ascribed to Plato and his followers.
In the *Republic*, Socrates declares that "both pleasure and pain
arising in the soul are a kind of motion." Aristotle and his school
interpreted this explanation of pleasure as *kinesis* in its literal
sense. So do the Utopians.[7]

How do the defenders of health answer the arguments of
their opponents? Their response is intimately connected with
the *second* of the two Utopian arguments which prove the
existence of health among corporal pleasures. Eating — which
admittedly involves motion — is nothing else than the battle
against hunger by health, which had begun to weaken but which
now enlists food as its fellow soldier in the war. As health gradually becomes stronger in the course of the conflict, the very
march (or movement) back to ordinary energy furnishes the
pleasure by which man is revived. In a word, the conflict is
pleasurable. But if health takes delight (*laetatur*) in the battle,
it ought unquestionably to be overwhelmed with gladness
(*gaudebit*) in the hour of victory. After having happily won
back its former strength — the only objective sought during the
whole conflict — indubitably it ought not to be stunned all at

once into insensibility (*obstupescet*), as the protagonists of the kinetic theory should logically claim, but rather it ought to recognize its own good and embrace it. Health, therefore, is aware and sensible of the pleasure it contains and imparts.[8]

What answer, therefore, do the defenders of health give to the argument of their opponents? In a sense, a simple and unequivocal denial. First of all, they more or less ignore the contention of the negative that pleasure can be felt only by reason of some contrary motion. They say simply that if the motion to some end is pleasurable, certainly rest in the end itself should be even more pleasurable. Secondly, they reach the heart of the dispute by limiting it to the all-important point: can health be felt at all (even in the absence of motion)? They answer that the statement that "health cannot be felt" is "nothing true" (*perquam procul a uero*, i.e., extremely far removed from the truth). Where is the wide-awake man — except, of course, the unhealthy fellow — that does not perceive and feel that he is healthy? Where is the man — except, of course, the insensible or the lethargic fellow — that does not confess that health is pleasant and delightful to him? Therefore, only the sick or the insensible or the lethargic man does not admit that health is a delight. "And what is delight but pleasure by another name?" Health *can* be felt as a distinct pleasure! Therefore, the argument of the negative falls to the ground.[9]

So much for the Utopian argument against the exclusively kinetic theory of pleasure. Basic to the other and earlier argument is the express assumption that everything, outside the state of insensibility or unconsciousness, is a pleasure (or begetter of pleasure) or a pain (or begetter of pain). For the Utopians the disjunction "either pleasure or pain" is complete: there can be a choice of no third member (*non datur tertium*). This is in complete agreement with the genuine doctrine of Epicurus. In Cicero's *De Finibus*, Torquatus the Epicurean describes Epicurus as affirming that "there is no such thing as a neutral state of feeling intermediate between pleasure and pain. . . . A man who is conscious of his condition at all must necessarily feel either pleasure or pain." This view of Epicurus and of the Utopians is opposed to the opinion of Socrates that there is "such a thing as a neutral state, . . . intermediate between them [pleasure and pain], and in the mean, being a quietude of the soul in these respects." Such is health to sick men and release from pain to the agonizing. Hence, it is not "right to think the absence of pain pleasure, or the absence of joy painful." The Utopians, however, presume that what is free from pain or inimical to pain must be a pleasure or a source of pleasure. In addition, it matters little whether one says that sickness is a pain or that there is pain from sickness; in either case, the sick man is in pain. In the same way, it matters little whether one maintains that health is a pleasure or that it necessarily begets pleasure, "as fire generates heat" (*uelut calor igni gignitur*); in either case, the man who is in health cannot be without pleasure. Since everything must be either a pleasure or a pain, and since health, all admit, is not a pain, health must be a pleasure.[10]

The core of the argument, however, is given in the sentence: "seeing that in sickness (say they) is grief, which is a mortal enemy to pleasure even as sickness is to health, why should not then pleasure be in the quietness of health?" Here the fundamental proportion is the following: sickness is to health as pain is to pleasure. Just as a basic relation exists between sickness and pain, so there is a fundamental connection between health and pleasure. The argument in form runs thus:

> Pain is opposed to pleasure.
> But sickness is pain (or begetter of pain, which to
>   the Utopians amounts to the same).
> Therefore sickness is opposed to pleasure.
> But health is opposed to sickness (and pain) which
>   is opposed to pleasure.
> Therefore health is not opposed to pleasure.
> But what is not opposed to pleasure is a pleasure
>   (or begetter of pleasure, which is the equivalent
>   to the Utopians).
> Therefore health is a pleasure.[11]

To resume briefly the section on health, one may say that almost all the Utopians consider health to be a great pleasure, if not the greatest of all pleasures. Health is a *pleasure*, first of all, because if the battle for health is pleasurable, the quiet possession of health must be joyful and gladdening; secondly, because, as pain accompanies sickness, pleasure must result from health; and thirdly, because the confession of every possessor of health that he is aware of experiencing a delightful pleasure refutes the contention of adversaries that health cannot be felt as a pleasure. Health is a *great* pleasure because its presence, by itself, makes life worth living and its absence leaves no room for the enjoyment of any pleasure at all.

Health is one of the two kinds of pleasure of the body. The other kind floods the senses with definitely perceptible sweetness (*sensum perspicua suauitate perfundit*). There are three varieties of this kind of bodily pleasure. The first variety occurs in the restoration to their original vigor of those portions of the body which have been exhausted in the consumption of physical energy. Food and drink accomplish this task of renovation. The second arises in disencumbrance from those things, e.g., faeces or semen, with overabundance of which the body is burdened. Such is the pleasure felt in excretion, or in sexual intercourse, or in the relief of any itch by rubbing or scratching. In the first variety of sensible pleasure, one gives the body what it craves, e.g., food or drink; in the second variety, one relieves the body of what pains it. The third variety, music for example, neither satisfies a desire nor removes a pain, but nevertheless titillates and affects one's senses with a certain hidden but well-defined motion, and makes one turn one's mind to it. Included in this third variety are "those pleasures which be received by the ears, the eyes, and the nose, which nature willeth to be proper and peculiar to man," namely, the vision of the beauty of the world, the appreciation of sweet odors, and the perception of the harmony of music. All these things the Utopians eagerly pursue as "certain pleasant rejoicings of life" (*iucunda quaedam uitae con-*

dimenta), which are to serve as the spice and seasoning, not the staple of existence.[12]

The Utopian attitude toward this third variety of sensible pleasure as the seasoning of life is clear. But what do they think of the first two varieties? These latter, they maintain, are the most abject and low of all pleasures insofar as they are the least unalloyed and unmixed with pain, for they never come on the scene unless accompanied by their corresponding pains. For example, hunger is always joined to the pleasure of eating, and this in altogether unequal proportion; for just as the pain of hunger is more powerful than the pleasure of eating, so likewise it is longer lasting. The pain is born before the pleasure and does not die until the pleasure dies with it. In fact, whatever is eaten after the satisfaction of one's hunger is not pleasant but painful, as More observes later in his *Four Last Things*: "The pleasure that the glutton hath in his viand can be no longer any very pleasure than while it is joined with hunger, that is to say, with pain. For the very pleasure of eating is but the minishing of his pain in hungering. Now all that ever is eaten after, in which gluttony beginneth, is in effect pain altogether." [13]

What argument do the Utopians use against the man who thinks he is perfectly happy (*beatus*) in the enjoyment of this kind of pleasure? Even the most blind, they argue, must see and admit that a life spent in never-ending hunger, thirst, itching, eating, drinking, scratching, and rubbing is not only a foul existence but also a miserable one. Yet the man who rejoices in sensible pleasures of this type must of necessity confess that he would experience the height of bliss (*se . . . fore felicissimum*) in a manner of life which consists in perpetual hunger, thirst, itching, etc. No sane man, to be sure, would ever make such a confession. Consequently, the inordinate lover of eating and similar pleasures stands self-confuted, or, at least, silenced. In the last years of his life, More was to use the same reasoning and the same examples in his *Answer to the . . . Book . . . Named "The Supper of the Lord"* (1533): "they that gladly would endure a

grief perpetually to have the pleasure of the continued swaging
[assuaging], have in their best wealth but a displeasant pleasure,
except men be so mad as to think that he were well at ease that
might be ever ahungered and ever eating, ever athirst and ever
drinking, ever scurvy and ever scratching." [14]

Having established the place of these activities in the Utopian
hierarchy of pleasures, one may still ask what precise function
such pleasures as eating and drinking perform. This question is
answered by determining their relation to health, for the Utopians
"give the preëminence to health" (*palmam sanitati deferunt*).
The pleasures of food and drink are certainly to be sought, they
believe, but only for the sake of health. Eating and drinking "of
their own proper nature be not pleasant" (*per se iucunda*): they
are pleasurable only insofar as they resist adverse health secretly
and stealthily creeping upon a person. As has been seen above
in one of the arguments for health as pleasure, food is a militant
aid to health in the battle against sickness, and the pleasure in
eating comes from the progressive advance toward the goal,
namely, the recovery of one's former unimpaired strength. Food
is a pleasant preventive medicine insofar as it resists sickness;
it is a gentle remedial medicine insofar as it restores health to its
pristine vigor. Indeed, More was to say in the *Four Last Things*
that the only reason one does not call the food which resists the
dissolution of the body by the name of medicine is "for none other
cause but for the continual familiarity that we have therewith."
To speak the truth, "What can be . . . more properly and more
verily a medicine than is our meat and drink by which is resisted
the peril and undoubted death that else should in so few days
follow by the inward sickness of our own nature continually
consuming us within?" As a matter of fact, hunger and thirst are
called later in the *Utopia* "daily diseases" (*cotidiani morbi*),
which, of course, imply the need of daily medicine. But just as
it is wiser to avert disease than to need medicine, rather victori-
ously to forestall pain than to receive relief, so it is better rather
to lack this kind of pleasure than to be gratified by it. As More

was to write in his *Confutation of Tyndale*: "if it might be provided that every man should be so well tempered that no man should by distemperance fall into disease, then were it better that the physician bestowed all his time about that part of physic that teacheth to preserve our health than to write any work of that part that restoreth it." Food and drink are pleasant medicines that at once preserve and restore health.[15]

The Utopians, therefore, conclude that such pleasures as eating and drinking are not at all to be valued in a high degree but only to the extent required by necessity (*nisi quatenus expetit necessitas*). Even though they rate them as lowly pleasures, however, they do not despise them but, on the contrary, take delight in them. Thus, one learns that the Utopian dinner is lavish and sumptuous (*lautum atque opiparum*) and that their desserts lack no delicacies of any sort (*nec ullis caret secunda mensa bellariis*). For this presence of pleasure in food, they gratefully acknowledge the tenderness of mother nature. For, with most alluring sweetness (*blandissima suauitate*), she entices her offspring to the performance of those necessary acts which must be done repeatedly. For example, men would live in extreme and weary distaste if medicines in the form of bitter poisons and drugs had to be used to drive away the diseases of hunger and thirst which recur daily, as medicines have to be used for other sicknesses which attack men less frequently.[16]

The truth that nature has surrounded man's necessary vital functions with pleasure in order to induce him to perform them has often found expression in philosophical literature. Two classic examples which More almost certainly read are found in St. Augustine and in Ficino. In the *City of God*, St. Augustine writes that to the offices of virtue belong living for one's country and begetting children for one's country. (In Utopia, even one sect of ascetics believe that "they cannot be discharged of their bounden duties . . . towards their native country without procreation of children.") Neither of these two duties can be performed without bodily pleasure (*voluptas*), for without bodily pleasure there is no taking of food in order to live and no lying together in order to propagate offspring. The elaborate and clear analysis by Ficino in his work *Pleasure* deserves lengthy quotation, but the citation of his conclusion alone will have to suffice: "We see that they [all animate beings] are moved by pleasure [*voluptas*] only as long as they are satisfying their craving, as if nature has given pleasure [*voluptas*] of the senses for the attainment of vital necessities and for the satisfaction of vital wants. Pleasure [*voluptas*], therefore, has been given both for the sake of preserving life and for the sake of propagating the species: it must not be sought for its own sake, nor as an end in itself." The similarity of the doctrine in these selections to that in the *Utopia* is so evident as to need no comment.[17]

For the existence of pleasure in vital and necessary functions, therefore, the Utopians feel very grateful to mother nature. They appreciate, but do not overvalue, pleasures like eating and drinking which are necessary and are possessed in common with brute animals. In contradistinction to these necessary animal pleasures there exist certain pleasures of eye and ear and nose which are distinctly human and which are intended to be the seasonings of life. Nature intended such pleasures to be proper and peculiar to man, for no other species of sublunary creatures recognizes the splendor and beauty of the world, or is stimulated by the fragrance of odors (unless in order to choose the right food), or distinguishes between harmonious and dissonant intervals in sounds. The very fact that these delights are special to man and are gifts of nature indicates that they are rational and hence natural. Consequently the Utopians may pursue them to their heart's content — always, of course, as seasonings. They provide even for olfactory pleasures at their dinners: they "burn sweet gums and spices for perfumes and pleasant smells and sprinkle about sweet ointments and waters." The only precautions are the usual ones: that lesser pleasures should not be an obstacle to a greater, that no harm or pain should come of them, and that one's neighbors should not be hurt unjustly.[18]

With proper qualifications, one may say that More himself followed the practice of the Utopians, at least if the words of Erasmus in the letter to Hutten are credible. After mentioning More's simple tastes in food and drink, Erasmus adds: "In other respects he is not in the least averse to all those things which bring harmless pleasure [*voluptas*] even to the body." This statement is not at all inconsistent with the penance and mortification in More's spiritual life. He realized that licit pleasures which aided positively in the more perfect fulfillment of his duties to God and man were not proscribed but even to be recommended. But mortification for him entailed abstinence, not only from evil pleasures with a view to the observance of divine law, but also from some licit pleasures with the intention of making his lower nature perfectly obedient to his will. Penance and mortification, therefore, seemed necessary only insofar as they resulted in most careful avoidance of sin and in most intimate union with God. This subordination of means to end is well expressed in Pico's commentary on Psalm XV translated by More: "a perfect man should abstain not only from unlawful pleasures but also from lawful to the end that he may altogether wholly have his mind into heavenward and the more purely intend unto the contemplation of heavenly things." [19]

Finally, the Utopians set a high value on beauty, strength, and agility of body. These are nature's own gifts, and they are agreeable ones. With this observation the discussion of the *kinds* of bodily pleasure comes to an end. But it may not be altogether unprofitable to attempt to arrange them in the order of ascending importance. Lowest in the scale are such pleasures as eating, drinking, excretion, copulation, and scratching or rubbing an itch. Next to these are pleasures which are described as the seasonings of life; for example, looking at the beauty of the world, smelling fragrant odors, or listening to music. Higher in value are beauty, strength, and agility of body. At the summit stands health, the highest and most important of corporal pleasures: with it life is pleasant; without it life is joyless.[20]

What do the Utopians think of the man who rejects all these bodily pleasures? How do they regard the man who despises beauty of form, who wears away his strength, who converts his agility into listlessness, who exhausts his body by fasts, who injures his health, and who refuses all "the other pleasant motions of nature" (*caetera naturae blandimenta*)? The last is a blanket designation for the whole class of pleasures in which "delectation is sensibly felt and perceived." The Utopians make a careful distinction here. If the man neglects his own interests in order to look after the interests of his neighbors and his country with a view to receiving greater pleasure (*uoluptas*) from God in compensation for his pains, he acts reasonably — and all is well. But — and here the Utopians hurl a dart at the upholders of virtue as the essence of happiness — it is the height of madness (*dementissimum*) to ill-treat one's own self, without benefit accruing to any one, just in order to achieve the empty appearance of virtue, or just in order to acquire greater ease in suffering misfortunes which perhaps may never come. It is highly significant that this emphasis on madness echoes the Utopians' viewpoint given at the very beginning of the debate on virtue and pleasure: "they judge it extreme madness [*dementissimum*] . . . not only to banish the pleasure of life but also willingly to suffer grief without any hope of profit thereof, . . . if a man . . . should have no reward after his death." Such conduct is an index, not only of utter insanity, but of cruelty of soul toward one's self and of black ingratitude toward mother nature, as if one disdained to be in her debt and scorned all her gifts.[21]

This passage in *Utopia* is similar in tone to the accusation launched in Lucian's *Cynic* which was translated by More himself. (Today the *Cynic* is generally viewed as spurious.) To the querulous interrogation of the Cynic as to why he blames his manner of life and denounces it as wretched, Lucian replies: "By Jove, for this reason. Nature, whom you worship, and the gods, too, have given us this world in common and have produced many good things in order that we may have a superabundance of all things, not only with a view to our necessities, but with a view also to our pleasure. But, as for you, you fail to avail yourself of all these things or at least of the greatest part of them, and take pleasure in none of them — in fact, no more than the wild beasts." The Cynic's long answer to the effect that choice is to be made from among nature's gifts according to one's need and station appears lame to Lucian. The final lesson of the Utopians, too, is that men should respect nature as their mother and should despise or refuse none of the gifts which she has put in this world for their use — and for their enjoyment. They are very insistent, however, upon the natural. If to despise beauty is unnatural, to use artificial means to enhance it is also un-natural: "as they count and reckon very little wit to be in him that regardeth not natural beauty and comeliness, so to help the same with paintings is taken for a vain and a wanton pride, not without great infamy." [22]

With the admonition against ingratitude toward mother nature, the whole discussion of the essence and object of human happi-ness comes to an end. It opened with the statement that the Uto-pians "reason of virtue and pleasure" (*De uirtute disserunt ac uoluptate*) — above all, they reason of the relations of each to human happiness. It closes, except for a brief confirmatory epi-logue, with the words: "This is their sentence and opinion of virtue and pleasure" (*Haec est eorum de uirtute ac uoluptate sententia*). At the beginning of the discussion, Hythloday had been cautious enough to safeguard himself by saying that the Utopians seem to be more inclined than was right and fitting (*propensiores aequo*) to the espousal of the cause of pleasure. In the course of his whole exposition he keeps reminding his listeners that this is the theory of the Utopians, not his own, especially by the constant use of "they say," "they think," and similar expressions.[23]

At the close of the discourse occur even more important quali-fications and reservations, coming from both Hythloday and the Utopians. The latter themselves confess that they believe in

their theory according to the light of human reason only. It is
man's unaided and unenlightened intellect which finds in "good
and honest" pleasure the essence of man's happiness. They join
a most important proviso to their theory: it is true unless the
spirit of religion, sent down from heaven into man, should inspire him with a more holy view (*nisi sanctius aliquid inspiret
homini caelitus immissa religio*). In other words, the Utopians
believe in the possibility and in the actuality of divine revelation. Thus, of the two ascetical sects among them, they consider
those men to be the holier (*sanctiores*) who in their apparently
unreasonable refusal of matrimony and of an easy life assert
that they are being led by religion (*religione duci*). Moreover,
the same provision implies that if a revealed religion — and this
was to be verified in Christianity on its propagation in Utopia —
should establish the falsity of their opinion, they were ready and
willing to bow their heads in submission.[24]

What is Hythloday's own opinion of the philosophy of the
Utopians? Hythloday refuses to divulge his own opinion. First,
he pleads lack of time; secondly, he disclaims any need for it,
since he has undertaken to narrate their ways of life and thought,
not to defend and support them. Yet it is not difficult to surmise
what would be his true opinion. In the discussion of communism,
Hythloday had answered More's theoretical objections, not by
lengthy argumentation, but by a direct appeal to the *fact* — to
the visible evidence that no other people anywhere else is so
"well ordered" (*recte institutus*), and this state of affairs prevails
on account of communism. On the question of pleasure also,
whatever might be the theory, the *fact* remains that "there is in
no place of the world nother a more excellent people, nother a
more flourishing commonwealth." In both cases, the proverb
obtains: "The proof of the pudding is in the eating." [25]

The country of the Utopians, for example, labors from two
difficulties. The first is that the soil is not uniformly fertile; the
second, that the climate is not very healthful. Against the first
handicap they employ great industry in remedying the deficien-

cies of the soil so that among no other nations is the harvest of grain richer and the increase of cattle greater. Against the second they defend themselves with temperance in their manner of eating and living so that nowhere else in the world are the inhabitants physically more vigorous and less subject to disease. In body the Utopians, who are of medium height, are agile and active. They are of greater strength than their height indicates. They are ardent lovers of leisure. They are capable, however, of enduring heavy corporal labors, but, in pursuance of their views on pleasure, they are far from seeking toil. In fact — and this is an example of More's broadest humor — they are so little fond of work that they have moved a whole forest to a more convenient place because it is much less labor to transport grain than wood by land! In addition to these qualities, the Utopians possess friendliness, humor, and intelligence. They may not love bodily toil, but, in accordance with the high estimation they set on mental pleasure, they are indefatigable in scholarly pursuits. As an example, Hythloday relates the eager welcome extended to the language and literature of the ancient Greeks.[26]

VIII

EDUCATION AND LEARNING IN GENERAL

How do the Utopians acquire their deep contempt for false pleasures, such as the insatiable hunger for wealth which is bringing Europe to moral ruin, and their deeper love for true pleasures, such as the testimony of a clear conscience and the contemplation of truth, which could help to lead western Christendom to a new golden age? Hythloday does not hesitate to say that they form their correct ideas "partly by education . . . and partly by good literature and learning" (*partim ex educatione . . . partim ex doctrina et literis*). The distinction which he draws between education and learning is not intended to be a serious or strict one. Education here seems to apply to discipline and training, often unconscious, received at home, in church, in public, at play, and at work, almost independently of all but the most elementary schooling. Learning appears to embrace especially knowledge imparted at lectures or gathered from books.[1]

First of all, the careful education of children is responsible for the right ideas of the Utopians. Boys and girls are brought up in a nation whose fundamental principles exclude the adoration of gold and the struggle for false honors. Once implanted in children, true opinions "do remain with them all their life after and be wonders profitable for the defense and maintenance of the state of the commonwealth, which never decayeth but through vices rising of [from] evil opinions." A deplorable example of such evil opinions rampant in Europe at the time was that man is of less value and importance than gold. Plato had called education and nurture "the one great thing" (ἓν μέγα). Erasmus had concurred by stating that "the source of every virtue is a careful and pious education." Wimpheling had declared: "The reformation of the Catholic Church according to its primitive holy morals should be begun with the youth since its deformation proceeds from their improper and wretched education." How close a proper education of children lay to the heart of More himself is clear from his letter (1518?) to the tutor of his own offspring, William Gonell. It is striking how much this passage is at once a parallel and a summary of Utopian views on false and true pleasures:

Therefore, my dear Gunnell, . . . I have often begged not only you, . . . nor my wife, . . . but all my friends, to warn my children . . . not to be dazzled at the sight of gold; not to lament that they do not possess what they erroneously admire in others; not to think more of themselves for gaudy trappings, nor less for want of them; neither to deform the beauty that nature has given them by neglect, nor to try to heighten it by artifice; to put virtue in the first place, learning in the second; and in their studies to esteem most whatever may teach them piety towards God, charity to all, and Christian humility in themselves. By such means they will receive from God the reward of an innocent life, and in the assured expectation of it, will view death without horror. . . .[2]

Next to environmental influences, formal instruction and wholesome literature are responsible for the sanity of Utopian views. There are, roughly speaking, three classes of students. The first are scholars by profession, a few talented persons who are freed from all other tasks to devote themselves exclusively to study. The second are all children of school age, because literary education is universal and compulsory in Utopia (*omnes pueri literis imbuuntur*). The third constitute a good part of the whole population, both male and female, who throughout their lives devote to literature those many hours which are free from manual labor. Great crowds, one learns, voluntarily attend the morning lectures,

in addition to the scholars who must be present. This passion for
knowledge, one must remember, prevails only because it is in
complete agreement with their philosophy of pleasure. Possessed
by the conviction that pleasures of the soul are superior to
pleasures of the body and persuaded that among mental pleasures the contemplation of truth begets true delight, the people
as a whole are tireless in intellectual pursuits. Literature is the
object of love because it is the source of great pleasure.[3]

What a contrast this zeal for learning offers to the disdain for
letters which often characterized nobles and gentlemen, even
as a class, in England and in Europe! Elyot in his *Governor* (1531)
rebukes "some which without shame dare affirm that to a great
gentleman it is a notable reproach to be well learned and to be
called a great clerk [scholar]." Shortly before the publication of
the *Governor*, John Palsgrave, who was the tutor of the Duke of
Richmond, the natural son of Henry VIII, wrote to Thomas
More to complain that "our shaven folk [tonsured ecclesiastics]
would in no wise he should be learned," and that they "let [cease]
not to say that learning is a great hindrance and displeasure to
a nobleman." The alternatives to the true pleasure of knowledge
are some of the selfsame false pleasures reprobated by the Utopians: "to hear a cry at a hare, . . . to kill a buck with his bow,
sometime with greyhounds and sometime with buckhounds, . . .
to see a flight with a hawk. . . ." In his *Benefits of Learning*,
Richard Pace tells Colet an anecdote about a gentleman whom
he met at a banquet. The latter was of the number of those persons who always carry a horn suspended from their back as if
they were going to hunt even during dinner. Infuriated at the
praise of literature, he burst out: "God's body, I would rather
have my son hanged than study literature. It befits the sons of
gentlemen to blow the horn roundly, to hunt expertly, to carry
and loose a hawk beautifully. But as for literary pursuits, let
them be left to the sons of rustics."[4]

In *The Tree of Commonwealth*, Edmund Dudley urges gentlemen and noblemen to bring up their children in "virtue and cun-

ning," and then continues: "For verily, I fear me, the noblemen and gentlemen of England be the worst brought up, for the most part, of any realm of Christendom." A kindred observation on the English attitude toward learning had been made a few years before by the Italian author of *A Relation of the Island of England*: "They [Englishmen] are gifted with good understandings, and are very quick at every thing they apply their minds to; few, however, excepting the clergy, are addicted to the study of letters." But the evil or defect was not confined to England. Castiglione in his *Courtier* avers that "the Frenchmen know only the nobleness of arms, and pass for nothing beside; so that they do not only not set by letters, but they rather abhor them, . . . and they think it a great villainy when any one of them is called a clerk." Thomas Niger makes the indictment universal. In a prefatory letter to the sermon delivered by Bernard Zane (or Zanni), Archbishop of Spalato, in 1512 at the Fifth Council of the Lateran, he complains:

A fine intellect and a high station rarely are joined together. How many of the crowd of nobles busy themselves with culture [*eloquentia*]? How many of them are learned or the patrons of learning? On the contrary, you may see a good many — I am speaking of the nobles and the more wealthy — who, at the very threshold of young manhood, give and devote themselves wholly to beastly pleasures. For them the school for the liberally educated is a prison, and the instruction a punishment. They scorn studies and they hate the studious.

The term *eloquentia* used by Thomas Niger was a complex term in the Renaissance. Basically it indicated the *perfect expression* of one's ideas. In particular, it was desirable to conform to the spirit and models of classical antiquity and to reveal one's ability to apply gracefully and forcefully to present circumstances the prudence and knowledge garnered from Greek and Latin sources. Consequently it connoted not mere academic or literary proficiency but fine address and practical *savoir-faire* in all pursuits of public and private life.[5]

To what subjects do even the common people in Utopia, in utter contrast to the ignorant or obscurantist upper classes of

Europe, devote themselves? What follows in the *Utopia* about
learning is an appraisal and criticism of contemporary Scholastic
education and, at the same time, a humanistic program of reform
for studies. The former expresses itself above all in a condemnation of the dialectical sophistry and subtle disputations of the
Schoolmen; the latter, in a plea for the intensive scrutiny of the
Greek classics. The two parts of the discussion are separated
by the disquisition on pleasure. One part is devoted to the body
of sane knowledge which the Utopians have acquired by their
own efforts and which is contrasted with decadent European
scholarship, often vapid and inane. The other part deals with
the Greek authors whom the inhabitants of Utopia now read
and study.

In the section which deals with the independent discoveries of
the Utopians, Hythloday admiringly reports that, in spite of the
fact that not even the names of the philosophers best known in
Europe had been heard on the island before his coming, the
Utopians have unearthed almost the same truths as "our ancient
philosophers" (*nostri illi ueteres* [*philosophi*]). The latter are
designated also as "the ancients" (*antiqui*) and "our old philosophers" (*ueteres philosophi nostri*). Since these men are contrasted with "our new logicians" (*nuperi dialectici*), the reference must pertain to non-Scholastic figures in philosophy who
had flourished in the classical world of Greece and Rome. It is
necessary to note that in More's use here, the term *philosophers* is
synonymous with seekers after knowledge of all things through
their causes. Natural philosophy, for example, embraces what
today is called the natural sciences.

The near equality of the Utopians with the ancient philosophers is especially manifest in their attitude toward the quadrivium: arithmetic, geometry, astronomy, and music. Since the
Utopians are philosophers, Thomas More appropriately gives them
the training and knowledge of philosophers, as outlined by his
mentor Plato. In the *Republic*, Plato had assigned the reasons for
studying the four subjects just mentioned. Arithmetic is intended

"for the uses of war and for facilitating the conversion of the soul itself from the world of generation to essence and truth." Geometry is suitable for the conduct of war. In addition, insofar as it is "the knowledge of the eternally existent, . . . it will draw the soul to truth." Astronomy is "serviceable, not only to agriculture and navigation, but still more to the military art." By means of astronomical problems, men "convert to right use from uselessness that natural indwelling intelligence of the soul." Finally, music is very important in education "because more than anything else rhythm and harmony find their way to the inmost soul and take strongest hold upon it, bringing with them and imparting grace, if one is rightly trained." In the *Laws*, too, Plato had prescribed for the freeborn, besides dancing and music, "three branches of learning": arithmetic, geometry, and astronomy.[6]

Where did the European university stand at this time in regard to the quadrivium? Concentrating on the University of Paris during the years 1507 to 1522, Ricardo Villoslada discovered that the program of clerics embraced only arithmetic, which was studied in the treatises of Boethius and Sacrobosco (Holywood or Halifax). If the other three were studied, astronomy was pursued in the works of Sacrobosco, Ptolemy, and Martianus Capella; music, in the books of St. Augustine and Boethius; and geometry, in the treatises of Euclid, Nicholas of Oresme, and Albert of Saxony.[7]

In particular, the Utopians are extremely skilled in astronomy, not only on its theoretical side, but also in its practical aspects. They have invented instruments for the very exact determination of the movement and location of all the heavenly bodies. In spite of their proficiency in astronomy, the Utopians have not even dreamed of the pseudo science of the astrologers. In this respect, they are true followers of Epicurus. Diogenes Laertius reports that Epicurus "rejects the whole of divination, . . . and says, 'No means of predicting the future really exists. . .'" Cicero also observes that "nothing provokes the ridicule of Epicurus so much

as the art of prophecy." The Utopians, too, "utterly despise and
mock soothsayings and divinations of things to come by the flight
or voices of birds and all other divinations of vain superstition,
which in other countries be in great observation." But in Europe,
astrology has assumed such an ascendancy that even popes and
emperors have their official astrologers. "The latter," observes
a marginal note, "rule as kings among Christians today" (*At hii
regnant inter Christianos hodie*). This astrological domination
of Christian life had taken place in spite of the doctrine of contemporary moralists. Angelus Carletus de Clavasio in his moral
digest declares: "Astrology contributes nothing to salvation but
rather conduces to error, and therefore it ought to be eschewed
by every Christian." Alexander the Englishman in his *Destruction
of Vices* pronounces astrology the most permissible of all forms
of divination but condemns it on the authority of Isaias, Basil,
Isidore, and Augustine. It is allowable to forecast physical phenomena like snow or rain, but it is futile and impious to attempt
to foretell with certitude human action and conduct which are
dependent upon free will — even if it be conceded (against the
truth) that constellations have an effect upon, and a significance
for, free acts. In particular, Alexander forbids, on the authority
of canon law and Augustine, the observance of ill-omened days
when no work or journey might be begun.[8]

It was not by the foolish study of astrology but by intensive
observations over the years that the Utopians have developed
another science: climatology. It is characteristic of More to give
special mention to climatology, for at this very time Linacre was
translating into Latin Aristotle's *Meteorologica*, the first treatise
of which dealt with climatology, and Alexander of Aphrodisias'
commentary on the work. The interesting explanation given of
scientific advance by Bishop Fisher seems verified in an eminent
degree in the Utopians. "Marveling was the cause why that the
philosophers came to so great knowledge as they had." Looking
around the world they saw earthquakes, thunder, lightning, rain,
snow, comets, eclipses, etc. "And those marvelous wonders,"

concludes Fisher, "moved them to search for the causes of the
same, and so by diligent search and inquisition, they came to
great knowledge and cunning, which cunning men called philosophy natural." Hythloday, however, observes that, while the
Utopians may have reached independently the level of knowledge of the ancient philosophers and scientists, they have not
advanced beyond them. When it is a question of the *causes* of
stellar movements and sublunary weather, of tides and salinity of
the sea, in a word, when it is a question of the origin and the
nature of earth and sky, they partly agree with the opinions of
the classic philosophers and partly disagree with them. When
Utopian scientists produce their own theories to explain natural
phenomena, there is wholesome difference of opinion on account
of the intellectual freedom which prevails in Utopia.[9]

As far as the quadrivium and allied sciences are concerned,
therefore, the inhabitants of Utopia have reached almost (*fere,
prope*) the same degree of knowledge as the ancient Greeks and
Romans. The qualifying words *fere* and *prope* are used designedly since otherwise the Utopians could not have profited
from the study of the "great books" in Greek, the commendation
and glorification of which was precisely one of the purposes of
the *Utopia*. From the rest of the masterpiece it is clear that all
the emphasis is on Greek, "for in Latin," declares Hythloday,
"there was nothing that I thought they would greatly allow
besides historians and poets." This statement is consistent with
the character of Hythloday who, having devoted himself entirely
to the study of philosophy, "knew that there is nothing extant
in the Latin tongue that is to any purpose, saving a few of Seneca's
and Cicero's doings." If the Utopians well-nigh equal the wise
men of the ancient world in the knowledge embraced in the
quadrivium, where do they stand in respect to the trivium (grammar, logic, and rhetoric)?[10]

No special word is said about grammar and rhetoric. In logic,
however, as in the subjects of the quadrivium, the Utopians "have
found out in a manner all that our ancient philosophers have

taught" (*tamen in . . . dialectica, . . . eadem fere quāe nostri illi ueteres inuenere*). The term *dialectic* is not employed here in the sense in which it is used in Plato's *Republic*. Shorey describes Plato's dialetic as "the closely reasoned argumentative discussion of the problems of ethics, politics, social life, philosophy and religion." As such, of course, Socrates could well term dialetic "the coping-stone" of all studies. In the *Utopia*, however, dialectic is simply that part of the traditional Aristotelico-Scholastic logic which deals with the laws and modes of reasoning. Since More's comment on dialectic is important toward the understanding of his attitude toward contemporary Scholasticism, a separate chapter will be devoted to a study of the background and to an explanation of this passage which is often obscure to modern readers.[11]

IX

LOGIC IN UTOPIA

When Hythloday equates the Utopians' mastery of logic almost
with that of the ancient philosophers, he undoubtedly intends
their logic to be almost the same as that contained, above all, in
the logical treatises of Aristotle. To these might possibly be
added such works as Porphyry's *Isagoge*, which the author of
Utopia mentions more or less favorably in his letters to Dorp
(1515) and to Lee (1519).[1]

What More and Erasmus desired, like other humanists, was
the end of interminable Scholastic caviling and the use of the
logical tracts of Aristotle unencumbered by medieval commentaries and accretions. The *Letters of Obscure Men* at this very
time uncomplimentarily lays the blame on the monks, who have
written endless commentaries on the philosophical classics and
"have thus submerged them in their comments" (*commerdave-
runt*, i.e., befouled with dung). Decades before, Aeneas Silvius,
later Pius II, in his treatise *The Education of Children* warned
against imitating professors in Vienna who put an end to their
study of logic, not by reason of its usefulness, but by reason of
their personal death. Reuchlin laments that a man who after the
study of the arts and philosophy has reached the heights of
theology should fall back again to rudiments of the sophism,
syllogism, etc., just in order to have the upper hand in garrulous
arguments. In one adage, Erasmus irritably insists that many

persons can judge correctly without dialectical rules and sophistical quibbles and then exclaims: "Mortals were wise even before the god of those fools, Aristotle, was born!" In more calm and irenic moments, however, as in his early work entitled *A Plan of Study*, he declares that if anybody makes up his mind to add dialectic to the curriculum he would not be altogether opposed on two conditions: provided that he learns it from Aristotle, not from that most loquacious tribe of Scholastic sophists, and provided that he does not settle down in dialectic permanently and grow old, as Gellius says, on the rocky isles of that siren. Years later, in his *Apology against the Dialogue of James Latomus*, he laments: "Would that we were content with the dialectic of Aristotle! Yet what vast supplementary material [*auctarium*] have we added to it, and are we still adding day by day!" [2]

The views of Thomas More are similar to those of Erasmus. Just at the time of the composition of *Utopia*, More was concerned with the problem of logic. In his letter to Dorp, he hails Jacques Lefèvre d'Étaples as "the restorer of a true dialectic and a true philosophy, especially that of Aristotle." If all the scholars at Paris and Louvain would only adopt the commentaries of Lefèvre on Aristotelian dialectic, both would find that subject less quarrelsome and a little more free of abuses. (More had visited Louvain and Paris in 1508, "the year of violent and stiff-necked rectors" in the latter university.) More marvels that Dorp should have mentioned in the same breath Louvain and Paris as upholders of Aristotelian dialectic, since they are so antagonistic to each other that they even affect the names of realists or nominalists. Both profess Aristotle, yet such a controversy on his mind and meaning rages between them that one knows not to which of the two to turn. If these quarrels on nominalism and realism *do* pertain to dialectic *but not* to Aristotle, a dilemma results: either one or both teach, not merely Aristotelian logic, but another kind of logic besides. If the quarrels do *not* pertain to dialectic, it would be extremely absurd to argue for so many years in the study of dialectic about matters not at all pertaining to dialectic. More is almost led to believe that a great number of the opinions concerning which, as for altars and hearths, a fierce battle has been raging for many years, either belong little to logic or help little in mastering it. Just as a few fundamental rules in grammar suffice for the speaking and writing of Latin, so a few basic laws in logic are enough to make dialectic a useful instrument adapted to employment in other branches. It was, More insists, to this important end that Aristotle looked in his treatises on logic. Both Aristotle and Porphyry, his commentator, avoided disputed questions by which unformed minds are retarded rather than helped. In fact, Porphyry acted thus professedly. How different from the present state of affairs! [3]

These paragraphs in this letter to Dorp, often entitled "Apology for *The Praise of Folly* by Erasmus," are of great importance because they are the best possible commentary on the passage in the *Utopia* under discussion. In them one listens to the plea for the uncontaminated logic of "our old ancient clerks," namely, Aristotle, Porphyry, etc. In them, as in clauses to be cited soon, one hears objections to the complicated precepts superimposed on the original Aristotelian foundation — "all those rules of restrictions, amplifications, and suppositions, very wittily invented in the *Small Logicals*." In them one hearkens to protests against the all-absorbing controversy over realism or nominalism, which involves the use of intentions and universals — the investigation of "the second intentions" and of "man himself in common." [4]

The appeal for a return to the works of Aristotle himself, not to his medieval commentators, is but a phase in the consistent policy of the humanists: *Ad fontes! Back to the sources!* Only a few years before *Utopia*, Alexander Barclay in his *Ship of Fools* (1509) had expressed his feeling of disgust with contemporary concentration on logic and sophistry and advised application to the authentic works and genuine doctrines of Aristotle or Plato:

> Leave off such study as is unprofitable,
> Without fruit outher [or] godly discipline;
> And give your minds to sciences laudable

Where ye may your heart set and incline:
To Aristotle's or Plato's doctrine,
And not always on logic or sophistry.
I will not say but it is a thing divine
And much worth to know philosophy.

On its positive side, similar aspects of More's thought will have
to be discussed in a separate chapter on More's "great books."
On its negative side, his program calls for (1) a rejection of the
Small Logicals and (2) a laying aside of the endless controversy
over the universals. Both of these two points will be discussed
in order.[5]

The Utopians, Hythloday tells his listeners, are equal — almost
— to the classic philosophers (and therefore to Aristotle also) in
logic, but they are far from being masters of the discoveries of
recent dialecticians (*nuperi dialectici*). In a word, Aristotle himself might not be a match for students of contemporary Scholastic
dialectic. As a matter of fact, a certain dialectician, who had a
reputation for great learning, had recently told More just that!
More tells Dorp that he is giving the man's own words as "a
shining flower of eloquence." "Aristotle wrote in a most unsubtle
manner. And there are now boys who are at present so solidly
grounded in their *Small Logicals* that I certainly believe that,
if Aristotle arose from his grave and began to dispute with them,
they would thoroughly vanquish him, not only in sophistry, but
also in his own logic." It is really worth while, continues More,
to see, not only the absurdity, but also the falsity of the petty
rules for the so-called suppositions, ampliations, restrictions, and
appellations. (The reverse order appears in *Utopia*: restrictions,
amplifications, and suppositions. In the *Small Logicals*, the order
is: suppositions, relatives, ampliations, appellations, restrictions,
distributions, and exponibles.) Thomas More then gives Dorp
examples taken from the *Small Logicals* itself. Students of More
are fortunate in knowing his views on dialectical subtlety, not
only in this letter to Dorp and in *Utopia*, but also from the treatise
of Vives, *Against the Pseudo-Dialecticians*. In a letter of great

praise, addressed to Erasmus about 1520, More writes about Vives as follows:

> Just as there is no work of his [Vives] which does not marvelously please all, so what he has written against the pseudo-dialecticians has filled me in particular with a certain special pleasure. This is so not only for the reason — although for this one also — that he has ridiculed their foolish subtleties with pleasant raillery, attacked them with strong arguments, and razed and overwhelmed them from the very foundations with unanswerable reasoning, but also because I see in that work certain aspects treated with almost the same methods which I myself had once thought of before I had read anything of Vives. . . . Now I find pleasure and delight above all in what follows. I see that the same argument engaged the mind and thought of both of us and that it has been so treated by both that in some things we bring forth, not only the same matter, but also almost the same words even, although done with greater elegance and detail on his part. As a result, I freely flatter myself that something of a kindred constellation unites our souls to each other by some occult force and harmony.[6]

What is the nature of the *Small Logicals*, which, as More satirically supposes, is called so because of the little logic in it? The *Small Logicals* is Tract VII of the *Summulae Logicales* ascribed to Peter of Spain, later John XXI (1276–1277), in which the first six tracts give a terse synopsis of the logical treatises of Aristotle, Porphyry, Boethius, and Gilbert de la Porrée which were then being studied. Only the seventh and final tract contains original matter in the form of the analysis of the properties of terms: suppositions, relatives, ampliations, appellations, restrictions, distributions, and exponibles. It is called by different names: *The Properties of Terms* (*De Proprietatibus Terminorum*), *Modern Logic* (*Logica Moderna*), or *Small Logicals* (*Parva Logicalia*).[7]

What is the meaning of the three terms used in the *Utopia*: suppositions, amplifications, and restrictions? To understand them, one must first know the definitions of *signification* and *supposition*.

Signification, according to Peter of Spain, is "the representation, established by convention, of a thing by an utterance."

Significations are of two kinds: that of "a substantival thing," which is "accomplished through a substantive noun, as 'man'," and that of "an adjectival thing," which is "accomplished through an adjective, as 'white,' or through a verb, as 'running'." *Supposition* is "the acceptance of a substantive term [which is already significant] as denoting something." [8]

The complexity of suppositions to an impatient mind is evident from the great diversity of types. With an eye to the explanation of *amplification* and *restriction*, one may show the relationship in the following outline:

Suppositions

I. Discrete: "Sortes," "this man"
II. General: "man," "animal"
    A. Natural: "man"
    B. Accidental: "man runs"
        1. Simple: "man is a species"
           a. As subject: "man is a species"
           b. As predicate in an affirmative proposition: "every man is an animal"
           c. As placed after an exceptive term: "every animal, other than man, is irrational"
        2. Personal: "man runs"
           a. Determinate: "a man runs," "some man runs"
           b. Indeterminate: "every man is an animal"
               (1) Indeterminate by the exigency of the sign or mode
               (2) Indeterminate by the exigency of the thing signified
           c. Restricted
               (1) By means of an adjective
               (2) By means of a verb
               (3) By means of a participle
               (4) By means of a subordinate clause

    d. Amplified
      (1) By means of a verb
      (2) By means of a noun or a substantive verbal expression
      (3) By means of a participle
      (4) By means of an adverb
            Etc.[9]

By *restriction* is meant "the contraction of a general term from a greater supposition to a lesser supposition" ("A *white* man is running"). There are numerous subdivisions of restriction, e.g., by means of an adjective ("*white* man"), by means of a verb ("A man *is running*"), by means of a participle ("A *running* man is arguing"), and by means of a subordinate clause ("A man *who is white* is running"). A number of rules are given for each kind of restriction. By *ampliation* is meant "the extension of a general term from a lesser supposition to a greater, as when one says: 'A man can be the Anti-Christ,' the term 'man' not only denotes men who exist but also men who will exist; therefore, it is amplified to include those who will exist in the future." Amplification may be accomplished by means of a verb ("A man *can* be the Anti-Christ"), by means of a noun or a substantive verbal expression ("*That man be the Anti-Christ* is possible"), by means of a participle ("A man is *able — potens —* to be an animal"), by means of an adverb ("A man *necessarily* is an animal"), etc., etc.[10]

The *Small Logicals* became of great importance in the history of logic, philosophy, and education in Western Europe. Duns Scotus and Ockham were among those to adopt and develop its distinctions. Realists and nominalists composed commentaries on the work. The universities of Paris, Cologne, Vienna, Freiburg, Leipzig, Ingolstadt, and Tübingen used it as a text. Jean Gerson wrote that in the classes in logic the *Summulae* of Peter of Spain were taught from the start and were to be committed to memory by the new boys even if they did not understand them at once.

The treatment of "modern logic" in the *Summulae* indirectly gave
an impetus to the nominalism which was to flourish after the
thirteenth century. The supremacy of the *Small Logicals* as late
as the two decades before and the two decades after the beginning of the sixteenth century is indicated by the great number
of printed editions, often accompanied by commentaries. After
1520, however, the work was rarely reprinted. This sharp decline
is due, at least in part, to the vigorous campaign of the humanists
against it. Typically humanistic and indicative of the trend is
the satiric attack launched in the *Letters of Obscure Men* against
dialectical abuse and Scholastic obscurantism:

> An old Magister of *Leipsic*, who hath been Master for these thirty
> years, told me that when he was a lad, then did the University greatly
> prosper: those were the days when there was not a Poet within twenty
> miles. . . . it was deemed a great scandal that a student should walk
> in the street without having *Peter of Spain* or the *Parva Logicalia*
> under his arm. . . .[11]

In Utopia, where reason and common sense reign supreme,
"they have not devised one of all those rules of restrictions,
amplifications, and suppositions, very wittily invented in the
Small Logicals, which here our children in every place do learn."
Perhaps, More is not so much attacking the *Small Logicals* itself
as the refinements introduced by the commentators, among whom
are such great figures as Arnoldus de Tungris, Georgius Brunel-
lensis, Johannes Major, Petrus Tartaretus, Johannes Versor, etc.
Certainly in his controversy with Tyndale, he does not hesitate
to argue "after an Oxford fashion with *concedo consequentiam
et consequens*." In another place Tyndale had said: "I would
fain wit in what figure that syllogism is made." More replies:

> But my syllogism is this. Every Christian man refusing to hear,
> believe, and obey the Church is to be taken as a heretic and an heathen.
> But so it is that Tyndale, being a Christian man and taking upon him
> in the understanding of Scripture to control and condemn the Church,
> refuseth to hear, believe, and obey the Church. Ergo Tyndale is to be
> taken as an heathen man and an heretic.
> This syllogism is mine. And this syllogism, if Tyndale would fain

wit in what figure it is made, he shall find it in the first figure and the third mode, saving that the minor carrieth his proof with him, which would else in the same figure and the same mode have made another syllogism.

In the same work, More makes reference to the classical sophism in the schools: "Mine ass hath ears, and thou hast ears, ergo thou art my ass." In his answer to *The Supper of the Lord*, he avails himself of the Scholastic axiom: "A posse ad esse non valet illatio." [12]

Turning from his strictures on the type of argumentation exemplified by the *Small Logicals* and its commentaries, More then directs his attention and attack to the primary subject matter of the dialectic of the Schoolmen, namely, second intentions and universals.

What is meant by *second intentions*? To understand second intentions, it is necessary to realize that logic is primarily concerned with beings of reason (*entia rationis*) or intentions (*intentiones*). These beings of reason exist only in the mind. Negative beings of reason have nonexistence included in their very definition, e.g., negations and privations. Positive beings of reason either have no foundation at all in reality (pure fictions) or do have a foundation in real things. Logic studies these positive beings of reason which have a remote foundation in reality and an immediate foundation in the mind in the manner of knowing.

Intention as understood here is the form in the mind which expresses the nature of the thing known; or, in other words, it is the form conceived in the intellect as a result of apprehension, expressing the nature of the thing known. This is the *first intention*. But after it has apprehended the thing according to its nature, the intellect can reflect in a threefold manner: upon itself, upon its way of apprehension, and upon the manner in which the nature consequently exists in the intellect. Through this threefold reflection the second intention is formed. The form which the intellect conceives as a result of the last named reflection is the *second intention*.

This second intention exists only in the intellect and therefore is a being of reason. The intellect abstracts the nature or quiddity of the thing known, and therefore the nature exists in the intellect without individuating conditions and yet with a uniform likeness to all individuals of its kind. But when the intellect reflects upon the abstracted manner in which the nature exists in the intellect and then compares it to the individuals, it perceives it to be applicable to many and similar to all. The relation of similarity of the apprehended nature to many inferiors is the intention of *universality*. It is the nature perceived as predicable of many inferiors which constitutes the essence of the universal.[13]

More uses the concept of second intentions in his reply to Friar Barnes in the *Confutation of Tyndale*. Barnes had said that some might object "that I feign such a Church as our logicians do *intentionem secundam*, that is, a thing that is nowhere." More answers that Barnes himself admits that the "pure and clean Church" he demands is so far from having been proved to exist that men rightly object that "he seemeth of his own brain to feign it, as logicians feign (saith he) the second intention — which is (he saith) nowhere."[14]

The intimate connection of universals with second intentions is clearly indicated in the *Utopia*, for the Utopians are so far from being capable of making inquiries into the second intentions that not one of them could see even man in common, although he is quite colossal and larger than any giant and although Hythloday and his companions pointed him out to them with their finger.[15]

This sentence seems certainly to be a disguised echo of two passages in Erasmus' *Praise of Folly*. In one place Folly speaks of philosophers who know nothing at all, and yet profess to know everything.

They do not know themselves, nor do they see sometimes a ditch or a stone in their path, either because the majority are blear-eyed or because their minds are wandering. Nevertheless, they proclaim that they see ideas, universals, separated forms, prime matters, quiddities, and ecceities, all of which are things so unsubstantial that even Lynceus, I suppose, could not perceive them.

In his notes, which first appeared in 1515 and in which Erasmus had a hand, Lister explains that Lynceus was an Argonaut who was endowed with such piercing vision that he could penetrate the very walls with his sight. He continues: "Our sophists have far better eyes than he because they see things which are nowhere at all." [16]

In another passage, Folly asserts: "there are innumerable λεπτολεσχίαι [i.e., nonsensical controversies], even much more subtle than the one mentioned: controversies on instants, on notions, on relations, on formalities, on quiddities, on ecceities, which no one can descry with the eye, unless he is so sharp-sighted [*Lynceus*] that he sees through the most dense darkness also those things which are nowhere at all." Lister observes: "No one, I think, is so stupid as to set any value on these foolish trifles. Nevertheless it is astonishing how they dispute about nothing else than second intentions, common natures, quiddities, relations, ecceities, and countless other questions even more trifling than these trifles. And because they dream of these monstrosities, they appear subtle in their own eyes and contemn with stern eyebrows persons who spurn these questions and penetrate to the real things themselves." One of the subtle questions which Erasmus holds up to scorn in his notes on I Timothy is the following: "Can God create and sustain in existence a universal nature without corresponding individuals?" [17]

Hundreds of passages similar to these in the *Utopia* and the *Praise of Folly* occur in the writings of the Renaissance. They reveal the hatred of the humanists for abstractions which are totally foreign or only tenuously related to reality, and their love for the concrete in thought and the practical in discussion. The Middle Ages have been arraigned for developing a philosophy which was "little more than an obstinate endeavour to solve one problem — the problem of the Universals." Although Gilson remarks that this "has often been said by historians, and not with-

out good reasons," nevertheless the statement is not true in an
exclusive sense since the Schoolmen discussed and solved many
other problems, such as the relations between faith and reason;
but the fact remains that the problem of universals, which, after
all, must be faced in all philosophies, was a major one in medieval
philosophy. The problem was not limited to its logical or epistemological phases, but was extended into the fields of psychology
and metaphysics where valuable contributions were made. The
four answers proposed for the problem were exaggerated realism,
moderate realism, conceptualism, and nominalism. At first glance,
on account of the implications of pointing with the finger to the
universal as a giant, More seems to be ridiculing the exaggerated
realists who followed Plato in maintaining a concrete existence
of the universal, but the context shows evidently that he wishes
to discourage all unreasonable argument over universals, which
are only second intentions viewed under the aspect of predica-
bility to many inferiors. More apparently does not wish to deny
that universals have a foundation in reality, but, by depicting the
Utopians as very happy and yet incapable of grasping such refinements, he wishes to divert the attention of learned men to
needed reforms and urgent problems.[18]

The great lesson which More wants his readers to draw from
this part of the *Utopia* is this: sanity and salvation for Europe,
even from the natural point of view, is not to be found in the
"subtle inventions" of the Schoolmen: their restrictions, amplifications, and suppositions, and their second intentions and universals. The logic of Aristotle, as contained in his own works
and those of his classical commentators, is an instrument sufficient
to meet all the exigencies of intellectual life. The refinements and
additions made by the Schoolmen to Aristotelian dialectic in such
books as the *Small Logicals* and its commentaries are to be condemned and rejected, unless perhaps some of the points are
found to be absolutely necessary for the discussion of really vital
problems — a condition hardly likely to be verified. The questions of second intentions and universals, which were once live

issues, have degenerated into mere quibble and sterile subtlety, and yet they continue to occupy the time and mind of scholars and teachers. The really important problems upon whose reasonable solution the fate of Europe depends are being ignored. The logical course of action is similar to the attitude of the Utopians: to confess that the whole question is too abstract for practical minds and too unrelated to real life, and to turn to such really important topics as happiness, pleasure, and virtue. The paramount branch of philosophy for the troubled Europe of that day should be that part "which entreateth of manners and virtue" (*de moribus*). What is the morality of poverty and wealth, freedom and tyranny, peace and war, superstition and religion? These questions, not the problem of universals, are the proper material on which the mind should work under its own native power aided by pure Aristotelian logic and unhampered by pseudo-Aristotelian dialectical overrefinements.[19]

In an appeal entitled "To Instructors on Teaching Youth Useful Matter," James Wimpheling gives such eloquent expression to the attack on Scholastic problems and to the practical and moralistic aspect of humanism that he might be quoted at length:

Forsooth, parents and their friends do not wish their children and descendants to be trained only in the more subtle problems of dialectic and geometry, nor only in the intentions which are termed first or second. They wish them to be educated also in those studies which conduce to the salvation of souls, the honor of God, and the glory of the country. . . . Therefore, do not exert yourself, do not pass your nights, do not be alert in speculative questions alone, nor in genera, species, and other universals alone, during your whole life, from tender years to advanced age. Do not let those infamous universals deceive, ensnare, and ruin your intellect, nor your sharp mind, to this extreme: as if the Christian religion grew out of them; as if our faith leaned on them; as if the worship of God, the veneration of our Lady, and zeal for souls had their foundation in the universals; as if all right and all justice, honest laws and equitable decisions relied on them; as if the pursuit of all the arts and sciences flowed from them; nay, just as if the remedy for body and soul, the administration of all kingdoms and principalities, the happy rule of all lands, the growth of governments, the defense of states, the splendor of the clergy, the honor of the orders, the reformation of the Catholic Church, the protection of the

Roman Church, the strength of the virtues, the thunderbolt of the vices, the glory of peace, the flight from war, the concord of Christian princes, the vengeance for the shedding of Christian blood, the repulse of the Turks and enemies of our religion, the goal of human life, and the preservation of the structure of the universe from collapse, depended upon the universals, consisted in them, revolved about them.[20]

On the other hand, the conservatives felt that the humanists were substituting the study of Latin, Greek, and Hebrew for Scholastic logic, philosophy, and theology and were recommending the three languages as the panacea for contemporary ills. James Latomus (James Masson of Cambron) in a dialogue on the subject has a wise old man censure the error of those who attribute the shameful and dire straits of Christendom to the neglect of languages, like sophists making a cause out of a non-cause. It is truer to say that avarice, luxury, ambition, and strife are the rapidly growing thorns which have choked the seed of the gospel; for, "if they lived entirely according to Christ's principles, even unilingual Christians would draw the world to themselves by the fragrance of their good lives." [21]

To return to the humanistic position. Vives, as has been seen above, had given such adequate expression to the humanistic objections to contemporary dialectic that More had hailed as his very own the views embodied in the treatise *Against the Pseudo-Dialecticians*. Equally important were Vives' later animadversions in *The Causes of the Corruption of the Arts*. Vives' works had found predecessors in Valla's *Dialectical Disputations against the Aristotelians* and in Agricola's *Dialectical Invention*. And, if he had gone back to the renaissance in the twelfth century, More would have read in the *Metalogicon* of John of Salisbury and in the letters of Peter of Blois an admirable criticism of too much emphasis laid in education on dialectical ingenuity and metaphysical subtlety. John of Salisbury, at once a humanistic philosopher and a literary statesman, extols dialectic as the chief subject of the trivium, but at the same time reduces it to an essentially subordinate role as an instrument in philosophical thought and expression. He subordinates subtlety to utility: "It is not a great thing if, according to the customary behavior of our people, dialectic constantly revolves around itself, travels in a circle, examines into its own mysteries, and dwells only on those questions which are useful neither at home, nor in military science, nor in public transactions, nor in the cloister, nor at court, nor in the church, indeed, nowhere at all except in school." The practical wisdom expounded by John of Salisbury finds expression also in a letter of Peter of Blois, who was among those who "were angry with the makers of the new *Summae*" and complained of the dialectical excesses of the schools. Positively, Peter makes a plea for the classics: "It was written that 'in the ancients is wisdom' [Job xii.12]. . . . For, one does not climb from the darkness of ignorance to the light of knowledge without reading over again and again with well-disposed zeal the writings of the ancients." [22]

John of Salisbury, Peter of Blois, and other advocates of the subordination of subtlety to utility echo and re-echo, with considerable freedom of quotation, the dictum that "nothing is more hateful than subtlety where there is nothing but subtlety" (*Nichil . . . odibilius subtilitate, ubi nichil aliud est quam subtilitas*). The original by Seneca the Elder or the Rhetorican reads: *Nihil est iniquius his qui nusquam putant esse subtilitatem, nisi ubi nihil est praeter subtilitatem*. His son, Seneca the Philosopher, of course, also has some acute observations on subtlety; for example: "Let me tell you what evils are due to over-exactness, and what an enemy it is of truth" (*Audi, quantum mali faciat nimia subtilitas et quam infesta veritati sit*). One result is that, like some Schoolmen contemporary with More, "they know more about careful speaking than about careful living" (*ut diligentius loqui scirent quam vivere*).[23]

X

THE CRITICISM
OF SCHOLASTICISM

It would be difficult to find a generation of Schoolmen in which
there was no one to protest against dialectical sophistry and
needless subtlety. A century before Thomas More, the great
Jean Gerson had voiced a plea for a return to the sanity of Bonaventure, Albert, and Thomas — a plea which was indicative of
independence of mind and soundness of judgment. In a sense,
it is not too far-fetched to say that the attitude of the humanists,
too, toward the greatest figures of the thirteenth century is a
gauge of their prejudice or a measure of their zeal for true reform and not bitter revolt. The widest awake of them all draw a
distinction between the excesses of the decades which immediately preceded their own and the sane brilliance of Bonaventure
and Aquinas.

The opposite attitude — extreme but not uncommon, especially in Italy — is found expressed in a letter of Aeneas Silvius
Piccolomini (Pius II). After urging Sigismund, Duke of Austria,
to read a list of pagan classics, Christian authors, and Holy Scripture, he declares that a learned non-Italian would censure him
for not including, among the recommended authors, Hugh of St.
Victor, Alexander of Hales, Albert the Great, Peter of Blois,
Nicholas of Lyra, Alain de Lille, and "this mob of newcomers"

(*hanc nouorum turbam*). He warns Sigismund against reading the fellows, for "although they are learned, they cannot for all that teach others." The savants of all Italy concur in this judgment. "Believe me [he concludes], learn nothing which must be unlearned, but exercise yourself in the more approved authors, for we ought always to take up the best for imitation." [1]

The great revival of Scholasticism in philosophy and theology in the sixteenth century, above all in Spain, was promoted by men who profited by the more sane criticism of Scholasticism on the part of humanists, who returned to the sources in Scripture, the Fathers, and the classical philosophers, and who followed the best methods and teachings of Aquinas, Bonaventure, etc. The result was the appearance of such great names as Vitoria, Soto, and Cano among the Dominicans, and Suarez, Vasquez, and Bellarmine among the Jesuits. In addition to these men, many others made decidedly original contributions to philosophy and theology. Mention should be made of Cajetan, Lessius, and the Salmanticenses, as well as of the studies in mystical theology by St. Teresa of Avila and St. John of the Cross. Although the movement as a whole was far from being exclusively Thomistic, it received its prime impetus from the renewed study of the *Summa Theologica* of Aquinas, which gradually replaced the *Sentences* of Peter Lombard.

Where do More and his friends, who saw only the dawn of the Scholastic reform and revival, stand in regard to the Schoolmen in general and to Aquinas in particular? The determination of this point is important to the understanding of the intellectual attitude given expression in *Utopia*. Unless it is borne in mind that More's silent opponent often is the unregenerate and reactionary Schoolman of his time, the full significance of many passages will not be as evident to the reader of today as they were to More's contemporaries in 1516. The ideal, in a sense, should be not only to receive the timeless import of More's *Utopia* but also to experience or recreate its topical or "timely" impact in order to capture its complete, permanent, and universal values.

The length of the present chapter is therefore necessary to get the "feel" of the charged atmosphere in which the *Utopia* first appeared.

Colet seems to have been of dominant authority in More's circle. Johan Huizinga sums up the views of biographers in declaring that it was Colet's influence that "definitely decided the bent of Erasmus' many-sided mind." More's great admiration and respectful friendship are evident from his words to Colet in one of his earliest extant letters, dated October 23, [1504].[2]

If one is to believe Erasmus, Colet considered the Scotists, who were popularly renowned for their subtlety, to be "dull and stupid, and anything but intellectual." His reason was that "it was the sign of a poor and barren intellect . . . to be quibbling about the words and opinions of others; carping first at one thing and then at another, and analysing everything so minutely." Colet never had friendly relations with his bishop, Richard Fitzjames, "a superstitious impracticable Scotist, and thinking himself on that account something more than mortal." In his condemnation Colet appears to have embraced not only the Scotists but all the Schoolmen, even the best of them. In fact, his antipathy and hostility were almost irrational. Erasmus could understand Colet's aversion for Aquinas, for example, only by confessing his ignorance of the cause (*nescio qua de causa*). A reading of the *Catena Aurea* had made Erasmus think that at least Aquinas among the Schoolmen was not to be despised because the work gave evidence of the careful study of Scripture and of the early writers and because it possessed some emotional warmth of spirit. Erasmus describes Colet's violent reaction to the praise of Aquinas as follows:

[O]n perceiving that I was serious in what I said, he broke out, like one possessed: — "Why do you preach up that writer to me? For, without a full share of presumption, he never would have defined everything in that rash and overweening manner; and without something of a worldly spirit, he would never have so tainted the whole doctrine of Christ with his profane philosophy." [3]

From his letter to Dorp at this time (1515), it is evident that Erasmus, too, objects strenuously to the "Aristotelization" of the pure Christian truths found in the Scriptures. Later, however, in his *Apology against the Dialogue of James Latomus* (1519), he clarifies his stand on the use of philosophical principles in theology as follows: "I am not adverse to philosophy, provided the mixture is made with prudence and moderation [*sobrie moderateque*]." [4]

Based upon a complete misunderstanding of the purpose and the spirit of such works as Aquinas' *Summa Theologica*, Colet's stricture is unjust. It gives expression, nevertheless, to some major humanistic objections to contemporary Scholasticism, which was predominantly Scotistic. Among these objections are, first, the Schoolmen's pretensions to the knowledge and definition of absolutely everything, and, secondly, their adulteration of the true teaching of Christ by the philosophical notions and opinions of Aristotle. A third objection has been implied in the words of Erasmus above: the cold barren intellectuality of the Schoolmen was devoid of all human glow of the heart. A fourth reason for dislike, which is implicit in Colet's words on the Schoolmen's "presumption," "rash and overweening manner," and "worldly spirit," and which will be developed in the course of the following paragraphs, may as well be enunciated here. It was the conviction of the humanists that the study of literature and science, philosophy and theology, should make the student and the teacher better men and better Christians, admirers of virtue and lovers of piety. The corruption in private life, the indifference to public duty, and the cold formalism in religion, which the humanists professed to see everywhere, were due to exclusive preoccupation with sophistical dialectic and metaphysical subtlety. Even if the latter did not totally corrupt men, nevertheless they did not make them any better. The words of Erasmus to Jonas sum up in their simplicity the attitude of a whole movement: "I may say that, whilst I have known many of this school [i.e., Scotists] whom I should not like to call bad men, I have

yet never to this day seen one who, in my opinion at least, could
be termed a real and sincere Christian [*nullum tamen adhuc
vidi quem mea quidem sententia possis vere pureque dicere
Christianum*]." To the mind of Erasmus, the only "true theologian
is the man who, not by syllogisms craftily turned, but in affection and in his very countenance and eyes and in his very life,
teaches that riches are to be scorned, . . . that injuries must
not be revenged, . . . that death is even to be longed for by
the devout as if it were nothing else than a passage to immortality." Such a character is a "great doctor." [5]

These four charges, which are consistently hurled against the
Schoolmen and which appear in humanistic works explicitly or
implicitly, in varying form and with varying emphasis, are common to nearly all the humanists. Their views are substantially
the same. The humanists differ among themselves insofar as
some make a wholesale condemnation of the Schoolmen and the
Scholasticism of every century, whereas others make exceptions
for the sane doctrine and method of Aquinas, etc. In a word, the
humanists agree on principles, but differ in their application of
these principles. Colet, for example, is at one with Erasmus in
his contempt and hatred for contemporary Scotism; he differs
from Erasmus, who is not devoid of admiration for St. Thomas,
insofar as he classes Aquinas with the objectionable Schoolmen
and condemns him along with all the others without distinction
or reservation. Colet, as is clear, has no use for the encyclopedic
knowledge, method, and spirit of the *summae*, even the *Summa
contra Gentiles* and the *Summa Theologica* of St. Thomas
Aquinas.

As a result of Colet's criticism, however, Erasmus' esteem for
Aquinas was somewhat lessened. Nevertheless, he was apparently
unable to shake off all admiration for the achievements of the
Angelic Doctor. As late as his note in the *New Testament* (1516,
1518, etc.) to the difficult passage: "who was foreordained Son
of God by an act of power, . . . by resurrection from the dead"
(Rom.i.4), he writes of Aquinas:

It is wonderful to see what twisting and turning marks this place in Thomas Aquinas, a man, in other respects, not great in his own century only. For, in my opinion, there is not one of the Scholastic theologians who has equal industry, who has a more wholesome character, who has more solid learning. He was wholly worthy to have had the knowledge of languages and other equipment of fine literature to grace him, since he used so skilfully the advantages offered by his own period.

This compliment bears the genuine stamp of the Renaissance: "Think of what that master mind could have achieved if he only had had Greek and Hebrew!" On one occasion Erasmus had not hesitated to call the knowledge of languages "even the greatest part of erudition." This praise of Aquinas is the more unusual since it comes from Erasmus as he speaks in his own chosen field. But, like a true humanist, he still objects to Thomas' style. In the same year as the *New Testament,* he published a prefatory letter to Jerome's works in which he writes: "Jerome never sinks so low as not to be more elegant than St. Thomas, even when the latter is at his rhetorical best." [6]

Erasmus describes Pico della Mirandola as "a nature simply divine, a genius made for all things." In his work *The Dignity of Man,* Pico proclaims that he has made up his mind to swear allegiance to no single school of philosophy, even Scotistic or Thomistic, but, on the contrary, to be all-embracive and extremely eclectic. As for More, Pace wrote in 1517: "There is no sect in philosophy which he does not approve in some respects, and he most admires each according to the points in which each most excels." Yet, in the translation of Pico's life written by his nephew, More points out that "of all these new doctors [i.e., Schoolmen] he [Pico] specially commendeth Saint Thomas, as him that enforceth himself in a sure pillar of truth." [7]

Thomas More, as is well known, had early taken as the model for his own life of *pietas literata* this Earl of Mirandola who, according to Stapleton, was "renowned in the highest degree throughout the whole of Europe for his encyclopedic knowledge, and no less esteemed for his sanctity of life." There can be no

doubt that, like Pico, More entertains the deepest veneration
for the solid learning of Aquinas. When Tyndale attacks "their
Duns, their Thomas, and a thousand like draff," More keeps
silent about Duns Scotus, but rises to the defense of "that holy
doctor Saint Thomas, a man of that learning that the great excellent wits and the most cunning men that the Church of Christ
hath had since his days have esteemed and called him the very
flower of theology and a man of that true perfect faith and Christian living thereto that God hath Himself testified his holiness
by many a great miracle and made him honored here in His
Church on earth as He hath exalted him to great glory in heaven."
In his earlier work against Luther, too, More had called Aquinas
"that most learned and likewise most holy man, St. Thomas
Aquinas." [8]

The campaign of the Christian humanists was to oppose the
contaminated theology of the Schoolmen with the pure Christianity of the Scriptures and the Fathers and early Doctors of the
Church. On the other hand, if he had not always held this view,
More had reached, by the time of his controversy with Tyndale,
the unshakable conclusion that "our Doctors of these eight hundred years last passed [i.e., the Scholastics], . . . do consent
and agree with the old holy Doctors of the other seven hundred
years afore." Tyndale objects, he claims, to the great Schoolmen
of the past eight centuries only because their writings convict
him of heresy. More keeps insisting upon the identity of doctrine
existing between the works of the Schoolmen and the writings
of the early centuries of the Church. Both, therefore, brand Tyndale as a heretic who stands against the constant teaching of
Christianity as a whole. Regarding those saints of the past eight
hundred years "whose faithful holy writings condemn his faith-
less heresy," More asserts that "every good man I dare say will
think them full unmeetly to be mocked and jested upon by such
a foolish fellow as this [Tyndale] is, which, while he setteth so
little by Saint Thomas, Saint Bonaventure, Saint Bernard, Saint
Anselm, and all such other men who have written in the Church

this eight hundred year, he seeth yet well enough that the reason which he mocketh was made by the holy Doctor Saint Austin four or five hundred year before that." (It may be significant that More again fails to approve Scotus by name.) A fundamental charge of Tyndale had been that the works of the Schoolmen, including Scotus and Aquinas, served as a kind of Talmud to falsify the Scriptures. More argues that just as the Talmud could be exposed by comparison with preëxisting expositors, so the medieval Schoolmen, if their teaching were false, could be unmasked by comparison with the early Doctors and Fathers of the Church. Strangely enough, Edward Lee had given a similar answer to Erasmus years before. When Erasmus in a note to Luke vi had said that Christ's eight beatitudes and not the subtleties of the Scotists or Ockhamists made true Christians, Lee claimed that there was no call for such a remark then and there. Lee's only desire was to defend their doctrine against the calumny that it was ungodly and opposed to Christ's doctrine. On the contrary, it was conducive to piety and in no way divergent from the institutes of the Christian faith nor from the doctrines of the old Fathers and Doctors of the Church.[9]

A good example of More's opinion and use of the Scholastic doctrine appears in his answer to Tyndale's treatise on the Blessed Sacrament. He maintains that the essential thing to do is to believe what the Church obliges one to believe, namely, the real presence of Christ as a revealed truth. The Church leaves one free to hold *how* Christ is present. Belief of the *fact* is obligatory: explanation of the *manner* is free. This quotation serves also to furnish a specimen of what the humanists termed a subtle, and hence useless, theological question. Each of the alternatives had defenders.

[A]s for the manner how the blessed body of Christ is in the Blessed Sacrament, whether with His dimensions as long, thick, and broad as He hanged on the cross; or with His dimensions proportionable to the form of bread as His blessed body was verily His body at the first moment of His holy conception as it ever was at His passion and yet was it then neither so thick, so long, nor so broad; or whether His body be there in His natural substance without any dimensions at all; or whether He be there in all His distinctions of the members of His holy body or there have His members without any distinction of place at all — these things and such other, in which learned men may moderately and reverently dispute and exercise their wit and learning, the Catholic Church in such wise leaveth at large that it bindeth not the people to any such straits in the matter but only to the points that we be bounden by certain and sure revelation to believe, that is to wit, that under what manner soever it be there, verily there it is: His very flesh and His very blood.

Against the cry of Tyndale that "the pope and . . . all the clergy . . . meddle philosophy with the things of God," Thomas More replies that this "is a thing that may in place be very well done, sith the wisdom of philosophy, all that we find true therein, is the wisdom given of God and may well do service to His other gifts of wisdom than that is." [10]

The attitude of St. John Fisher is similar to that of More. In his *Defense of the King's Assertion*, he objects to Luther's opprobrious attack on St. Thomas Aquinas whom men of outstanding learning and erudition have always venerated as the "Flower of Theology" (*Theologiae Flos*). Christians ought to believe St. Thomas, and other pious and learned men like Peter Lombard and Nicholas of Lyra, rather than Martin Luther. Again, in his *Confutation of Luther's Assertion*, he protests against Luther's depreciation of Aquinas whom most biblical scholars have usually called the Flower of Theology. The pope, of course, has not approved his entire doctrine to such an extent that all must believe each and every point in his writings. Neither has the Church ever endorsed the teachings of Augustine or Jerome or any other author without allowing disagreement with them on some issue or other. "Tell me," Fisher challenges Luther, "who has ever become a heretic from reading Thomas or who has lifted an heretical error from Augustine alone?" The fault lies not in Thomas or Augustine, but in the perverse mind and will of the heretic. If a man progresses in the study of theology without the aid of Augustine or Thomas, Fisher has no doubt that he will reach the same conclusions in regard to the substantial tenets of the faith as those held by Augustine and Thomas. If he disagrees with the latter two on points of faith, he should know that he has not drunk the Holy Spirit because He is the Author of unity and concord, not of schism and discord.[11]

The clearest exposition of Fisher's stand on Scholasticism occurs in his work against Oecolampadius entitled *The Reality of Christ's Body and Blood in the Eucharist*. Fisher wishes to show that the Schoolmen were not deficient in their study and exposition of Holy Scripture. To this end, he mentions only the "Princes" of the Schoolmen, praising each of them by means of a succinct and revealing characterization. His list is full and almost surprising: Alexander of Hales, Bonaventure, Albert the Great, Thomas Aquinas, William of Paris, William of Ware, Giles of Rome, Henry of Ghent, Richard of Middleton, Duns Scotus, François de Meyronnes (Franciscus Maronis), William of Ockham, Durandus, Pierre de la Palu, John of Baconthorpe, and Gregory of Rimini. "Even though they be wanting in style," Fisher declares, "they are not wanting in learning." Cicero himself does not expect style from philosophers. Knowledge of truth is distinct from elegance of expression and can be a separate gift. Fisher would not deny that a philosopher is better off if he has both, and especially if he possesses piety as well. "The man who lacks piety," he continues, "even if he has knowledge of all truth and can also express it with Ciceronian eloquence, is not worth a pin in Christ's eyes." Consequently, it is better to be lacking in elegance of expression than in knowledge of truth or holiness of life. Since the Schoolmen mentioned above were not wanting in zeal for holiness nor knowledge of truth, Christians ought not to reject their authority altogether. After all, even Paul did not preach salvation with "wisdom of words" (I Cor. i.17).[12]

In another section in the same work, Fisher admits to Oecolampadius that the Schoolmen were lacking in style but not in skill in the Scriptures. Even those who are considered masters of style, such as Erasmus who is certainly "a man of admirable judgment," have lauded Thomas Aquinas for his knowledge of the Bible. Pico della Mirandola, too, has words of praise, not only for the Flower of Theology, but for Duns Scotus, Giles of Rome, François de Meyronnes, Albert the Great, and Henry of Ghent. It is only on account of his pride of intellect that Oecolampadius makes them of less than no importance.[13]

It is in *The Reality of Christ's Body and Blood in the Eucharist* that Fisher defends the necessity of exercise in the Scholastic method for theologians. An ordinary theologian may be expert in the three languages (Latin, Greek, and Hebrew), but, unless he has been practised in the Scholastic method, he will set forth his opinion and that will be the end of it. He will be incapable of establishing his opinions and of combating the errors of others. The chronicles prove that few heresies have arisen since the coming of Scholasticism, whereas before they used always to plague the Church. Fisher admits that certain heresies have arisen afterwards, but by the assistance of the man who in the great pride of his heart contemned the Schools, namely, Wyclif.[14]

The attitude of More and Fisher toward the learning of the Schoolmen was shared by the more sane and the more constructive intellects among the humanists. Wimpheling, who defended the theology of the Schoolmen against the attacks of Locher (the Latin translator of Brant's *Narrenschiff*), was afraid that Erasmus might think that he was criticizing adversely *The Praise of Folly*. Consequently, he wrote to Erasmus in 1511:

Although I consider that the noble philosophy and subtle logic of Aristotle, as well as his metaphysics and modern theologians [i.e., the Schoolmen], are not altogether useless to younger men of still active intellect for the exercise of mental sharpness and for the refutation of heresies, yet I cannot approve a course of action in which they become involved and entangled, even to the moment of death, in those studies alone to the consequent neglect of the teaching of Christ and Paul and the four luminaries of the Church.[15]

This concise statement summarizes also the views of Erasmus. The latter insists upon such purity of doctrine as is to be found in the New Testament, the Fathers of the Church, and the Doctors of the Church. At the same time he expects the purity of doctrine to be reflected and expressed in the purity of one's personal life. In a long note to I Timothy i.6 on "vain babbling" or "vain speculations" he gives his opinion of the Schoolmen, including a long list of uselessly subtle questions, and then concludes:

The purpose of all I have said is not to persuade the condemnation of the dialectic and philosophy which are taught in the schools; my disapproval rests on the excessive concentration on frivolous subjects. And those who blow in our faces the smoke of Cabalistic and Talmudical studies are no less to blame. . . . "Time is getting short," says Paul, and this is a question of serious business. Why does this loss and waste please us? Let only the best be taught, and that only insofar as it seems profitable. Let superfluous subjects be cut off. . . . Yea rather, let us be occupied with the things by which we may be transformed into Christ.[16]

Christ appears in Christians, not if they engage in thorny disputes over instants, relations, quiddities, and formalities, but if they hold what Christ taught and do what He did. Erasmus maintains that he has no intention of condemning the zeal of those who, not unlaudably, exercise their powers of intellect in subtleties of this kind; but he is convinced that the gospels and epistles are the best sources for the true and undefiled philosophy of Christ. If anyone devoutly philosophizes on these books, with prayer and not with argument, with desire for transformation and not with plans for future dialectical battles, he will discover therein the proposal, discussion, and solution of every problem which pertains to human happiness and the conduct of the present life. If this is true, the subtleties of the Schoolmen are unnecessary. "Where in the Scriptures do you find a statement of Aristotle or Averroës? where any mention of first and second intentions? where any mention of ampliations and restrictions? where any mention of formalities or quiddities or even ecceities, with which everything is now crammed full?" Yet Erasmus keeps insisting that he does not want Scholastic philosophy and theology to be driven out, but that he desires such studies to be accompanied by others and to be treated in a reasonable and moderate fashion (*sobrie casteque*). "It is enough for me," he writes to Nicholas Beraldus, "if theology be handled more soberly [*magis sobrie*] than heretofore, and if what hitherto the majority of us used to draw from pools not altogether unpolluted, be now sought at the gospel sources." [17]

Erasmus' personal remarks, annotations, and scholia in his edition of Jerome's epistles (1516) are pointed and trenchant. At the end of Jerome's catalogue of ecclesiastical writers, for example, he tells his reader that these great authors have been succeeded by that sordid "tribe of commentators on the *Sentences*, compilers of summaries, gatherers of nosegays, and makers of mirrors" (*genus sententiariorum, summulariorum, fasciculariorum, speculariorum*), and other epitomists, the very remembrance of whom nauseates well-born and well-bred temperaments. This sad situation ought to stimulate all devotees of great writers to read what remains the more avidly according as the destroyer time has caused less to survive. If Jerome objects to the faulty style of Ruffinus, which seems even eloquent to many, and complains loudly that he has worked harder at understanding him than at answering him, what would he do if he had to deal with the Ockhamists, or Scotists, or those like them? It is the Fathers like Jerome who have the true theology, which is far more conducive to Christian learning and piety of life than the theology which now is everywhere offered in the universities. The latter is so crammed with Aristotelian principles, sophistical trifles, and inane little questions that, if Jerome or even the apostle Paul returned from the grave, he would seem to know no theology at all. Erasmus has no doubt that Jerome would have thundered unreservedly against this type of theology which is contaminated, or rather ruined, by Aristotelian axioms and laws. "Jerome does not absolutely disapprove of the knowledge of these things," Erasmus continues, "provided it is moderate, but he condemns those who attribute more than warranted to pagan sciences and almost place their principles on a par with Christ's principles." Jerome traces all heresies to the writings of the philosophers and declares that the purity of Christian wisdom is defiled, not aided, by their teachings. Erasmus asks:

But why is not Jerome summoned to the bar by certain infamous theologians who think that nothing in God's Scripture can be understood unless you consume a good part of your life on Aristotle — who think that it is an unspeakable shame to deliver a sermon about Christ before the people unless you know Aristotle's *Physics* and *Metaphysics* to the letter? They think everything unscholarly unless you intrude the philosopher Aristotle a hundred times. They think that the Christian religion is done for, if a person rejects the principles of Aristotle. . . . I do not say these things in order to impugn the study of Aristotelian philosophy or any study at all, provided it springs from true culture, but I do not wish to have the defense of the sacred doctrine of Christ lie in the profane doctrine of pagans.[18]

Even on a philosophical basis, Erasmus might have argued against narrow Scholastics from the nature of a philosopher, as defined, for example, by Valla, who had exerted a powerful influence on his life. According to Valla, Pythagoras termed himself a lover of wisdom (*philosophus*), not a wise man (*sophos*), and after him no one called himself a wise man. Philosophers had always possessed the liberty of expressing strongly what they thought, not only against the leaders of other schools, but even against the leader of their own. This was even truer of persons who had joined no particular school. How intolerable, then, are those recent Peripatetics who forbid even the follower of no school the liberty of disagreeing with Aristotle, as if the latter were a wise man (*sophos*), and not a philosopher (*philosophus*).[19]

To return to the most serious charge of Erasmus and other humanists against the Schoolmen. In his dialogue on the three languages, the conservative James Latomus summarizes the charge as the Schoolmen's contamination and leavening of theology with Aristotelian philosophy. A wise old man declares that one must read the Schoolmen selectively just as one should the older writers. If Thomas and Scotus are disagreeable because they appear too Aristotelian, Bonaventure should be more acceptable because he grants less to Aristotle. If Bonaventure is still too Peripatetic, the following Schoolmen are less and less Aristotelian in descending order: Altisiodoreus (= William of Auxerre), William of Paris, and Armachanus (= Richard Fitz-Ralph). Talented young men should imitate Pico della Mirandola who testifies that he had devoted six whole years or more to the study of Thomas, Scotus, and Albert alone. A man of divine genius, he would not have done so unless he rated them as good authors. Nothing offended by their humble and Scholastic style, he sought in them truth and not verbal ornaments, and he actually did find in them solid truth with which to feed his mind. When an interlocutor asks what caused the Scholastics to mix Aristotle and his metaphysics and natural philosophy with theology, the reason given is that many students flocked to theology insufficiently instructed in philosophy just as today professors are forced to treat grammar and philology in lectures on Holy Scripture.[20]

In his *Paraclesis*, Erasmus has a carefully worded statement to the effect that he is minimizing Scotus, Thomas, etc., only in relation to Christ and His Scriptures. Elsewhere he concedes that truth comes from the Scholastic disputations as fire from flint, but demands measure and selection (*modus ac delectus*). The many things worthy of knowledge in the Schoolmen are to be tasted with moderation (*modice*) and to be treated in a temperate and restrained manner (*sobrie casteque*). Toward the end of his life, Erasmus answered the attack of certain Spanish monks as follows: "Against sophistical theology and useless questions I frequently say something which is most worthy of being heeded. Nowhere do I condemn Scholastic theology, but frequently approve of it. Let my books be my witness." [21]

The judgment of the great theologian Vitoria upon Erasmus is well worth noting. When Erasmus' books were under examination at Valladolid in 1527, Vitoria wrote: "It seems to me that Erasmus approves the true and Catholic sense but does not sufficiently reprove the opposite and foreign sense" (*mihi videri Erasmum verum et catholicum sensum probare, sed non satis alium et alienum improbare*). Vitoria supports Erasmus' rejection of certain curious and useless Scholastic questions, but he adds that, if Erasmus wishes to condemn the controversies by which the holy Fathers safeguarded the unity of essence with trinity of persons against the heretics, his opinion is scandalous and injurious to the Fathers and the Church. "Indeed," he concludes, "I should not like to think this about Erasmus who is a Catholic but certainly it cannot be denied that he has given much occasion to his readers for thinking so." [22]

At any rate, Erasmus' emphasis upon moderation and tolerance in disputation and study is worthy of the wisdom of Utopus, who, in a far more serious matter, declared it "lawful for every man to favor and follow what religion he would, and that he might do the best he could to bring other to his opinion so that he did it peaceably, gently, quietly, and soberly, without hasty and contentious rebuking and inveighing against other" (*placide ac modeste, . . . non . . . acerbe*).[23]

A primary objective of the humanists, as was stated early in this chapter, was to mend the divorce between head and heart, intellect and emotions. The result of the preoccupation with dialectic, or rather sophistry, in the schools was to equip the student with invincibility in dispute, but "in the discussion of divine literature and in the delivery of sacred orations, O immortal God, how spiritless, how cold, nay more, how lifeless we see them! Yet the principal function of Scripture and sermons is to inflame the heart." The profession of theology should consist rather of affection than of subtleties; the latter are derided by pagans in their own pagan philosophers and are execrated by Paul in Christians. Hence, in the colloquy entitled "The Religious Banquet," Eusebius declares: ". . . I had rather lose Scotus, and twenty more such as he, than one Cicero or Plutarch. Not that I am wholly against them neither, but because, by the reading of the one I find myself become better; whereas I rise from the other I know not how coldly affected to virtue, but most violently inclined to cavil and contention. . . ." In his *Benefits* of *Learning*, Richard Pace makes a similar observation. The fruit of the study of philosophy should be the maintenance of integrity, the shunning of infamy, the flight from vice, and the pursuit of virtue. For reading, one should select the best, e.g., Paul, Jerome, Augustine, Gregory, Ambrose, and similar men, and eschew Scotus and his followers, who apparently have more verbose subtlety than true and salutary doctrine.[24]

This, therefore, is most definitely an important part of education and philosophy: that a man rise from his study, not a better disputant, but a better man in private and in public. And the fact that the ancient classics, especially the Greek, perform this function and produce this result is one of the primary reasons for their recommendation, perusal, and study.

It might be for good reasons, therefore, that Hythloday's Christian name is *Raphael*, which is interpreted as "the healing of God," or "God hath healed," or, as Warham says in a letter to Erasmus, "the physician of health" (*salutis medicus*). By his description of Utopia, Raphael Hythloday is to bring health and salvation to Christian Europe and to free it from the demon of Scholastic subtlety (cf. Tobias xii.14). This achievement was to be accomplished by proper education and learning.[25]

XI

INTELLECTUAL SALVATION

Hythloday's exposition of learning and education in Utopia,
as has been pointed out in Chapter VIII, is divided into three
parts. The first directly outlines the branches of knowledge
developed independently of European influence and indirectly
deplores the preoccupation of scholars in Europe with sophistical
logic and with abstruse and subtle questions. The second section
constitutes a long digression on pleasure and happiness which is
given as a specimen of the earnest and practical discussion of
ethical problems by the Utopians. The third part describes the
eager welcome given to Greek by the Utopians. Here More
offers a remedy for the intolerable intellectual situation in Europe: an intensive and extensive study of the Greek language and
literature. The seven liberal arts are to be retained by Europeans
just as they are among the Utopians; even much-abused logic is
not to be excluded, but to be reduced to its true role as instrument, not as end. But the most choice treasures of the human
intellect and heart, in their most pure and original Greek sources,
are to be studied, first, as supplements and developments of the
knowledge already possessed, and, secondly, as independent
and invaluable contributions to human life and culture.[1]

The success of the program depends upon the attitude of the
Europeans. At the time of the composition and publication of
Utopia, the attitude of some Schoolmen was one of extreme con-

servatism and extreme dislike, if not hatred, of innovation and
progress. Their last retort was like that of the king's councilors
described by Hythloday: " 'These things . . . pleased our forefathers and ancestors: would God we could be so wise as they
were' . . . [as if] it were a very dangerous matter if a man in any
point should be found wiser than his forefathers were." Nevertheless, as Hythloday caustically observes, such men will have
nothing to do with the wisest principles of their progenitors,
but they will hold tenaciously to less prudent ancestral ordina-
tions. The Utopians, on the other hand, are glad to hear of what
is going on in all other countries. Hence they welcome with open
arms any stranger who is blessed with native intelligence or any
traveler who is gifted with the knowledge of many lands. Of
this Utopian trait Hythloday offers an amazing instance. Twelve
hundred years before his arrival, a number of Romans and Egyp-
tians had been shipwrecked on the coast of Utopia. The Utopians
either learned from these people all the arts and crafts of the
Roman empire which were of any use or developed them from
the hints and suggestions which they received. Another example
of the latter gift would be the perfecting of the crafts of paper-
making and printing merely from the meager information imparted by Hythloday and his fellows. If any Utopian by similar
misfortune had reached Europe, his presence had been buried
in utter oblivion, just as that of Hythloday would be. What a
difference between Utopians and Europeans! At a single en-
counter the former had made their own the best institutions of
Europe; yet, as Hythloday sighs, "it would be long before we
would receive anything that among them is better instituted
than among us." This superb open-mindedness and extreme
willingness to profit by the experience of others, to accept the
best in human discoveries, and to welcome progressive innovations, is "the chief cause why their commonwealths be wiselier
governed and do flourish in more wealth than ours." [2]

Ingrained conservatism and hatred of change on the part of
many at this time in Europe is marked especially in education and

scholarship. In his letter to a monk, printed in 1520, More answers at some length the obscurantist monk's argument borrowed from Scripture: "The old is better" (*Vetus melius est*; Luke v. 39). In the preface to his notes to the New Testament, Erasmus makes the observation that, as the result of typical human behavior, novelty, if displeasing in all things, is offensive particularly in studies. In arguing for application to languages for the purpose of acquiring knowledge at its very sources in Latin, Greek, and Hebrew, he contends that, if it is only the novelty that is obnoxious, one must remember that the old (i.e., Scholasticism) was once new and the new (i.e., humanism) was once old. One late passage from his *Adages* is so significant that it merits quotation in spite of its length:

They call new the things which are very old, and they call old the things which are new. In the ancient doctors of the Church the knowledge of the sacred books was joined to skill in languages and humanistic literature. We see the same in the ancient philosophers, physicians, and lawyers. Where are Aristotle or Hippocrates guilty of solecisms? Are Plato and Galen not full of eloquence? . . . It is new, for boys being taught grammar, to be forced to learn the modes of signification and to be lectured on insane glosses which teach nothing else than faulty language. It is new to admit to the study of philosophy, law, medicine, or theology a youth who, on account of ignorance of the language, understands nothing in the old authors. It is new to bar from the doors of theology all except the fellow who has perspired long over Averroës and Aristotle. It is new to inculcate in the young students of philosophy sophistical trifles and certain trumped-up difficulties, mere racks for the intellect. It is new in the universities to give different answers according to the system of Thomists and Scotists, of nominalists and realists. It is new to exclude from discussion arguments taken from the sources in the sacred books and to accept only those drawn from Aristotle, from decretal letters, from the teachings of the Scholastics, from the glosses of professors of canon law or generally chilling parallels from civil law. If we find new things offensive, these are the things that are really new.

In the same adage, Erasmus parodies the secret instruction of the enemy of humanism to his young charges: "Beware of the Greeks, lest you become a heretic; fly from Hebrew literature, lest you become like to the Jews; throw away Cicero, lest you

be damned with him." Budé, too, in his *Study of Literature*
laments the recent rise of a few theologians who have been
preaching with popular success that skill in Greek, which is
really "the mistress and restorer of all fine literature," is the
originator and defender of evil opinions.[3]

In no English literary work of the time is the conflict between
the new Greek learning and the old Latin Scholasticism more
clearly depicted than in Skelton's *Speak, Parrot*, a poem written
a very few years after *Utopia*. In spite of their length, the important pertinent passages must be quoted to show the conservatism of even a writer not wholly averse to Greek:

> Let Parrot, I pray you, have liberty to prate
>   For *aurea lingua Graeca* ought to be magnified . . .
> . . . .
> *In Academia* Parrot dare no problem keep,
>   For *Graece fari* so occupieth the chair
> That *Latinum fari* may fall to rest and sleep,
>   And *syllogisari* was drownéd at Stourbridge Fair;
>   Trivials and quatrivials so sore now they impair
> That Parrot the popinjay hath pity to behold
> How the rest of good learning is roufled up and trold.

After describing how the old Scholastic textbooks, including
"Albertus de modo significandi," have been driven from the
schools, Skelton continues:

> Plautus in his comedies a child shall now rehearse,
>   And meddle with Quintilian in his *Declamations*,
> That Petty Caton can scantly construe a verse,
>   With *Aveto in Graeco*, and such solemn salutations,
>   Can scantly the tenses of his conjugations:
> Setting their minds so much on eloquence
> That of their school matters lost is the whole senténce.[4]

It is well to remember that the languages and the classics
never lacked champions, whether few or many in number,
whether unreserved or cautious in their approval. Antoninus,
Archbishop of Florence (1446–1459), for example, maintained
the usefulness and propriety of the knowledge of various languages, especially Greek and Hebrew, on the part of the the-

ologians with a view to the conversion of infidels and the fuller understanding of Sacred Scripture. In a letter to the students at the College of Navarre, Jean Gerson (1362–*ca.* 1428) extolled the advantages to be gained from the study of the Doctors, such as Augustine and Jerome, but by no means disapproved of a cursory perusal of pagan writings for good reasons: the abundance of moral sentiments, the style and distinction of language, the human experience in poetical and historical works, and finally a certain delight in the variety of reading.[5]

In contrast with such figures, Colet in his exposition of the First Epistle to the Corinthians lays such emphasis upon the Scriptures and upon Christian writers that in the writings of the ancient pagans he finds "nothing that savours of Christ, nothing that does not savour of the Devil":

If we seek to feed on the wisdom of the heathens, which is devilish, not Christian, we lose the principles of our Lord. For no one takes food at their tables, that is, their books, unless either doubting or despising the Scriptures. . .

It is unreasonable to plead that pagan authors help in the interpretation of the Bible since thereby one reveals one's patent lack of confidence in understanding Holy Writ "by grace alone, and prayer, and by the help of Christ, and of faith."

Those books alone ought to be read, in which there is a salutary flavour of Christ; in which Christ is set forth for us to feast upon. Those books in which Christ is not found, are but a table of devils. Do not become readers of philosophers, companions of devils.

In accordance with his own admonitions and principles, the *Statutes of St. Paul's School* declares: "I would that they were taught always in good literature both Latin and Greek and good authors such as have the very Roman eloquence joined with wisdom, specially Christian authors that wrote their wisdom with clean and chaste Latin." Accordingly, Colet prescribes the study of Mantuan and Erasmus (represented by his *Copia* and *Institutum Hominis Christiani*) among the moderns, and Lactantius, Prudentius, Proba, Sedulius, Juvencus, etc., among the ancients. These are the only authors assigned by name in the statutes. The Latin style to be taught, of course, must be that used by masters like Cicero, Sallust, Vergil, and Terence, and practiced by Jerome, Augustine, Ambrose, and other Doctors.[6]

Lupton tries to explain Colet's attitude toward heathen authors as a reaction against the excesses of the Italian Renaissance. This rationalization is hardly necessary in view of Colet's extremely high standards of Christian ethics and perfection and in view of what he could easily find objectionable, on the score of danger to faith and morals, in the classics themselves. He evidently was a man who wanted all truth, not half-truths, and all morality, not half-morality, in reading and study. *Malum ex quocumque defectu* seems to have been a principle of thought and action with the Dean of St. Paul's. In a word, if he found anything which had the least defect or the least lack of the perfection necessary to it, he felt that it was bad and hence to be eschewed.[7]

What would be the answer of More to these strictures of his friend and guide? The former's response, in substance not tone, would be similar to that given in his epistle to the University of Oxford in answer to the obnoxious Lenten preacher who had "babbled, not only against Greek literature and Latin belles-lettres, but exceedingly liberally against all the liberal arts." Not even the most ardent humanist would dare to affirm that a man could not be saved without knowledge of letters, profane letters included. But learning, even so-called secular learning, prepares the soul for virtue. This is its major role. However matters may stand, no one can doubt that letters are almost the one and only reason for the large attendance at Oxford, since any good woman herself could, not in the worst possible manner, teach her children a kind of unrefined and unlettered virtue.[8]

On this point there is complete agreement between Erasmus and More. In the *Enchiridion* the former had written: "You must think that whatever truth you hit upon anywhere at all belongs to Christ." The Christian soldier is to pick out all the best portions from the books of the pagans. Following the example of the tiny bee, he is to fly around all the little gardens of the ancients, by-passing the poisons and extracting only the healthful and excellent juice. The use of the arms furnished by the pagans is by no means to be contemned by the soldier of Christ. The same conviction later finds eloquent expression in the colloquy entitled "The Religious Banquet" when Eusebius pleads:

Whatever is pious, and conduces to good manners, ought not to be called profane. The first place must indeed be given to the authority of the Scriptures; but nevertheless, I sometimes find some things said or written by the ancients, nay, even by the heathens, nay, by the poets themselves, so chastely, so holily, and so divinely, that I cannot persuade myself but that when they wrote them, they were divinely inspired; and perhaps the spirit of Christ diffuses itself farther than we imagine; and that there are more saints than we have in our catalogue.[9]

Even to Colet's admonition against association with pagan philosophers, Erasmus would answer, as he answered Luther later, that Christians possess in common with pagan philosophers many truths, such as the freedom of the will, the creation of the world (Plato), the immortality of the soul (Plato), the sanctity of marriage (Aristotle), and numberless others. Far from impairing the authority of Christian dogmas, the fact that their light of reason saw some things which God's Scriptures give to Christians, rather strengthens it. "But we do not believe the philosophers unless they agree with Scripture." Nevertheless, in spite of the many truths shared by pagan antiquity and Christianity, Erasmus most probably agrees with Bulephorus and Hypologus in his *Dialogue on Cicero* that, far from any pagan philosopher being so gravely learned as to be preferred to any Christian, "the whole of Greek philosophy is but a foolish dream and a futile trifle in comparison with the philosophy of Christ." In the same dialogue, such excesses of the Renaissance as the application of pagan titles to God, Christ, the Incarnation, etc., are severely criticized. Bulephorus tells Nosoponus the Ciceronian: "It is paganism, believe me, Nosoponus, it is paganism which is persuading our ears and hearts to do such things. We

are Christians in name only. Our body has been bathed with the
holy water of baptism, but our mind is unwashed; our forehead
has been signed with the cross, but our heart abominates the
cross; we confess Jesus with our tongue, but we bear the high
and mighty Jupiter and Romulus in our heart." [10]

On this very score Erasmus has serious objections to the union
of Aristotelian philosophy and Christian theology. "We have
reached such a point that the whole of Aristotle is accepted in
the heart of theology, in fact, accepted to such an extent that his
authority is almost more sacred than that of Christ. For, if he
says anything that is little in keeping with our Christian life,
it is permissible to distort it by a clever interpretation; but the
man who dares even slightly oppose his oracular utterances, is
downed on the spot. From Aristotle we have learned that the
happiness of man is imperfect without the addition of the goods
of body and fortune. From Aristotle we have learned that the
commonwealth in which all things are common cannot flourish." [11]

The Utopians, in contrast with the Christians, are not placed
face to face with the task of the reconciliation of a heathen literature with a Christian morality and revelation. Not only the problem of the pagan classics, but also the problem of the study of
Greek even for Christian philosophy and theology, was very
acute at the time of the composition and publication of the
Utopia. It engaged much of More's attention, and it would be
surprising if a matter so close to his heart had not found expression, even in a disguised form, in his truly golden little work
(*libellus uere aureus*). Two important letters reveal More's mind
at this period. The first, dated October 21, [1515], is addressed
to Martin Dorp, president of the College of the Holy Spirit at
Louvain, and is headed in More's *Lucubrationes* (1563): "An
apology for Erasmus' *Praise of Folly*, in which is also taught how
necessary is the knowledge of the Greek language." One of the
principal points of this letter is the necessity of the study of
Greek for the understanding of both the Holy Scriptures and
theological questions. The second letter, bearing the date March

29, [1518], and addressed to the University of Oxford, undertakes the protection of the humanities against a virulent attack
of a university Lenten preacher and the defense of Greek against
the self-styled Trojans, the opponents of Greek at the university.
These two letters furnish a valuable commentary and background to the pages in *Utopia* on the Greek classics.[12]

In view of the fact that the epistle written to the University of
Oxford is more fertile and more germane to the present topic,
it may well furnish the basis for this discussion. The function of
even profane learning at a university, as has been seen above,
is to prepare the soul for an advanced and enlightened virtue.
In addition, at the university a man should acquire prudence in
dealing with human affairs, without which — and this is an in-
nuendo pointed against the Lenten preacher — even the theologian will shout nonsense to the ordinary people in his congregation. This prudence and experience can be drawn most
abundantly from the poets, the orators, and the historians of
antiquity. (Note Hythloday's words in *Utopia*: "in Latin there
was nothing that I thought they would greatly allow besides
historians and poets.") The preacher condemns philosophy and
the liberal arts by the name of secular or worldly literature;
nevertheless, there are some who, by this very means, make
their way to theology, despoiling, as it were, the women of Egypt
for the adornment of their queen. But More fails to see how they
can attain to theology, the mistress of the sciences, without skill
in language, whether Hebrew or Greek or Latin. Of course, they
might limit themselves to theological books written in English
— a ridiculous supposition at this time — or to the very little
Latin sufficient for arguing about those Scholastic questions
which, they think, hedge in the whole of theology. But More
persists in denying that theology, the august queen of heaven,
is encompassed in such narrow confines alone, so that in addition
to these Scholastic questions she does not sojourn and abide in
the Sacred Scriptures and from there wander through all the
dwellings of the most ancient and holy Fathers: Augustine,

Jerome, Ambrose, Cyprian, Chrysostom, Gregory, and Basil.
These, and others of the same kind, were responsible for the
study of theology for more than a thousand years, before those
subtle petty questions, which now are almost the only ones discussed publicly, came into being. Whoever boasts that he understands the works of the Fathers without more than an ordinary
command of their language, will ignorantly have to boast a long
time before scholars believe him.[13]

Dorp, argues More, had said with much truth and wisdom
that each language is outstanding and superior to the extent that
it happens to have a greater treasure of arts and sciences in its
letters as in jewel caskets. Using this single reason of Dorp, every
one must come to know and admit that Greek is the language
which all mortals, and especially Christians, ought to embrace,
since it is the tongue from which all the branches of knowledge,
including almost the whole of the New Testament, have come
down to us.[14]

In theology itself, as in all the other sciences, the men who
either discovered whatever was best or who handed down most
carefully what had been discovered, were the Greeks. In philosophy, except for what Cicero and Seneca have left, the Latin
schools of thought possess nothing but what has been brought
over from the Greek. (Hythloday, who had devoted himself
entirely to philosophy, "knew that there is nothing extant in the
Latin tongue that is to any purpose, saving a few of Seneca's and
Cicero's doings.") The New Testament was first written almost
entirely in Greek. The most ancient and learned interpreters of
the Holy Scriptures were Greeks who wrote in Greek. Not even
half of these Greek books have been translated. The translations
have recently been better, but no translation can equal knowledge of the original for greater accuracy and more fruit. For this
reason Jerome, Augustine, Bede, and many other Doctors of the
Latin Church devoted themselves assiduously to the thorough
study of Greek, in spite of the consideration that more books
were then translated than are now read by many who appear very

erudite in their own eyes. In fact, these Fathers not only learned the language, but also counseled posterity, especially those who wished to be theologians, to do the same.[15]

The same ideas are close to the heart of Erasmus. "None of the branches of knowledge," he declares, "is more dependent on the study of languages than theology, provided that we think the exposition of the Sacred Books to belong to theology." In *Ecclesiastes* he advises the preacher to read scriptural interpreters selectively and judiciously. "In general," he counsels, "the Greeks surpass the Latins, and the ancients the moderns, in the genuine discussion of the Scriptures. For the gospel came first to the Greeks before the Latins, and the race itself has always excelled in fortunate geniuses." Fisher agrees with Erasmus. Although Latin Catholics ought to esteem the four Latin Doctors of the Church next to Christ's apostles, they ought, nevertheless, to embrace and venerate whatever the Greek Doctors have rightly taught, and this for three reasons: (1) their antiquity and nearness to apostolic times, (2) their extreme learning and singular eloquence, and (3) their language, on account of which one must have recourse to them in many things. One must be free, of course, to depart from the Greek Fathers where they depart from the common opinions of the Church.[16]

In pursuance of these ideas, More had told Dorp that it would take an infinite amount of time to explain what the man ignorant of Greek is missing. He admits that, without the knowledge of Greek, Dorp, as well as others, has advanced to heights of learning to which many, even possessed of Greek, could not climb with all their sweating and panting. But he ventures to assert that, if Dorp added Greek literature to the rest of his knowledge, he would then surpass even his own self as much as he now excels others, even those expert in Greek. When Erasmus had made Dorp much the same promise, Dorp had answered that such humanists as Joannes Campanus (Giannantonio Campano) and Pomponius Laetus (Pomponio Leto), and even Valla who studied Greek only as an old man, had attained to great pro-

ficiency as Latinists without the aid of Greek. But Erasmus'
fundamental plea in defense of his *Praise of Folly* had been this:
instead of reading certain authors only with the idea of carping
at them, instead of rending and being rent in turn, instead of
thus losing one's leisure and that of others, how much better it
would be to learn Greek or Hebrew or certainly Latin literature!
The knowledge of these languages is such an advantage to the
study of sacred literature that Erasmus fails to see how anyone
ignorant of them can shamelessly arrogate to himself the title of
theologian.[17]

In regard to Greek, Erasmus speaks from the depth of his
experience. In 1501, he wrote to Antony of Bergen that he now
realized what he had very often read in the most learned authors,
namely, that Latin learning, however considerable it might be,
was defective and cut in half without Greek. "For, among us
Latins there hardly are turbid pools and rivulets; among the
Greeks are most pure fountains and rivers rolling gold." And,
three years later, he wrote to Colet: "I now see by experience
this one thing: we amount to nothing in any field of knowledge
without Greek." According to his *Ecclesiastes*, it is not only because the Old and New Testaments existed in the Greek before
the Latin that the Greek language evidently possesses a most
extensive usefulness, but also because all philosophy and almost
all the liberal arts have reached us through the Greeks in the
Greek language. Without Greek letters, he told Simon Pistorius,
"all erudition is blind." One great advantage of Greek, he explained to James Latomus, is that in the very study of the Greek
language as such the learner acquires a wealth of knowledge.
It is impossible for a beginner to struggle with Greek lessons
without drawing immediate profit: in literature by reading
Homer, etc., in philosophy by reading Aristotle and his commentators, in theology by reading the New Testament and its Greek
interpreters, in medicine by reading Hippocrates and Galen,
etc. In a word, to cite his *Plan of Study*, if almost all knowledge is to be sought in Greek authors, whence can one draw it

more purely or more quickly or more pleasantly than from the very sources in Greek? [18]

The opinions of Guillaume Budé and Richard Pace at this time are similar to those of Erasmus and More. For Budé, Greek is like a writer of tragedy or comedy, and Latin is merely like an actor that executes the play. Again, Latin plays the role of ape to Greek. "Without knowledge of the Greek language," he states, "Latin is deficient and weak, something that none of the more learned will deny." In his *Benefits of Learning*, Pace tells Colet, whom Erasmus' *New Testament* has stirred to a desire for Greek, that Greek literature would add so vastly to his previously great learning as to make him judge his past knowledge little or none. Pace then cites the example of William [= John?] Stokesley who regretted the devotion of many years, before he learned Greek, to such imaginary trifles as "restrictions and second intentions, which even the Utopians never allowed." Even oratory and history which seem to belong peculiarly to the Latins were borrowed from the Greeks. Philosophy is so much wanting among the Latins that nothing could be more foolish than the comparison of Latin philosophers with Greek. In conclusion, Pace declares: "If any person, without Greek erudition but by the gift of nature, reaches some degree of learning, it will undoubtedly be doubled by adding Greek." Ignorance of Greek causes one to consume upon trifles the amount of time which could make one an extremely erudite man, as is proved by the case of Erasmus.[19]

The way to our conclusion has been long, but necessary, for the full significance of the section on Greek studies in the *Utopia* is now evident: Europeans should adopt Greek with the same willingness and the same open-mindedness with which the Utopians welcome the language. The Utopians plead to learn Greek; the least that Europeans can do is not to organize a campaign against it and to give it an experimental trial. Why cannot Europeans be as progressive as Utopians? The only motive of the Utopians was a love of knowledge and a desire for improvement.

The reasons which should induce Europeans to study the language are a thousand times more weighty. First of all, the roots of Christianity lie in Greek, for the New Testament, the best scriptural commentaries, and the works of the first and greatest theologians are written in Greek. It is impossible to know the whole, the best, and the purest of Christianity without Greek. Let theologians give heed to this declaration. Secondly, all the liberal arts and sciences which flourish in Western Europe owe their origin or their transmission to the men and the language of Greece. Philosophy itself is Greek. The universities of Europe possess a great deal of knowledge in these branches, but, in comparison with the Greek sources from which it comes, it is adulterated or contaminated, deficient or buried under accretions. By turning to the Greek sources, European men of learning will at once purify their knowledge from alien or extraneous corruptions and advance it with many new improvements.

Being a non-Christian people, the inhabitants of Utopia cannot set the example for Christian Europe in the study of Scripture and theology in Greek. It would have done violence to More's original conception of the Utopians as a thoroughly reasonable race unblessed by revelation. Nevertheless, More is far from failure to make his point. The Utopians are models, perhaps less in the matter of study, than in the spirit of study. If one must be eager to study in Greek all the arts and sciences which depend upon reason, how much more ardent and desirous one must be of examining in the original language Scripture, the word of God, and theology, the queen of the arts and sciences!

It is not only in theology and philosophy, however, but in all the arts and sciences that Greek is useful and necessary. Here the Utopians definitely set an example for Europeans. The degree of education and learning which has been reached without Greek appears to be much the same for Utopians and Europeans. The former, Hythloday tells his listeners, "in all things be almost equal to our ancient clerks," meaning Greek and Roman men of learning. These words must not be taken too broadly because the Utopians would then receive no benefit or profit from the study of Greek. It may be best to restrict their proficiency to the subjects mentioned by name: music, logic, arithmetic, geometry, astronomy, climatology, and ethics. This leaves room for Latin and Greek poets and historians, Greek medical books, etc. Nevertheless, Hythloday's words are clear: *antiquos omnibus prope rebus exaequant.* Europeans in the person of the Schoolmen profess to be able to give some kind of opinion on everything knowable (*de omni scibili*). Nothing is said directly concerning the superiority of Greek-less Utopians to Greek-less Europeans, except that the Utopians have not even dreamed of suppositions, second intentions, and universals, nor of the superstitions of astrology. Nevertheless, it would be against More's purpose at this stage to make the Europeans markedly inferior to the Utopians. This would have been at once insulting and discouraging to the scholars of Europe. Rather, he seems to place both of them at the same level of knowledge. The Utopians respond with initiative and zeal to Greek knowledge, and consequently make great advances. Some Europeans thus far have greeted it with resentment and hostility; what *should* they do now, but imitate the reasonable Utopians? [20]

The pages in the *Utopia* on knowledge and learning, one must conclude, are not a whimsical display of humanistic predilection, but an important document in the struggle over Greek in the early sixteenth century. This inference is confirmed by the writings of Erasmus and More at this time, especially by More's letters to Dorp and to the University of Oxford. Indirectly, the section on Greek studies constitutes an answer to the captious critics of Erasmus' *Novum Instrumentum* in particular and embodies an invitation to drink deep from the pure fountains of the Christianity of the Greek exegetes and Fathers of the Church. This urgent request to read the documents of early Christianity in their context, and not in compilations or anthologies, extends, as a matter of course, to all the sources or *fontes*, including the Latin ecclesiastical writers and the Latin Fathers, especially

Jerome and Augustine. As has been seen, even Hythloday allows for Latin historians and poets and for two Latin philosophers, Cicero and Seneca. This study of scriptural and patristic sources, especially Greek, is at once the substitute and the remedy for the insane absorption in abstruse and unreal questions in theology. More immediately, the object of these pages in *Utopia* is twofold: first, to argue for a spirit of tolerance and progress such as makes the Utopian welcome all knowledge, especially Greek learning; and secondly, to plead for a basic knowledge of Greek literature such as contained in the list of Hythloday's books. "Be eager, even impatient, to welcome the best," begs More. "But the best is in Greek. Therefore, receive Greek with open arms." Once, in the distant past, England and Europe knew and loved Greek. In a sense, England and Europe trace their intellectual origins to Greece just as Hythloday conjectures that the Utopians take their racial beginnings from the Greeks. The Greek language and learning must come back to all Europe, especially England, as it came back to Utopia.[21]

XII

THE GREAT BOOKS
IN UTOPIA

The twofold aspect, the one negative and the other positive, of the humanistic program for intellectual and educational reform is well exemplified in the *Utopia*. On the negative side, More cleverly derides the engulfment of contemporary Scholastic philosophers in "all those rules of restrictions, amplifications, and suppositions," "the second intentions," and "man himself in common." But he does not wish to substitute merely literary equivalents, taken from among the classics, for the philosophical controversies of the Schoolmen. His ardent desire is the elimination of abuses only. Even in logic, for example, he advocates "all that our ancient philosophers have taught," especially the methods found in the logical treatises of Aristotle, but unencumbered by medieval commentaries and additions. For More, as for the other humanists, a few simple principles and rules of logic are necessary — and sufficient. For the excessive and insane preoccupation with sophistical dialectic and epistemological subtlety, the teachers and scholars of Europe have a most useful and absorbing substitute in the study of the Greek language and literature. The latter constitutes the positive side of More's humanistic campaign.[1]

Does More offer any program of "Great Books" for those European men of learning who are willing to study the language and

literature of Greece, and thus to broaden their knowledge of all
the secular arts and sciences? The volumes which Hythloday and
Tricius Apinatus carry with them and share with the inhabitants
of Utopia might well serve as the basis for a list of required
reading, but a few titles would be lacking for the perfect education. This is evident from the fact that Hythloday tossed into
the ship only "a pretty fardel of books" (*librorum sarcinam
mediocrem*). The list, however, does represent what Hythloday,
an ardent student of the Greek tongue and a devotee of Greek
philosophy, must have considered as an essential minimum of
the most valuable Greek books, since he "intended to come again
[back to Europe] rather never than shortly" (*quod mecum plane
decreueram nunquam potius redire quam cito*). Hythloday's
catalogue — and More's — can be filled out and completed by the
various enumerations of recommended books made by More's
lifelong friend, Erasmus. Of these the most important is the
selection of authors which appeared only five years before *Utopia*
in his *Plan of Study* (1511). There are a number of remarkable
resemblances, which can hardly be due to pure coincidence,
between the *Utopia* and the *Plan of Study*. Erasmus' *Plan* may
be supplemented by his *Apology against the Dialogue of James
Latomus* (1518), by his *Ecclesiastes* (1535), and, to a less extent,
by his *Method of True Theology* (1519). The net result of such
a study is proof for the great influence exerted by Erasmus over
his friend More, at least in literary matters, as well as a clear
picture of the early Renaissance in England.[2]

In general, Erasmus maintains that, just as bees collect different
substances from different flowers and plants, "so one must not
seek everything in the same author, but must take from each one
what is most useful: verbal splendor from poets and orators,
argumentative subtlety from dialecticians, knowledge of nature
from philosophers, and moral precepts from theologians." Aeneas
Silvius (Pius II) had used the same simile of the bees in his
Education of Children.[3]

Hythloday begins the list of his Greek books, as one might

well expect from a philosopher, with the writings of three great philosophers: "the most part of Plato's works, more of Aristotle's, also Theophrastus' *Of Plants*." In his *Plan of Study* Erasmus informs his readers that "the best teachers of philosophy will be Plato, and Aristotle, and the disciple of the latter, Theophrastus." The order of mention, it will be noted, is the same in both works.[4]

As for Plato, little need be said of his preëminence and influence during the Renaissance in England. However large or small More's debt to him in the *Utopia* may be, the spirit of Plato hovers over the work. In the introduction to his *Adages*, Erasmus had pointed out: if it is true the greater the number of adages in an author, the greater his erudition and eloquence, "nothing could be more aphoristic than great, not to say divine, Plato." And Elyot was to write later in his *Governor*: "above all other, the works of Plato would be most studiously read when the judgment of a man is come to perfection."[5]

The second author, Aristotle, who was often under attack as the god of the Schoolmen, was far from being unappreciated among the English humanists who were More's friends. Both Grocyn and Linacre, for example, were pronounced Aristotelians. In a letter to Aldus in Linacre's *Sphere of Proclus*, Grocyn declares of Aristotle and Plato: "For my part I think the difference between these great philosophers is simply that between πολυμαθῆ and πολυμυθῆ [*sic*] [a world of science and a world of myths]."[6]

As an example of the profit to be gained from the knowledge of Greek, More could use Aristotle himself, the god of the Schoolmen, in his letter to Dorp. How few of the works of the Greek poets, orators, philosophers, and Fathers of the Church have been translated into Latin — and barbarous Latin at that! Other than sorry fragments in Latin, even the great Aristotelian commentators — Alexander of Aphrodisias, Themistius, Ammonius Hermiae, Simplicius, Philoponus, Olympiodorus, etc. — must still be read in Greek, with the exception of Themistius. As for Latin translations, they are such poor Latin that they are almost less

understandable than the Greek originals! Most telling argument
of all is the consideration that Aristotle himself in his entirety
cannot become known to his disciples without the command of
Greek. Erasmus, too, complains in his *Method of True Theology*
that all natural science cannot be learned from the eight books
of Aristotle's *Physics* which alone are now being studied in the
universities. Much more can be learned from Aristotle's other
very erudite works: the commentaries on animals, *Meteorology,
On the Earth, On the Soul, On Sense and the Sensible, On Memory and Reminiscence,* and *Problems.*[7]

More has no intention of stressing the point that no translation is so good that it can put in the shade the influence and
power of the original Greek over the mind and heart, nor of
pressing home the consideration that certain works of Aristotle
extant in Greek are not even known by name among the Latins.
Of the works which they do have, they have some in a way in
which it would be better not to have them. In this sorry plight
is Aristotle's *Meteorology,* which deals also with the very science
at which the Utopians are so expert: "[r]ains, winds, and other
courses of tempests . . . [and with] the causes of all these things,
of the ebbing, flowing, and saltness of the sea." More believes
this to be extremely lamentable; he knows of no work of the man
more worthy of knowledge, since it acquaints its readers with
the mysteries which surround them and yet which remain unknown and perplexing. This deplorable deficiency, however, will
soon be remedied by the clear and elegant translation which
Thomas Linacre is soon going to publish, not alone, but accompanied by the excellent commentary of Alexander Aphrodisiensis
on the work. Here More relates a confirmatory incident. While
Linacre was giving him a prelection and interpretation of the
Meteorology in Greek, More glanced now and then, for the sake
of experiment, at the current popular translation. The latter
seemed so translated that it seemed not at all translated; in fact,
to the extent that what More understood excellently in the Greek
was unintelligible to him in the translation. Nor could any help

to Aristotle's thought be expected from the Latin commentators. Even Albert the Great who professes to be Aristotle's "periphraser" (apparently a commentator who gives a relatively full explanation of the text) is in this work more truly his "paraphraser" (merely a commentator who gives the meaning in other words); and yet, instead of echoing the sense of Aristotle in other words as he ought, he produces doctrines diametrically opposed. Even the influential Paduan Averroist, Gaetano Tiene (Gaietanus de Thienis, d. 1465), gives not a bit of Aristotle's true meaning. This woeful state of affairs could be remedied completely by the study of Aristotle and his commentators in the original Greek. More does not mention the fact that in 1501 and 1504 had appeared *Paraphrases of the Entire Natural Philosophy of Aristotle*, including four books of the *Meteorology*, with the paraphrases by Jacques Lefèvre d'Étaples and the commentary by Josse Clichtove. Moreover, in Lefèvre's separate paraphrase of the *Meteorology*, published in 1512, John Cochlaeus says that he had not wished to tire students by unnecessary circumlocutions since the Aristotelian text was clear but that he had nevertheless added materials from other authors.[8]

Turning from the philosophers, Hythloday mentions Constantine Lascaris and Theodore Gaza, both fifteenth-century Greeks, as grammarians, and Hesychius of Alexandria (fourth century or later) and Pedanius Dioscorides (first century) as lexicographers. The latter's work *De Materia Medica* was for centuries the standard authority in medicinal substances and in botany. A letter from Josse Bade to Erasmus in August 1515, reveals that Jehan Ruelle (Joannes Ruellius or a Ruella) was preparing this work for printing; in fact, his translation was published in April 1516. Erasmus in his *Method of True Theology* refers to Dioscorides as one of the sources to be studied in natural science. There seems to be no special mention of Hesychius in the works of Erasmus. In the *Plan of Study*, however, Erasmus writes of Lascaris and Gaza: "There is no one who does not yield first place to Theodore Gaza among the Greek grammarians; Con-

stantine Lascaris, in my judgment, claims the second place for
himself in his own right." Erasmus' translation of the first book
of Gaza's *Grammar* was published in July 1516, a few months
before the *Utopia*. In his dedicatory epistle to John Caesarius,
he praises Gaza for his brevity, his order, and his simplicity. The
translation, on account of its superior usefulness, was a great
success. The translation of the fourth book of Gaza by Richard
Croke appeared in Leipzig in 1516.[9]

Two authors are singled out for special commendation: Plutarch and Lucian. The Utopians hold the writings of Plutarch
very dear. This is probably less for his *Parallel Lives*, since Hythloday would otherwise have included him among the historians,
than for his *Moralia*. Strange as it may seem, Plutarch is not
among the recommended authors in Erasmus' *Plan of Study*. He
receives mention, however, in the *Apology against the Dialogue
of James Latomus* and, especially, in *Ecclesiastes*. In the latter,
Erasmus claims that "no one has written more happily on morality
than Plutarch, whose writings are worthy of being learned word
for word." His *Adages* speaks of Plutarch as "a weighty and holy,
and almost forbidding, author"; indeed, no one is holier than
he among pagan philosophers. Finally, in "The Religious Banquet," Eusebius points to one of his volumes as containing "some
of the choicest of Plutarch's books of morals. . . . I find in them
so much purity of thought, that it is my amazement how such
evangelical notions should come into the heart of a heathen." [10]

Lucian has captivated the Utopians with his flashes of wit
and pleasantry. As might be expected from the devotion of More
and Erasmus, the latter in the *Plan of Study* places Lucian first
in the list of the three authors who unite excellence of style with
wealth of matter. In the preface to his translation of Lucian's
Gallus (1506), Erasmus cries out that, if anybody ever attained
Horace's ideal of winning all votes by the union of pleasure and
usefulness, it was Lucian. Without peevish querulousness he
touched everything with subtle pleasantry, ridicule, and wit.
Above all, he used, with the best right in the world, every weapon

against the philosophers, especially the Pythagoreans and the Platonists on account of their deceptive juggling and the Stoics on account of their intolerable arrogance, for "what is more hateful and less bearable than roguery parading under the mask of virtue?" No comedy and no satire ought even to be compared with Lucian's dialogues on the score of profit as well as pleasure. In the same year in a letter to Thomas Ruthall, which serves as a preface to his own translations, More praises Lucian, in whom he took special pleasure in his youth, for the same virtues as Erasmus: "If there was ever a man, most learned friend, who fulfilled the Horatian precept of joining profit and pleasure, it is my firm conviction that Lucian succeeded in doing so preëminently. Keeping clear and free of the arrogant rules of the philosophers and the too lax jests of the poets, he exposes and inveighs against mortal vices with most virtuous as well as cleverly facetious sallies of wit." [11]

The name of Lucian occurs just after that of Plutarch in Erasmus' *Apology against the Dialogue of James Latomus*. In his *Plan of Study*, Erasmus for moral reasons advises a careful selection of Plautus' comedies for young people. Oddly enough, he does not do so for Lucian's dialogues. Thomas Elyot is far more cautious. After having the child begin with Aesop's fables, he then recommends "some quick and merry dialogues, elect [selected] out of Lucian, which be without ribaldry or too much scorning, for either of them is exactly to be eschewed, specially for a nobleman, the one annoying [troubling or injuring] the soul, the other his estimation concerning his gravity. . . . [T]hus much dare I say, that it were better that a child should never read any part of Lucian than all Lucian." [12]

After Plutarch and Lucian, Hythloday reveals the poets, epic and dramatic, whom the Utopians now have: Aristophanes, Homer, Euripides, and Sophocles. The same order, except for the absence of Sophocles (who, however, is named later), is found in Erasmus' *Plan of Study*. "Among the poets," he writes, "I should give the first prize to Aristophanes, the second to

Homer, and the third to Euripides." Later, he calls Homer "the father of all fables." The inspirational value of Homer in the eyes of the humanists is well propounded by Elyot as follows: "in his books be contained and most perfectly expressed not only the documents martial and discipline of arms but also incomparable wisdoms and instructions for politic governances of people, with the worthy commendation and laud of noble princes, wherewith the readers shall be so all inflamed that they most fervently shall desire and covet, by the imitation of their virtues, to acquire semblable glory." There is no word of banishment or disapprobation of Homer's works in the *Utopia* such as is found in Plato's *Republic*. In fact, More later defends against Tyndale the study of poetry by arguing: "albeit poets been with many men taken but for painted words, yet do they much help the judgment and make a man, among other things, well furnished of one special thing without which all learning is half lame, . . . a good mother wit." [13]

The historians follow the poets. They are three in number: Thucydides, Herodotus, and Herodian. Of these three, only Herodotus is recommended in Erasmus' *Plan of Study*, where he is ranked next to Lucian and Demosthenes for an excellent combination of style and subject matter. Thucydides, as well as Herodotus, is mentioned in Erasmus' answer to James Latomus. Erasmus' friend, William Herman, was reading Thucydides in Valla's translation, perhaps as early as 1493. There is no outstanding reference to the history of Herodian in the works of Erasmus.[14]

Galen and Hippocrates, who are mentioned next in the *Utopia*, will be given special treatment below. To Latomus' objection that in the study of Greek nothing is learned but the language, Erasmus answers: "What if a physician reads Hippocrates and Galen in Greek? Will he learn nothing but the language?" [15]

While Herodian is not an author of such magnitude or popularity as to merit a place in such a distinguished group of authors, Demosthenes seems to be the only major author, extolled and

praised by Erasmus, whose works Hythloday did not carry with
him. This is strange in view of the importance which Erasmus
gives to the Athenian orator. He is the only writer to appear in
the three principal works which have been used here, namely,
Ecclesiastes, A Plan of Study, and *An Apology against the Dialogue of James Latomus.* The only other non-Christian Greek
authors recommended by Erasmus in the pertinent passages in
these works are Aesop, Menander, Xenophon, Athenaeus,
Ptolemy, Strabo, Eratosthenes, Libanius, and Aristides. The last
two are recommended as authors of exemplary declamations.[16]

Hythloday was such a devotee of Greek that he seems to have
carried only Greek books with him and spoke to the Utopians
only of Greek literature and learning. On account of the advanced
intellectual stage of the Utopians, he thought that "in Latin there
was nothing that . . . they would greatly allow besides historians
and poets." Earlier the reader is informed that in philosophy "he
knew that there is nothing extant in the Latin tongue that is to
any purpose, saving a few of Seneca's and Cicero's doings." This
emphasis on the excellence of Greek is completely in accord with
More's primary purpose in this part of the *Utopia*: to foster
interest in, and enthusiasm for, Greek.[17]

Again the best analogue for these historians, poets, and philosophers would be Erasmus' *Plan of Study.* For form and substance, among the poets (and, in fact, among the Latin writers
in general) Erasmus gives first place to the comedies of Plautus
and Terence, second place to Vergil, and third place to Horace.
Caesar and Sallust are best for Latin history. As for grammarians
and rhetoricians, the outstanding are Quintilian, Donatus,
Diomedes, Nicolaus Perottus, Antonius Campanus, and Lauren-
tius Valla. Ovid is a good source of mythology. As mines of useful
miscellaneous information, Pliny, Macrobius, Gellius, and Pomponius Mela are worth reading. In his advice to the Christian
preacher in *Ecclesiastes,* Erasmus recommends Vergil for the
mild emotions and the tragedians for the strong passions. He
praises Livy for eloquence and prudence and Tacitus for pene-

tration and number of speeches. In the *Method of True Theology*, he includes Pliny and Macrobius, although Latins, among the Greeks as fine sources of natural science. In a very early letter (1497?), written by Erasmus for Henry Northoff to be sent to his brother Christian Northoff, the authors Macrobius, Gellius, Apuleius, Catullus, Martial, Campanus, and Politianus are designated as suitable for lighter moods.[18]

As for the Latin philosophers, Cicero and Seneca are the only two who merit consideration. Cicero, but not Seneca, receives notice in the *Plan of Study*, though he is given only fourth place among Latin men of letters. In *Ecclesiastes*, however, Cicero, together with Demosthenes, is one of the two authors to be studied above all others by the preacher. In the same work, Seneca is praised for his witty, elegant, and even violent satire of human vices. In October 1516, Erasmus wrote to Peter Gilles a letter urging him to make Seneca and Plato his friends, for frequent conversation with these two would not suffer his soul to grovel in the dust, but would raise it to great achievements.[19]

It is interesting to compare Elyot's program of classical studies with Hythloday's catalogue and Erasmus' recommendations. Elyot recommends only four authors present in the list in *Utopia*: two, Lucian and Homer, to be learned before the age of fourteen, and two, Plato and Aristotle, to be studied after that age. The other Greek authors are Aesop, Demosthenes, Hesiod, Hermogenes, Ptolemy, Strabo, Dionysius of Halicarnassus, and Xenophon. Among the Latin writers Cicero is most prominent, being represented by his orations, *Topica*, *De Partitione Oratoria*, and *De Officiis*. The Latin poets to be read are Vergil, Ovid, Horace, Silius Italicus, and Lucan; and the Latin historians, Livy, Quintus Curtius, Caesar, Sallust, and Tacitus. Other writers to be used are Quintilian, Solinus, and Mela. The only two figures of the Renaissance represented are Agricola and Erasmus. The student is to read the former's *Topica* and the latter's *Copia* and *Institutio Principis Christiani*. The proverbial and historical books of the Bible also are to be studied.[20]

More closes the list of Hythloday's books with medical works: "certain small works of Hippocrates and Galen's *Microtechne*." In medicine the knowledge of Greek is imperative. In one passage Erasmus confesses that it is not his office to decide whether lawyers, physicians, and mathematicians need Greek books, but he holds the incontrovertibility of the fact that many professing skill in these subjects have committed deplorable errors, precisely on account of their ignorance of Greek. Certainly, as far as medicine is concerned, he should find confirmation of this view in the undeniably outstanding and leading physicians of the time: Nicolaus Leonicenus, Ambrosius Nolanus, William Cop, and Thomas Linacre, all of whom value the Greek medical authorities. In the explanation of an adage, Erasmus does not hesitate to affirm that "medicine is a distinguished science, but without the knowledge of the languages and books of the ancients it is almost blind." It is for the same reason that Pace in his *Benefits of Learning* urges medical students to combine the study of Greek with that of Latin. "For, just as other sciences in which the Latins have left written records issue from Greek sources," he writes, "so you can hardly achieve anything in medicine if you are ignorant of the Greek language. If you contemn the latter, you will be classified in the number of those physicians who are accustomed to kill people with impunity!" [21]

The prominence given to medicine among studies in this part of the *Utopia* is undoubtedly a compliment to Thomas Linacre and an appreciation of his efforts. More's letter to Dorp reveals that the more urgent translation of Galen was calling Linacre away from his translation of Aristotle and Alexander Aphrodisiensis at the time of the composition of the *Utopia*; and in fact, the translation, *De Sanitate Tuenda*, appeared in August 1517. Budé falters not a whit in saying that, if all of Galen's "works (which I consider worth all other medical lore put together) be in time translated, the want of a knowledge of Greek is not likely to be seriously felt in our schools of medicine." To him Linacre is "that pillar of the British name in all that concerns good learning." When Linacre established two lectureships in medicine at Oxford, the university wrote to him as follows: "For how can you deserve better of our commonwealth, . . . than in favouring and promoting the liberal arts. . . . [Y]ou have chosen the science most subservient of all others to the necessities of mankind. For who even of the most potent has suitably requited the physician? The life we take from God, we retake from him: to his care we owe the preservation of the gift of existence, which we have received from the great Creator of all things, and the restoration of it when in a state of decay." [22]

Like Linacre, Budé, and the other humanists, the Utopians have the books of Galen, as well as those of Hippocrates, "in great estimation." Of all the nations in the world, they need the art and science of medicine perhaps least of all. This state of affairs is altogether in accord with Plato's theory that the excessive need of medicines and physicians is a sign of degeneracy in a people, for simplicity and moderation in diet and gymnastics are enough to keep a man in health. Nevertheless, no race holds medicine in greater honor than the Utopians. This view is thoroughly consonant with their conception of health as the greatest of bodily pleasures. But the basic reason given by Hythloday is that, in the hierarchy of knowledge, they rank the science of medicine among those subjects in philosophy which are of the highest beauty and greatest usefulness. For, in medicine, if in any science, the secrets of nature are subjected to a probe and scrutiny which give at the same time pleasure to the investigator and glory to God. In his early work, *The Praise of the Medical Art*, Erasmus had exclaimed eloquently: "[A]fter penetrating to the bowels of the earth and examining the secrets of all nature everywhere, to search out efficacious remedies for all the ills of human life from all herbs, shrubs, trees, animals, gems, and finally from very poisons, and to seek their appropriate use from a multitude of authors and sciences and from the very stars: to pry, I say, into these deep secrets with solicitude, to overcome these great difficulties with one's own mental powers, to hold so much in the memory, to produce for the common good so many things necessary for the preservation of the human race: does all this not seem to be a thing more than human and something wholly divine?" [23]

The Utopians are acutely aware of this divine quality, not only in medical research, but in all scientific investigation. In fact, penetration into the mysteries of nature assumes an aura of religious duty and devotion to the deity. "They think that the contemplation of nature and the praise thereof coming is to God a very acceptable honor" (*Gratum deo cultum putant naturae contemplationem, laudemque ab ea*). Only man, in all visible creation, has the intellect and the power to appreciate the marvelous structure and beauty of the universe as it comes from the hands of God. Therefore, the more man grows in knowledge of the secrets of nature, the more he grows in the praise of the Creator; the more curiosity and wonder he shows in the contemplation and employment of creatures, the more love the "Author and Maker thereof" displays towards him. The man who "without sense or moving hath no regard to so great and so wonderful a spectacle" is "like a very beast without wit and reason." It must be recalled here that this investigation and contemplation is the source of even bodily pleasure, insofar as it is among "those pleasures which be received by . . . the eyes . . . which nature willeth to be proper and peculiar to man (for no other kind of living beasts doth behold the fairness and the beauty of the world)." [24]

There cannot be much doubt that this passage in the *Utopia* embodies a latent invitation to Europeans to imitate the conduct of the Utopians in their devotion to natural philosophy, that is, to natural science. It is a plea to widen, and even to extend, the frontiers of such knowledge. The first and most important step is to master the corpus of classical, and especially Greek, science.

The description of the manner in which Greek can help to the knowledge of Aristotle and philosophy and also aid in the study and practice of medicine, furnishes only two solitary examples.

The same can be done, with remarkable results, in all the other arts and sciences.

The pages in *Utopia* on Greek, therefore, are a plea for a basic knowledge of Greek literature such as contained in the list of Hythloday's books. Here lies the release from the sterile pre-occupation of European thinkers and scholars with dialectic and universals. Hythloday, who "had given himself wholly to the study of philosophy" (*totum se addixerat philosophiae*), could well serve as a model for the philosophers of Europe insofar as he is conversant, not only with the great philosophers, but also with the classical poets, historians, moralists, etc. The latter statement might be applied to More himself. Richard Pace, writing a short time after the publication of *Utopia*, praises him as being outstanding, not in mere knowledge, but in "varied knowledge, so that wherever you turn, there is nothing of which he seems ignorant." [25]

In conclusion, one may say that Thomas More's program of Greek studies is an important document in the history of the early Renaissance in England. The views of Erasmus in regard to a new educational program seem to have carried great weight with More. In this matter More could be expected to defer to the judgment of Erasmus since the man of affairs, Thomas More, could hardly have the time and energy to draw up a cultural plan absolutely independently of the humanistic genius who was his close friend.[26]

More's program shows that by 1515 the Renaissance in England had reached the stage where great emphasis was placed on the introduction of Greek. In Greek was written all that was worth knowing and worth preserving. Hence comes the reason for the heavy stress laid on the return to the *sources*. The cry was ever "Ad fontes!" Even the Schoolmen, who prided themselves on their logic and dialectic, could profit themselves and their disciples by abandoning medieval commentaries and supplements, which were unnecessarily and needlessly complex, and by returning to the original treatises of Aristotle and his classical commentators, which contained all that was essential and significant. Why should the Schoolmen, moreover, not earn their title of Aristotelian by studying *all* the works of their deified Aristotle — in Greek, of course? Why should they not broaden their horizons by intensive reflection, not only on books of philosophy, but also on works of history, natural science, lexicography, poetry, drama, etc.? Proof of the profit to be gained from this procedure could be found in the advances made in medicine on account of the study of Galen in Greek. For those who reasonably could not be expected to learn Greek, translations should be made available in elegant *Latin*. It was reserved for succeeding generations in this same century to see the need and desirability of translation into *English*.

More's list of the best books in Greek is very revealing when compared with contemporary lists of great books. Such "popular" favorites as Aristophanes, Aristotle, Euripides, Herodotus, Homer, Plato, Plutarch, Sophocles, and Thucydides are common to both. Notable is the omission of such names as Aeschylus, Aesop, Demosthenes, Pindar, and Theocritus. With a "more advanced" list, such as that of St. John's College, Annapolis, More shares the works of Galen, Hippocrates, and Lucian. Significantly absent are, beside the *Enneads* of Plotinus, the astronomical or mathematical books of Apollonius of Perga, Archimedes, Aristarchus of Samos, Euclid, Nicomachus, and Ptolemy. Proper to More are the Renaissance grammarians Lascaris and Gaza, the lexicographers Hesychius and Dioscorides, the philosopher Theophrastus, and the historian Herodian. As far as a list of Latin writers is concerned, it has already been noted that More praises as worth while, in addition to the Latin poets and historians whose names he fails to mention, only two philosophers, namely, Cicero and Seneca. Consequently, it is evident that More, although advocating the perusal of great standard authors, adapts his list to what he considers the peculiar need and taste of the hour.[27]

The hour, according to Villoslada, was characterized and animated by two great desires. The first was the yearning for simplification, which manifested itself in mental life by rebellion against the great ideological systems and in social life by revolt against the great politico-ecclesiastical system. Individualism triumphed over hierarchy and complexity. The second was the longing for criticism, reform, or purification. Old habits were to give way to a primitive simplicity. The ideal of the gospel was to be stripped of man-made traditions. The prototype was sought in the rejection of counterfeit imitations. Old translations were abandoned, and new and better ones were secured in order to discover the original text and genuine thought. Men wanted immediate contact with the sources and in natural consequence prepared exact and critical editions. It was the union of philology with humanism, according to Augustin Renaudet, that was new in the Renaissance. Philology discovered, analyzed, and interpreted texts, and thereby orientated the efforts of humanists toward their goal: "the definition and the realization of the most complete and the most lofty type of human being and of human existence, in the individual as well as in society." [28]

XIII

GREEK, PLEASURE, AND COMMUNISM: THE LINK

Strange as the assertion may seem at first glance, there is an intimate connection between Greek, pleasure, and communism in the *Utopia*. The link between two of them, pleasure (as their philosophy) and Greek (as a favorite branch of learning), has been discussed. In brief, having once established in the course of their history the nature and criteria of true pleasure and false pleasure by using their keen but practical intellects, the Utopians perpetuate the truth among children and adults "partly by education . . . and partly by good literature and learning." And of all "good literature and learning" they have just discovered the best and highest — in Greek. Europeans, too, are thus indirectly urged to find their intellectual salvation and advancement in Greek — in the Great Books.[1]

Significantly, it is the name of Plato that heads Hythloday's list of great Greek authors. Of all of Plato's great books it must be the *Republic* which the Utopians find most stimulating and profitable — for its communistic principles. But nothing can illustrate better the independent and original use made of classical models by the best spirits of the Renaissance than a glance at a few evident differences between Platonic communism and Utopian communism in the application of principles. The common life prevails only among the soldiers and guardians in the *Repub-*

lic, but among the whole people in the *Utopia*. In the former, too, the soldiers and guardians are exempt from manual work, but in the latter, all except a handful are farmers and craftsmen. Most important of all, the form of government in the *Republic* is aristocratic, but in the *Utopia* it is democratic and casteless. Finally, in the actual conduct of affairs, there is in the *Utopia*, often but not always, a sweet and humane reasonableness which is lacking in the *Republic*.

One notable result of the introduction of Greek into western Europe was at least analogous to that in Utopia: the intellectual rediscovery and revaluation of Plato and his *Republic*. The latter Great Book raised in thoughtful reforming circles the question of communism, at least theoretically. The issue appears briefly here and there in many humanistic works, but the most important treatment is undoubtedly Thomas More's *Utopia*.

It is indicative of his artistry that More does not introduce communism as a social, political, and economic system with no relation to philosophy and learning. If he had done so, the unity of concept of the *Utopia* would certainly have suffered. But the connection of education and learning with communism has already been indicated. It is true that the connection is more or less extrinsic since the Utopians study in the original Greek Plato's advocacy of a high form of communism and since they use instruction and lecture to propagate and perpetuate their ideal system and its principles. The connection of communism with philosophy, however, is far from being merely extrinsic: the total communistic system is intrinsically and intimately related to Utopian hedonism. The whole matter is so important for an appreciation of both the thought and the art of the *Utopia* that it merits more detailed elaboration.

The "end and felicity" of human life and activity is pleasure according to the Utopians, who appeal to nature, reason, and religion for proof and confirmation. The pleasure espoused, however, must be "good and honest." Hence, the inordinate appetite for riches which is ruining England and Europe can be labeled only as an evil and false pleasure. On the other hand, a due esteem for physical well-being and an ardent devotion to the arts and sciences, especially in their non-Scholastic and Greek form, are simply the laudatory pursuit of "true and natural" pleasure. But what chance for the enjoyment of health and study could the ordinary Utopian have had if, like the Englishman dispossessed of land or bereft of employment, he had been forced to wander with his family through the country begging and stealing for survival, or if, in a situation almost as bad, he had been compelled to work from dawn to dark for a rackrent land-owner or at starvation wages for an avaricious capitalist? The Utopians feel that the inordinately rich who in Europe fight to gather money and land "by right or wrong" are violating a most important decree of nature. The latter draws one and all to the love of pleasure: "in that that nature doth allure and provoke men one to help another to live merrily, . . . verily she com-mandeth thee to use diligent circumspection that thou do not so seek for thine own commodities that thou procure others' in-commodities." Pride alone "measureth not wealth and prosperity by her own commodities but by the miseries and incommodities of other." [2]

What is meant by *commodities*? Nothing else is intended, to use a most simple description, than food and drink, clothing and shelter, field and forest, leisure and work, in their thousand and one varieties and forms. By extension the term is made to include everything that is necessary or advantageous to man: from medi-cine and music to gold and Greek. For the Utopians, all the *commodities* of life constitute "the matter of pleasure" (*materia uoluptatis*).[3]

The fact that the Utopians view the commodities of life as *the matter of pleasure* is extremely important for an understand-ing of their adoption and retention of the communistic form of government. Since it counsels and urges all men to lead a care-free and joyful existence and to help their fellows to a similar existence, nature has ordained all men to a life of natural and reasonable pleasure. Consequently it wants no individual to secure his own advantage and pleasure at the price of his neighbor's disadvantage and pain. From this decree of nature, the Utopians draw a practical moral conclusion: public laws dealing with the partition of the commodities of life must be observed. These laws may either be promulgated in the spirit of justice by a good prince or be ratified by the common consent of the people, not forced by tyranny or circumvented by fraud, but fully informed and wholly free. The Utopian system for the distribution of commodities enjoys the distinction of a double approval: first of all, promulgation by Utopus who "brought the rude and wild people to that excellent perfection, . . . wherein they now go beyond all the people of the world," and, secondly, subsequent ratification by the people themselves who have made a law to keep their magistrates from attempting "to change the state of the weal public." In the monthly religious services, the individual Utopian, too, reiterates his approbation by thanking his "Maker" and his "Governor" publicly that "through the favor of God he hath chanced into that public weal which is most happy and wealthy." [4]

The laws framed by Utopus and the Utopians, of course, are related to their basic principle, namely, pleasure. In their eyes, all the commodities of life are to be viewed fundamentally and essentially as the *matter* of pleasure. The significance of the term *matter* may be made clear as follows. Food, for example, as the matter of pleasure is the undetermined, but determinable, raw substance which potentially can give pleasure to the few or the many. When this food as "good and fine fare" ([*prandium*] *lautum atque opiparum*), accompanied by sweet music and fragrant incense and agreeable perfumes, is served in halls for thirty families apiece day after day, it receives — to retain the Aristotelico-Scholastic terminology — its *form* as a communistic meal, as distinct from a banquet served to a few wealthy men. In the former case, the laws concerning "the partition of the commodities of life, that is to say, the matter of pleasure," look principally to the common good of the whole people, whereas in the latter case there is "nothing but a certain conspiracy of rich men, procuring their own commodities under the name and title of the commonwealth." These rich men, "not only by private fraud but also by common [i.e., public] laws, do every day pluck and snatch away from the poor some part of their daily living." The Utopians, on the contrary, strive to secure the blessings of pleasure for all their citizens according to the prescript of mother nature. They have therefore adopted and sanctioned a system of organization in which the matter of pleasure, that is, the commodities of life, is held in common, with a view to the common ownership of the means of production and to the equal distribution of the products of human labor. In a word, the Utopians prefer public ownership to private property in order to secure an equitable and just participation of all the people in the matter of pleasure.[5]

In passing, one might note an assertion of Diocles in Diogenes Laertius' *Lives of Eminent Philosophers*. Diocles says of Epicurus and his friends: "Epicurus did not think it right that their property should be held in common, as required of the maxim of Pythagoras about the goods of friends; such a practice in his opinion implied mistrust, and without confidence there is no friendship." If this is true, the statement discloses another difference between the ideas of Epicurus and the Utopians, not so much in regard to theoretical principles as with respect to their applications, practical but important and far-reaching.[6]

Communism, not private property, therefore, is the answer of the Utopians to the division of goods among their citizens — so that all might attain a maximum of pleasure and a minimum of pain during their earthly life. The result is that, "all things being there common, every man hath abundance of everything," or, to look at the matter on its negative side, "seeing they be all thereof [i.e., of the 'store and plenty of all things'] partners equally, therefore can no man there be poor or needy." Accordingly, Hythloday does not hesitate to proclaim of the Utopian state that, in his reasoned opinion, "the form and order of that

commonwealth . . . is not only the best but also that which
alone of good right may claim and take upon it the name of a
commonwealth or public weal." [7]

On the other hand, the state which is founded upon private
ownership and capitalism cannot be outstanding for equity, justice, and prosperity. This is the firm judgment, based upon observation and experience, of Hythloday and the Utopians. Hythloday says: "wheresoever possessions be private, where money
beareth all the stroke, it is hard and almost impossible that there
the weal public may justly be governed and prosperously flourish." This is true, Hythloday adds almost cynically, unless one
thinks that justice obtains where all the best things are in the
grasp of the worst men or that prosperity reigns where all things
are divided among a handful of men. In Utopia, no man has any
possessions of his own, and yet all are rich according to the Utopian philosophy of life because they "live joyfully and merrily
without all grief and pensiveness." Their own livelihood, as well
as that of their wives and families, is assured, and even old age
holds no terrors for them on account of the certainty of public
support. This is true equity: to reward generously the hard labors
of the workers and artisans who are necessary to the commonwealth. In comparison with Utopia, no other country shows even
the slightest trace of equity and justice. At least, so it appears
to the critical eye of Raphael Hythloday. England, for example,
repays the idleness or unnecessary business of bankers, usurers,
etc., with pleasure and wealth, but condemns to a poverty-
stricken and labor-laden life and to a miserable death the farmers
and the workingmen without whose necessary toil the commonwealth could not last one year. Yet "for the most part it chanceth
that this latter sort is more worthy to enjoy that state of wealth
than the other be, because the rich men be covetous, crafty, and
unprofitable; on the other part, the poor be lowly, simple, and
by their daily labor more profitable to the commonwealth than
to themselves." [8]

This view of rich and poor had often found expression in

literature. In Plato's *Laws*, the Athenian maintains that "it is impossible for them [the people] to be at once good and excessively rich." Plutarch quotes the following verse from a fragment: "For often evil men are rich, and good men poor." Lucian in his *Cronosolon* complains of the injustice which makes reprobate and crime-laden men superabound in wealth and alone enjoy delights, while very many learned men lead their lives in want and poverty. The *Adages* of Erasmus are especially wealthy in observations of this kind. One adage, which mentions Plato and St. Jerome, runs: "The rich man is either an unjust man himself or the heir of an unjust man." In another adage he writes: "It has been remarked that this nearly always happens to men who have deserved well of their country: they receive from the populace a most wretched reward for their good deeds." (Note the similarity between Erasmus' *Adages*: *hoc fere accidere viris de repub. bene meritis, ut pro benefactis pessimam gratiam retulerint a populo*, and More's *Utopia*: *optime de Republica meritis pessimam referre gratiam*.) "The good," Erasmus observes in still another adage, "nearly always are wedded to poverty, and are forced to undergo many sufferings." Finally, he examines in the *Adages* Aristotelian reasons for the poverty of the good and the riches of the wicked.[9]

Far more germane to the special social problems in the *Utopia*, however, are the indignant words of Erasmus: "It is against nature, as Aristotle has written in his *Politics*, that money should beget money. But today the practice is so far accepted among Christians that, while tillers of the soil, the class of men most innocent and most necessary to the commonwealth, are the object of scorn, usurers are almost numbered among the pillars of the Church." And this obtains in spite of the fact that usury is restrained or condemned by the ancients, pagan regulations, Hebrew laws, patristic authority, and pontifical decrees. Erasmus continues: "Above all, if you analyze the morality of our time, I would sooner approve the usurer than that sordid class of business men who by means of trickery, lying, quackery, and dissimulation hunt down the profit of a few pennies. They buy up here in order to sell for more than double there, or they rob the miserable people by monopolies. Nevertheless, we consider men who do nothing else than this in life as almost the only reputable people in the nation." In his commentary on Psalm XXXIII Erasmus reveals the spiritual and intellectual poverty of these rich scoundrels.[10]

The inequity and injustice apparent in this reward of wicked and selfish profiteers and this affliction of innocent and useful citizens is one of what Peter Gilles calls "the original causes and fountains . . . whereof . . . issueth and springeth the mortal confusion and utter decay of a commonwealth." What is the remedy for this "conspiracy of rich men procuring their own commodities under the name and title of the commonwealth"? [11]

The obvious and immediate answer, of course, is an "equal and just distribution of things." How is this distribution to be accomplished once for all? Hythloday's answer is prompt and emphatic: certainly not by such halfway measures as he himself had once suggested to Cardinal Morton — the rebuilding of agricultural homesteads and towns, the restriction of monopolies, the prevention of rearing persons in idleness, the restoration of farming, the rehabilitation of the wool-weaving industry, etc. Neither would the limitation of the land or money to be possessed by an individual, or the prohibition of the sale of public offices, or any similar enactments, be of permanent help. The only way that these evils "may be perfectly cured and brought to a good and upright state" and that "perfect wealth shall ever be among men" is through the abolition of private property and the introduction of communism. This form of government insures a true *commonwealth* which looks to the common interests of the many, not the few, and which secures a just distribution of the commodities of life — "that is to say, the matter of pleasure" — especially for the virtuous and hard-working members of the nation.[12]

There can be no doubt that Hythloday, like the Utopians, is persuaded that communism is the answer to the social, economic, and political evils of the day. But what is the real attitude of Thomas More himself toward communism? Which of the following does the author of *Utopia* consider communism to be: a practical remedy? an impossible ideal? a desirable, but unattainable, ideal?

XIV

HUMANISM AND COMMUNISM: THE BACKGROUND

The current study naturally and necessarily limits itself to Thomas More and the Renaissance insofar as it concerns *Utopia*. But to say that the present cannot be understood satisfactorily without the study of the past is a platitude. This is true also of the attitude of the humanists toward communism. A knowledge of the past is necessary for an appreciation, not only of humanist criticism of late Scholastic conceptions, but also of humanist recourse and appeal to classical, scriptural, and patristic authority. After a succinct treatment of communism in ancient and medieval thought, this chapter will concern itself in greater detail with the views of the humanists of the late fifteenth and early sixteenth centuries.

Erasmus in his books of apophthegms includes the dicta and enactments of Lycurgus and the Spartans. For example, he writes:

. . . everyone, unlike the practice in other countries, not only had jurisdiction over his own children, servants, and possessions, but also enjoyed as much right over the children and possessions of his friends and neighbors as over his own, so that they had everything as much as possible in common and everyone took no less care of his neighbor's goods than his own. This people realized how much advantage arose from a common participation, not inflicted under compulsion, but springing from a mutual benevolence. For they desired the famous saying of Pythagoras that friends have all things in common to hold sway as widely as possible in their commonwealth. All citizens, after all, are one another's friends.

In Utopia, too, as in every communistic state, the assumption is that "where nothing is private, the common affairs be earnestly looked upon" (*ubi nihil priuati est, serio publicum negotium agunt*).[1]

The predilection of many humanists for Plato must have encouraged a reëxamination of the accepted concepts of private property and communism. The communism of the guardians in the *Republic*, for whom Plato had prescribed that "none must possess any private property save the indispensable," is too well known to need description. Its foundation is the principle: "That city . . . is best ordered in which the greatest number use the expression 'mine' and 'not mine' of the same things in the same way." In the *Laws*, it is necessary to remember, Plato retains the completely communistic state as an ideal, but reluctantly abandons it in a more sober moment, since "such a course is beyond the capacity of people with the birth, rearing and training we assume." In *Politics*, Aristotle objects that Plato's attempt to produce uniformity is destructive of the state, which depends upon diversity of occupation, rank, etc. Common ownership, moreover, produces not harmony, but discord, for it generally leads to quarrels and litigations. It reduces the individual's interest in what is common, and waters down the force of family affection. This pithy summary of objections based on common sense and knowledge of normal human nature is to reappear in various form and phraseology throughout future centuries.[2]

To understand the relations of the Platonic and Aristotelian doctrine on communism to the Christian concept through the ages — and especially to the attitude of the Christian humanists at the time of the composition of the *Utopia* — it is essential to grasp clearly the practice of Christ and the early Christians. There can be no doubt that Christ Himself imposed upon His chosen band of apostles and disciples a strict and obligatory poverty and communism (Matt. x. 9–10; Mark vi. 8–9, x. 21; Luke

ix. 57–58, x. 4, xiv. 33; John xii. 6, xiii. 29). But this common poverty was wholly voluntary, since a certain rich youth could refuse His gracious request to join this restricted group (Matt. xix. 22; Mark x. 22; Luke xviii. 23), and was directed solely to the perfect fulfillment of an apostolic life of teaching and preaching. "It was not an attempt at a social revolution for the benefit of the 'proletarians' of Palestine." In a word, the invitation to a life of communal poverty was *not* a *commandment*, but a *counsel*.[3]

In spite of frequent misinterpretation of the pertinent texts in the Acts (ii. 44–45, iv. 32–35), the Christians in the church of Jerusalem did not practice a strict community of goods; they were free to retain their property or to sell it in order to give the proceeds to the poor. As for the Fathers of the Church, they in their genuine writings praise the voluntary communism among the monks, but condemn the heretics wishing to make it compulsory and universal; they assert the right of the individual to private property, but oblige the rich to the alleviation of the needs of the poor. [4]

Of special importance are the texts on the common life in Gratian's *Decretum*. Gratian gives as an example of the natural law "the common possession of all things," and later reiterates that "by the natural law all things are common." The right of private property arises from custom or positive human enactment. As St. Augustine maintains in his commentary on St. John, even the Church holds its goods, not by divine right, but by human right. The spurious epistle of Clement is quoted in its entirety in the *Decretum*. This epistle gives six reasons, ranging from the natural law and Plato's authority to texts in the *Acts*, to prove that all things ought to be common to all men, and explains that it was "through iniquity" that private ownership entered the world. The glosses on the assertions on communism in the *Decretum* are extremely interesting for their sense of the purely theoretical nature of the discussion and for their defense of the existing system of private property. There was agreement among the Scholastics, however, that if Adam had not sinned, things would have remained common. There was also agreement on salient points in regard to the justice of private property.[5]

The doctrine of Aquinas in its baldest form is the following. Private ownership is not against the natural law, for it is a necessary addition made to the natural law by human reason. As a right, it belongs, not strictly to positive human law, but to the *ius gentium* (Law of Nations), which, in the words of Drostan Maclaren, "lies as an intermediary between natural law and human positive law" and which "consists of precepts derived from the primary precepts of the natural law in the same way as conclusions are derived from their premises; without the *ius gentium* it would be impossible for man to live peacefully in society." Private property is best because man takes more care of his own than of the community's possessions, less confusion results, and greater order is effected since altercations are fewer. Goods, however, remain common at least in respect to *use*, insofar as the owner must be ready to share his goods with others in time of need. Aquinas views the common life of the early church in Jerusalem as only a temporary expedient for a particular church. The Utopians, of course, claim that communism begets greater care of common property, perfect order, and no lawsuits.[6]

Following the lead of earlier Scholastics, Duns Scotus tries to reconcile the texts of Gratian, Augustine, and Clement by developing the theory that in the state of innocence all things would have been common by a precept of the law of nature or of God, but in the state of fallen nature private property is a just right which is founded, not on the natural law (since it had determined human nature to common ownership), nor on divine positive law, but on human positive law. The natural or divine precept of community of possessions was revoked after the fall for the sake of greater peace and order and for the protection of the weaker members of society. Private property is natural, therefore, in the sense that it rests upon the general principle that a community or a commonwealth must have peace. This aspect is true of almost all positive laws. Scotus explains that there is always some principle which serves as the basis for establishing other (or positive) laws or rights. The latter, however, do not follow simply and absolutely from that principle but declare or explain that principle in regard to definite, particular circumstances. These explanations, of course, are in close accord with the general natural principle. Thus, private property, according to Scotus, is not a simple and absolute necessity; but, in view of the weakness and acquisitiveness of most men, the system is most suitable for peaceful existence. From such statements it is clear that, except for a different approach and terminology, Scotus is in substantial agreement with Aquinas for all *practical* purposes — and so is almost every Scholastic.[7]

In summary, one may say that the Schoolmen were ardent defenders of the theoretical right of private property. Strict communism on an extensive popular level, according to both Thomists and Scotists, was impracticable in existing conditions, whatever might have been the rule before the fall of man. Hence they rejected the social errors of the Apostolics who defended obligatory communism, the Manichaeans who viewed all matter as evil, the Albigensians who reprobated any attachment to material things and hence to property, the Waldensians who extolled landless poverty, the Spiritual Franciscans or Fraticelli who declared poverty to be of universal obligation, Wyclif and his followers who upheld the Dominion of Grace, John Ball who was one of the leaders in the Peasant Revolt of 1381, and the Beguines and Beghards who defended and practiced poverty and communism in the Netherlands.[8]

This rapid survey of the medieval background would hardly be complete without a word on another group in the Netherlands, the Brethren of the Common Life, the educators and inspirers of many northern humanists, including Erasmus. During their first days, the Brethren were attacked for presuming to lead the common life without religious vows taken in an order or congregation. In reply to these enemies, Gerard Zerbolt of Zutphen

(1367–1398) wrote a treatise on the common life, entitled *The Manner of Life for a Society of Devout Men* (*De Modo Vivendi Devotorum Hominum Simul Commorancium*), in which he collected all the pertinent arguments: Christ's advice to the rich young man (Matt. xix), the apostolic church in Jerusalem (Acts ii, iv), the recommendation of Fathers and Doctors of the Church, communism in the state of original innocence, the authority of pagan philosophers like Pythagoras and Seneca, the nature of men as social and mutually helpful animals, etc. Erasmus may have formed some of his ideas from the reading of Zerbolt's treatise or from conversation with the Brethren about the common life.[9]

English literature before *Utopia* offers interesting side lights on the whole question of communism. In the second half of the fourteenth century, the author of *Piers Plowman* denounces the friars for teaching communism to the people in spite of God's command not to covet one's neighbor's goods. Reginald Pecock in the middle of the fifteenth century tries to prove to the Lollards that the practice of the common life in the church of Jerusalem was a matter of counsel, not of precept. Early in the sixteenth century, Alexander Barclay, following Locher, speaks of the original golden age in which all things were common. A petition in the middle of the sixteenth century gives as a reason for putting an end to the original communism of the Church the fact that the idle and slothful need an incentive to work, namely, private ownership and profit.[10]

What are the views of More's humanistic friends and acquaintances in respect to communism and private property? The views of John Colet, who exerted great influence on Erasmus and More, should prove interesting and revealing. Before the coming of Christ, the majority of fallen mankind lived, not according to revelation, but according to "the *law of nature*: — not the law of simple, holy, and inviolate nature (for that state of innocence was in paradise alone), but of a defiled and corrupted nature." It was this law, under the aspect of the law of nations, which "brought in ideas of *meum* and *tuum* — of property, that is to say, and deprivation; ideas clean contrary to a good and unsophisticated nature: for that would have a community in all things." Colet, therefore, seems to hold that man's real nature is man's nature in the state of original justice, which inclined him toward common possession of all things. This natural inclination to communism remains, even though private property is now best in view of the weaknesses or evil propensities which afflict human nature at present. If Colet in the quotation given above really means to identify the natural law (even though it now is the "law of a corrupter nature") with the law of nations (which is "resorted to by nations all over the world") — the two are usually distinguished — he disagrees with Scotus in making the natural law, and not positive human enactment, the source of rights of property. But he does concur with Scotus in emphasizing communism for the state of original justice.[11]

The question is: does Colet advocate Christian communism? It is impossible to give a categorical reply. One must use the distinction between three states: the first, original justice (*status iustitiae originalis*), the second, fallen nature (*status naturae lapsae*), and the third, nature fallen and restored (*status naturae lapsae et reparatae*). The last is that of the regenerated Christian in the state of grace. Needless to say, Colet holds communism to be the best system for the state of original justice. For the state of fallen nature, private ownership is the inevitable order. As for the state of nature fallen and restored (but not restored to the complete simplicity and integrity of the state of original justice, since mortality and concupiscence remain in the regenerated man), Colet would probably say that for perfect followers of Christ communism is the ideal but that practically private property, animated by a spirit of generosity and self-sacrifice toward the poor and needy, is best for this state; for, though a redeemed nature is restored to justice, it remains, in certain respects, a fallen nature, and therefore a nature subject to weakness and defect. For this reason, Lupton can rightly maintain that the *Utopia* echoes the teaching of Colet who "expressed approval, though briefly and guardedly, of a Christian communism." [12]

Another English humanist, Thomas Elyot, believes that in the beginning the people "had all things in common, and equality in degree and condition," but that now "the best and most sure governance is by one king or prince, which ruleth only for the weal of his people to him subject." He apparently can conceive of a communistic state only as a "communalty" without order and without distinction of superior and inferior. He insists that *respublica* should be translated *public weal*, not *common weal*. The persons who think that it is called the *common weal* because "every thing should be to all men in common, without discrepance of any estate or condition," are led to this opinion "more by sensuality than by any good reason or inclination to humanity." Elyot has no more than these few words to say on communism.[13]

As one turns back a few years from England to the continent, one finds interesting views in the writings of Ficino. In his summary of the fourth book of the *Republic*, which had exerted influence on the *Utopia*, Ficino tells how Plato descends by degrees to "his mystery." This "mystery" is nothing else than the common possession of all things, so that some do not have more property with consequent luxury, pride, and indolence, and so that others do not have less with resultant envy, lying, and thievery. Even more significant of his attitude is the passage in a letter to Angelo Poliziano:

> God wished the water to be common to all aquatic creatures and the earth to be common to all terrestrial beings. Man alone, unhappy soul, separated what God had joined together. He contracted to a narrow compass his overlordship which by nature was spread far and wide. He introduced into the world *mine* and *thine*, the beginning of all dissension and wickedness. Therefore, not without justice did Pythagoras decree that all things are common among friends; and Plato, among fellow citizens. . . . [T]hey are just and happy, who, established in immense wealth, consider themselves to be the servants of God, the guardians of the poor, and the dispensers of great sums of money.

Basic to Ficino's conception of property and wealth is the notion
that God originally wished all things to be common. Man thwarted
that plan. The best that the wealthy — who, after all, receive
their wealth ultimately from God — can do practically is not to
get rid of their riches and establish a communistic society, but
to behave as the stewards of God and protectors of the poor.
They are to regard their property not as absolute owners but
as Christian administrators. Ficino, therefore, is something of an
eclectic philosopher. With Scotus he lays stress on communism
as the proper order in the state of innocence; with Aquinas he
believes in the communism of use, not of ownership, i.e., he
advocates that in the present condition of mankind the rich view
themselves as the dispensers of God's common bounty, especially
in time of need. [14]

The opinion of Guillaume Budé, if one is to judge from his
letter to Thomas Lupset first prefixed to the Paris edition (1517)
of *Utopia*, is less conservative. The island of Utopia, according
to Budé, "is said, . . . by what must be owned to be a singular
good fortune, to have adopted Christian usages both in public
and in private; to have imbibed the wisdom thereto belonging;
and to have kept it undefiled to this very day" (*Vtopia vero
insula . . . mirifica utique sorte . . . Christianos vero ritus ac
germanam ipsam sapientiam publice priuatimque hausisse
perhibetur, intemeratamque ad hunc usque diem seruasse*).
There is a certain ambiguity about this statement. In Budé's
view, did the Utopians have Christian rites and wisdom only
after the coming of Christianity? Certainly the phrase "to have
have kept it undefiled to this very day" has little significance if
it applies merely to the slightly more than a decade which has
elapsed since Hythloday's arrival in Utopia. The phrase must
apply rather to the rites and wisdom of the Utopians, curiously
similar to those of the Christians, prevalent before the missionary
endeavors of Hythloday. Later on, Budé marvels that avarice
and covetousness have failed to penetrate Utopia "for so many
ages" (*tot seculis*), a phrase which indicates that the Utopians

had Christian practices and wisdom before the introduction of Christianity. Budé's comparison thus gains immensely in strength: pagan Utopia, unlike the Christian West, has clung tenaciously to "three divine institutions": (1) "the absolute equality, or . . . the civil communication of all things good and bad among fellow-citizens"; (2) "a settled and unwavering love of peace and quietness"; and (3) "a contempt for gold and silver." One may well speculate whether Budé designedly used the term *divine* instead of *Christian*. If he did, it would mean that such were God's plans for man from the very creation and that the Utopians have recaptured and preserved these three ideals independently of the preaching of Christ's gospel, which, of course, reëstablishes and perfects God's original designs. The three institutions are directed against crying evils of contemporary Europe: the first, against the great inequality of rich and poor, nobles and commons, among Christian peoples; the second, against the uninterrupted wars of Christian princes; and the third, against the greed for wealth which was corrupting Christian countries. If Europeans had as firm convictions on these points as the Utopians, there would be an end to all fraud, deception, avarice, pride, and litigation. Hence, Budé cries out: "Would that great Heaven in its goodness had dealt so kindly with the countries which keep, and would not part with, the appellation [i.e., Christian] they bear, derived from His most holy name!" [15]

Christ, Budé writes, was the founder and dispenser of all possessions (Matt. xxviii. 18; I Cor. xv. 24–27, etc.). What disposition did He make of property? As far as His followers were concerned, He established among them "a Pythagorean communion and love" (*Pythagoricam communionem et charitatem*), a reference to the early Christians in Jerusalem where they held "all things in common" (Acts ii. 44, iv. 32). Budé seems to believe that these Christians not merely shared all their goods but actually practised a loving communism such as prevailed among the Utopians. For Christ showed what a heavy sanction He laid on His law by making an impressive example of the case of

Ananias, whom He condemned to death for violation of the law
of communion (*ob temeratam communionis legem*). Evidently
Budé holds that Ananias was not punished for telling a serious
falsehood (as exegetes generally hold), but for violation of the
communism of the church in Jerusalem. Nevertheless, he does
not make even an academic plea for the adoption of communism,
but draws out of Christ's law a more immediate and practical
lesson for Christians: the abolition of the thousand and one un-
edifying litigations about property in both the civil and the
ecclesiastical courts. Instead of making the noble law of love
and communion, enunciated by Pythagoras and proclaimed by
Christ, the guiding principle of their lives, Christians have low-
ered themselves to the ignoble norms and increasing tyranny of
the civil and canon laws.[16]

In summary of Budé's view, one may say that theoretically
he sees a mutual sharing of all things, if not strict communism
itself, as the ideal state for contemporary Europeans as it was
for the earliest Christians and as it is now for the Utopians, who
are Christian in all but name. Practically, he descends to a concrete and particular application of the law of love and communion: he wants the simple precepts of Christ set forth in the
gospel to displace the intricate and specious laws of church and
state on property and possession.

Christ and Pythagoras and Plato are often linked together as
religious teachers in the minds and works of many humanists,
just as they are in Budé's letter. In the introduction to his *Adages*,
Erasmus declares that, if one examines thoroughly the saying of
Pythagoras on the community of all things among friends, one
will find therein the whole of human happiness in a nutshell.
Plato did nothing else than advocate this community and friendship among the founders of his republic. If he had been success-
ful in his plea, war, envy, and fraud would have departed forth-
with from the city; and, to be brief, the whole mass of human
plagues would have left once for all. Erasmus continues: "What
else than this did Christ, the head of our religion, do? In fact,

He gave to the world only a single commandment, that of charity, teaching that the whole of the law and the prophets depended upon it. Or what else does charity urge upon men but that all things must be common to all men?" Erasmus then reinforces his point with an appeal to the doctrine of the mystical body of Christ.[17]

This espousal of Christian communism by Erasmus is continued in the commentary on the very first of his *Adages*: "Friends have all things in common" (*Amicorum communia omnia*). He points out the use of this proverb by Aristotle and Plato. Plato, for example, realizes that the citizens of the best and happiest commonwealth, like friends, must have all things in common and must not utter the word *mine* and *not mine*. Yet it is wonderful to mark what displeasure Christians show toward this communism in Plato, in fact, what violent criticism they launch against it, although nothing has ever been said by a pagan philosopher more in accordance with the mind of Christ. Even Aristotle, who moderates Plato's communistic thought by assigning ownership and goods to definite private persons, wishes all things to be in common under the aspect of free and unhampered *use*. Gellius is Erasmus' authority for the statement that Pythagoras not only was the author of the saying on the community of all things among friends, but also introduced among his followers a communism of life and resources, "such as Christ wished to exist among all Christians." Whoever had been initiated into the company of Pythagoras' disciples, put into the common stock whatever he possessed in the way of money and household. In the second of his *Adages*, however, Erasmus observes that communism is not to be carried to the extent of giving things equally to old and young, learned and ignorant, stupid and wise, but goods are to be distributed in accordance with everyone's office, dignity, etc.[18]

The *Praise of Folly* even makes humorous use of this famous axiom of Pythagoras. Folly singles out "certain Pythagoreans, in whose eyes all things are common — to such a degree, in fact, that whatever they light upon that is lying around loose they carry off with a tranquil spirit, as if it passed to them by inheritance." Lister in a note explains that the joke is about thieves who take things from all as from their friends, for "among friends all things are common." [19]

Erasmus thus seems to have had a settled conviction that Christ had wished communism — not merely the communism of use or alms, but the communism of joint ownership — to be the proper state for His followers. Here is yet another point of conflict between the humanistic Erasmus and the Aristotelian Schoolmen. The author of the *Adages* does not spare the latter in his denunciation of their amalgamation of the doctrines of Aristotle and Christ, which to him are as incompatible as fire and water. Here are his indignant words:

We have reached such a point that the whole of Aristotle is accepted in the heart of Christian theology, in fact, accepted to such an extent that his authority is almost more sacred than that of Christ. For, if he says anything that is little in keeping with our Christian life, it is permissible to twist its meaning by a clever interpretation; but the man who dares even slightly oppose his oracular utterances, is downed [and silenced] on the spot. From Aristotle we have learned that the happiness of man is imperfect without the addition of goods of body and fortune. From Aristotle we have learned that the commonwealth in which all things are common cannot flourish. We keep trying to amalgamate the principles of Aristotle with the doctrine of Christ, that is, to mix water and fire.[20]

The whole implication of this passage is that for the Christian philosopher Aristotle's criticism of Plato's communism should be invalid. Christians should follow, not Aristotle's condemnation of joint ownership and his defense of private property, but Christ's doctrine which enjoins communism for the entire Christian community, not merely for monks and friars. In spite of his strong words in the *Adages*, however, Erasmus strangely has little to say on the practices of the early church in Jerusalem in his notes on the crucial texts in the Acts of the Apostles, either in his New Testament or in his paraphrase of the Acts.

In the preceding citations, Christ's law of love and community is linked to that of Pythagoras and Plato. On another occasion Erasmus found a bond between Christ and the Spartan Lycurgus. In his *Apophthegms* Erasmus writes:

It was customary [among the Lacedaemonians] to use the slaves of neighbors, if anyone had need, as one's own. The same held for dogs and horses, unless their master had occasion to use them. What is more, in the country, if anyone needed anything, he opened the doors and took away from its possessor what was necessary for his present task; he merely marked the place from which he had taken anything and then went his way. In the midst of customs of this kind, where could insatiable avarice find a place? where the rapacity of men who appropriate other people's property as their own? where the arrogance springing from riches? where the cruelty of robbers who cut the throat of an unknown and innocent traveler for a few pennies? Would you not say that this was a genuinely Christian custom if they had obtained Christ, instead of Lycurgus, as a maker of laws? [21]

Here, it is true, is found a communism of use, rather than of ownership, a concept which is more in the Aristotelian tradition, but it is a use carried so far that it amounts, for all practical purposes, to a communism of ownership.

Erasmus' whole concept of the strict communism which should prevail in Christendom must have received a severe jolt in the early years of the Reformation. Except on a purely theoretical basis, he seems hardly to have conceived of Christian communism on a large scale. If it had come peacefully and gradually, Erasmus would have welcomed the transformation and change. The violent espousal of total communism, as on the part of some Anabaptists, was quite another matter. Erasmus admits that for some time in the apostolic period at the origins of the early Church a community of all goods prevailed, but not even at that time among all Christians. For, with the spread of the gospel far and wide, communism could not be preserved, for the reason that it would have ended in revolt. He seems to be referring to distressing disagreements and conflicts, from which even the primitive church in Jerusalem had suffered in a small way: "Now in those days, as the number of the disciples was increasing, there arose a murmuring among the Hellenists against the Hebrews that their widows were being neglected in the daily ministration" (Acts vi. 1). His final decision is expressed thus: "More in accord with harmony is the following policy: the ownership of goods and the right of administration should be in the hands of lawful proprietors, but the use of these goods should be made common by charity." Face to face with hard reality, even the scholarly idealist has to admit that the sane judgment of Aristotle and Aquinas, after all is said and done, is the best: private ownership with common use inspired by Christian love.[22]

The author of *Utopia*, too, in the heat of conflict indirectly asserts against the Anabaptists the right of private property. One of the worst charges he can launch against Tyndale is that the latter has added to his own heresies those of the Anabaptists, who say "that there ought to be no rulers at all in Christendom, neither spiritual nor temporal, and that no man should have anything proper of his own, but that all lands and all goods ought by God's law to be all men's in common, and that all women ought to be common of all men." [23] Did More, in a way similar to Erasmus, suffer a change of opinion in regard to Christ's view of communism?

XV

THOMAS MORE AND
COMMUNISM: THE SOLUTION

The wisdom of Christ, Hythloday declares toward the end of
his discourse in *Utopia*, was so great that He could not be ignorant of what was best for humanity, and His goodness was so
immense that He could not but ordain what was best for men.
If it had not been for human pride, the Savior "would have
brought all the world long ago into the laws of this weal public,"
the very foundation of which was communism. Needless to say,
not the least of the attractive features which drew the Utopians
to Christianity was the fact that Christ had been pleased to establish the common life among His followers. This common life
was still in vogue among the most genuine of Christian communities, namely, the enclosures of monks and friars. Here there is
more than a tinge of regret that what Christ had instituted for
all should be practiced by only a few.[1]

The notion that Christ has tried to call His followers back to
the communism originally instituted by God finds even stronger
expression within four years or less after the publication of
Utopia in More's letter to a monk, which appeared first in *Epistolae Aliquot Eruditorum Virorum* (1520). More writes: "God
manifested great foresight when He instituted all things in
common. Christ, too, manifested great foresight when He made
the attempt to recall mortals again from what was private to
what was common. He was fully aware, there can be no doubt,

that our corrupt mortal nature does not cherish lovingly what is private without detriment to what is common." All experience verifies this last statement. Whatever a man calls his own, whether his plot of land, or his sum of money, or his family, divorces his feelings from concern with what is common. Examples which More derives from religion are the following: the emphasis on private rather than official fasts, the preference of one saint to another, the exaltation of the ceremonies of one religious order over those of another, and the glorification of monastic observances over the practices common to the whole Christian people, such as "those plebeian virtues: faith, hope, charity, fear of God, humility, and others of the same kind." [2]

Similar statements are echoed by humanists and Scholastics. In his *New Testament*, Erasmus asks why Benedictines, Augustinians, and Franciscans attribute more to a rule written by a man (Benedict, Augustine, and Francis) than Christians do to their rule, which Christ gave to all and which all have equally professed in baptism. On an even more general plane, Vives in his *Help of the Poor* insists that "all things were given to us by God, to some for the sake of the others." What liberal nature has given to be common, men maliciously make private; what she has made visible and accessible, they carry off, lock up, guard, and keep from others by doors, walls, bolts, iron, weapons, and laws. "Thus, our avarice and wickedness impose scarcity and hunger on the abundance of nature and cause poverty amid the riches of God." For Alexander the Englishman in his *Destruction of Vices*, false Christians make common goods private property. This he finds especially true of so-called religious who appropriate for their own use the tithes and offerings which justly ought to be common property for distribution to the needy poor. On the testimony of experience, religious and pastors and prelates are defrauding the poor and spending such revenue on personal vices and worldly pleasure and vain pomp.[3]

The dominant attitude toward Christian communism, with the resultant stress upon what was peculiar and proper to an individual or group, was symptomatic of a general disease which was affecting the very vitals of Christendom. Instead of the pure Christianity which Christ taught in His life and in the pages of His gospel, people were living a Christian life perverted by the doctrines and authority of Aristotle or watered down by clever moralists to the low standards of contemporary life. If he could not speak of Platonic and Utopian communism and other institutions in the royal council as well as anywhere else, Hythloday feels that logically "we must among Christian people wink at the most part of all those things which Christ taught us and so straitly forbade them to be winked at that those things also which He whispered in the ears of His disciples He commanded to be proclaimed in open houses." The discrepancy between the doctrine of Christ and the conduct of Christians has been glossed by cunning preachers who practice More's advice: "that which you cannot turn to good, so . . . order it that it be not very bad." Only with the greatest reluctance do men suffer the adaptation and adjustment of their morality to the standards of Christ. In order to make the two agree in some way or other, preachers "have wrested and wried His doctrine and like a rule of lead have applied it to men's manners" (*doctrinam eius uelut regulam plumbeam accommodauerunt ad mores*). What is the result? They have succeeded in nothing, except to allow men to feel more secure in their evil-doing.[4]

The convenient accommodation of Christian morality to the low practices of the day was the object of vehement attack by persons with the welfare and reformation of the Church at heart. In the very first sermon delivered in May 1512, before the Fifth Council of the Lateran, the brilliant Egidio of Viterbo had declared that it was only right and just that men should be changed by religious observances, and not religious observances by men. Erasmus, too, almost from the time of his earliest published works, cries out against the manifest absurdity of persons who "strive to bend, not the morality of men to Christ, but Christ to the life of men." He sees a race of men reigning supreme in the world, who do not measure and regulate their religious devotion by the rule of Christ (*Christi regula*), but by their own emotional predilections. They attribute an aura of sanctity to whatever they love passionately, with the result that they flatter themselves astonishingly in regard to things which are most sinful by nature. They publish that they are wearing such and such a holy cincture. "Why? Because they want, on account of a little effort, to be taken for saints. But they have no desire to live either soberly or chastely, or to suffer injuries. Why so? Because it is too hard and too difficult." [5]

The ideological source of such unfortunate and disastrous attitudes is exposed by Gerard Lister in his notes (1515) to Erasmus' *Praise of Folly*. The lofty doctrines of Christ and the corrupt values of the world, he points out, are as compatible as fire and water. The purpose of Christ's incarnation was to pluck out depraved opinions and to implant new and unprecedented ones. Thus, Christ wanted His followers to be rich, not in worldly possessions and influence, but in the contempt of all earthly goods. He wanted His own to be powerful, not in strength of body and weapons of war, but in the contempt of death. He wanted His own, finally, to be blessed with exile, imprisonment, persecution, and death. And here Lister drives home his point: "These recent theologians of ours, however, wish to effect a union between Christ and the world, and label as Christian those things which are done by the overwhelming majority, that is to say, by the world; they admit as allowable pleasures, war, weapons, two garments, and all other worldly things, provided only they are used, as they say, with moderation." [6]

The word *moderation* is a clue to the principal complaint of the humanists. They feel that the prestige of Aristotle and the Aristotelization of theology have contributed much, although not all, to the contamination of the pure teaching of Christ and to the abasement of the high moral standards of Christ. As has been seen above, Erasmus declares that the union of Aristotle and Christ is like a mixture of fire and water. Yet Christians hardly

dare to deny a single doctrine of Aristotle and go to great lengths
to twist his words, even those most un-Christian, to some sort of
compatibility with Christ's principles. An extremely pertinent
example is the maintenance of the impossibility of a communistic Christian society — in the very face of the example of Christ
and His disciples and His early Church. It is from Aristotle, not
from Christ, "we have learned that the commonwealth in which
all things are common cannot flourish." [7]

But Aristotle is not the only source of offense. No less to blame
is human law, whether ecclesiastical or civil. In his letter to
Lupset, Budé trenchantly expresses the clash between the law
of church and state and the law of God and Christ as follows:
"in the decrees of the canonists, the divine law differs as much
from the human; and, in our civil laws and royal enactments,
true equity differs as much from law; as the principles laid down
by Christ . . . and the usages of His disciples, differ from the
decrees and enactments of those who think the *summum bonum*
and perfection of happiness to lie in the money-bags of a Croesus
or a Midas." In his famous Adage 3001 (*Sweet Is War to the Un-
initiated*), Erasmus concentrates on the civil, or Roman, law. On
account of the civil law's appearance of justice, men twist and
turn and stretch the teachings of the gospel to the utmost allowable limits in order to make it agree with the civil law. The latter
permits the repulsion of force with force and the prosecution of
every right by every individual; it approves of big business; it
legalizes usury, provided the latter is moderate; it exalts war
as a glorious thing, provided it is just. And what is a just war? A
just war is defined by the civil law to be one declared by the
prince, however puerile or stupid. Christ and His sacred writings
receive little or no hearing. Erasmus rises to an indignant grand-
eur as he continues:

To sum it all up, the whole doctrine of Christ is so contaminated by
the writings of pagan dialecticians, sophists, mathematicians, orators,
poets, philosophers, and lawyers that the greatest part of one's life
is consumed before one has time for the examination of the Sacred

Books. When at length you come to them, you are bound to approach
them tainted with so many worldly opinions that either you are re-
pulsed altogether by the principles of Christ or you twist them to suit
the views of those pagan authors. And this state of affairs is so far
from being subjected to censure that to speak of the writings of Christ
is a crime for anyone except the man who has stuffed himself, as they
say, even to the ears with Aristotelian, or rather sophistical, nonsense —
as if the teaching of Christ were such that it could not be as common
as possible to all men, or that it could in any way agree with the wisdom
of pagan philosophers. [8]

As one studies all these views of the humanists, one cannot
escape the conviction that there is an underlying consistency in
the attitude toward Christian communism in Hythloday's views
as propounded in *Utopia*, in More's mind as revealed in his
letter to a monk, and in the writings of such humanists as Budé,
Lister, and Erasmus. In its most simple terms, this common attitude may be expressed as follows. God originally intended communism to be the social system best suited for human beings.
Fallen man, however, divided up possessions hitherto held in
common, and introduced the right of private property. When
He came upon earth, Christ tried to recall at least His followers
to the original arrangement made by God. This attempt is evident from His own practice and that of His apostles and disciples, as well as that of the early church in Jerusalem. Except
for the triumph of the common life in certain select companies
(the so-called religious orders), Christ's endeavors had but little
success. His program of reform was a failure, not because He
Himself was deficient in any respect, but because He required
the free coöperation of His creatures. Man's wickedness (in the
form of pride and avarice and other monsters, according to
Hythloday) led him to frustrate Christ's plan for his happiness
by way of the common life. Christians were aided in this thwart-
ing of Christ's wise provision by the authority of Aristotle and
the ingenuity of clever preachers who trimmed Christ's doctrine
to suit the evil times.[9]

As far as the introduction of communism in Christian nations
and contemporary conditions is concerned, it is most important

to note, there is nothing here but wishful thinking. There is not
a single definite statement to the effect that England, or France,
or Germany should become communistic. The humanistic re-
formers apparently do not entertain any immediate practical
hope on this score. They are content to contemplate the ideal
commonwealth in all the glory of its common life, and then to
come dazzled down to earth again to suggest such measures as
are suggested by Hythloday himself and are suited to human
weakness: the restoration of the commons, the rebuilding of
farms and villages, the abolition of monopoly, the limitation of
acreage legally possessed, the prohibition of the sale of offices,
etc. This assertion does not overlook Hythloday's conviction that
what Christian nations need is not the temporary medicine of
parliamentary statutes but the perfect cure of the common life.
Yet even he proposes the communistic state as a general ideal,
without urging particular countries to adopt communism as a
program of practical and immediate reform. In his heart he realizes that, given the general run of Christians, his commonwealth,
like the republic of Plato, will never exist in the Christian West.[10]

Does this compromise mean that humanists like More are false
to their ideal? By no means. Even Christ had extended His invitation to communal poverty only to the man who ardently desired to be perfect (Matt. xix. 21). The common life for all Christians remained the ideal for the humanists, but they realized
that, in order to have perfect communism, one must have perfect
Christians — or, at least, Christians as perfect as those of the
early church in Jerusalem who sold their possessions for distribution of the proceeds to the poor by the apostles. As long
as the mass of Christians is imperfect, even though striving after
perfection, private property is best, with a view to the maintenance of peace and order against those merely nominal Christians
who would abuse the privileges of communism. In the midst of
an imperfect world, Christ gave a blessing to the poor *in spirit*
(Matt. v. 3) as well as to the heroes who chose actual poverty
for His sake. The important lesson of *Utopia*, too, is that every

person in England and all Europe must acquire the *spirit* of common life. This spirit manifests itself above all in a detachment of heart from wealth and rank and in a passionate attachment to the cause of justice and the poor.

But is not this critical view of More's attitude toward communism really noncommittal? Is More's real attitude shown in the program of communism espoused by Hythloday *or* in the objections to communism put in his own mouth by More? More's personal attitude is manifested absolutely and unconditionally in neither, but in both. "It all depends," More himself would say. His ideal will always remain that of a common Christian life for a whole Christian nation, but the realization of this ideal depends upon the character of its citizens, who must be as perfect in their Christianity — or as eager in their pursuit of Christian perfection — as the Utopians are in their rationality. There is basically nothing heretical, dangerous, or even offensive to pious ears (*piis auribus offensivum*) in the enunciation of this proposition. The imperfection, alas, inevitably connected with man's existence, even with his spiritual life, makes the condition attached to the ideal almost impossible of fulfillment. On the other hand, if Christians are to be taken as they actually exist, the objections offered to Hythloday's opinion by More in his own person are valid. Hythloday represents More's ideal views; he himself voices his practical judgments in his own person. In a word, if he regards communism abstractly or academically (according to the *philosophia scholastica*), More favors communism. If he looks at it in concrete circumstances as a practical statesman who knows what is in man (according to the *philosophia ciuilior*), he defends private property.[11]

More's objections to communism are fundamentally the Aristotelian objections. First, the promised abundance of all goods will not materialize since every man will try to get out of work. He will shun labor because the prospect of personal gain is not present to spur him on and because the foolish confidence he has that other citizens will do the necessary work will make him lazy.

Secondly, when consequent poverty begins to afflict the people and when no man can defend according to the law the common property given for his personal use, the result will be continual slaughter and revolt, with the stronger taking over the portion of the weaker. Hythloday the idealist, it will be noted, does not even attempt to answer these arguments, because they are unanswerable if one takes human nature as it actually exists. His only reply is indirectly to appeal to the principle that no line of argumentation is valid against an actual fact (*contra factum non valet illatio*). What is Hythloday's *fact*? Nothing else than the island of Utopia. Because of communism, "you never saw people well ordered but only there." But Utopia exists only in More's brain; so, too, the communistic Christian commonwealth exists only as an ideal in his mind and heart.[12]

But More does not surrender the thought of the realization of his communistic ideal without a shot. Toward the very end of *Utopia*, he speaks of many customs and laws of the island as being extremely absurd institutions, especially "the community of their life and living without any occupying of money" (*uita . . . uictuque communi, sine ullo pecuniae commercio*). What is the result of the existence of such communism in a nation? By this one feature, "all nobility, magnificence, worship, honor, and majesty . . . utterly be overthrown and destroyed" (*qua una re funditus euertitur omnis nobilitas, magnificentia, splendor, maiestas*). Yet nobility, magnificence, splendor, and majesty are the true embellishments and ornaments of a commonwealth in the opinion of the populace (*ut publica est opinio*). This last expression, used as it is parenthetically, embodies the most skilled and subtle irony: it is a stroke worthy of a master of rhetoric. For the whole purpose of *Utopia* has been to prove that these are *not* the qualities which should distinguish a commonwealth. The success of a commonwealth is to be measured by the well-being and happiness of its people, not by external fame and glory. The ideal commonwealth is much like that of the Polylerites: "their life is commodious rather than gallant [*splendide*] and

may better be called happy or lucky than notable or famous
[*nobiles aut clari*], for they be not known as much as by name, I
suppose, saving only to their next neighbors and borderers." It
is the mad striving for nobility and majesty, magnificence and
splendor, which is bringing Christian princes and peoples to
their downfall and which is causing the poor and needy to suffer
unutterable hardships. If suffering and ruin are the price of
glory, farewell magnificence, welcome common life! [13]

But the common life must not be purchased at any price or
any cost. Injustice must not be committed, for the right of private
property, even if based on human law, is just insofar as it proceeds from the civil power with God-given authority. Violence
must be eschewed, for the common life as lived by unwilling
members is intolerable. Such reasons as these show why the doctrines of the Anabaptists "that there ought to be no rulers at all
in Christendom, neither spiritual nor temporal, and that no man
should have anything proper of his own, but that all lands and
all goods ought by God's law to be all men's in common" savor
of heresy.[14]

In his description of the errors of the Anabaptists, More links
together their concept of Christian freedom and their espousal
of communism. By the year that More published his work against
Luther (1523), the communistic experiments of Muenzer, Pfeiffer,
Rothmann, and John of Leyden had not occurred. But the concept
of faith as the supreme and only law for Christians, with a resultant depreciation or denial of all human laws, had been em-
phasized almost from the earliest days of the Reformation. According to the exegesis of the innovators, the "freedom wherewith
Christ has made us free" (Gal. iv. 31, cf. Gal. ii. 4, v. 13; 2 Cor.
iii. 17; Jas. ii. 12, etc.) lay in immunity from every bond of every
law, not merely in liberation from the slavery of sin (John viii.
31 sqq., Rom. vi. 17 sqq.), from the state of servile fear (Luke
i. 74), or from the yoke of the extremely heavy ceremonial and
judicial law of Moses (Acts xv. 10, Gal. iv. 21–31). It was the
law of faith in the gospel alone which could bind the disciples

of Christ. It is in his discussion of the emancipation of the Christian from human law in his attack on Luther that More in passing gives his views on private property and communism.[15]

More labels as manifestly absurd the contention of Luther in *The Babylonian Captivity of the Church* (1520) that good and prudent magistrates would administer the government much better under the guidance of nature than by the agency of laws. The reason given by More against this view is that a good magistrate is not more just in pronouncing judgment (where the chances of corruption are usually numerous) than in passing a law. In fact, More goes so far as to claim that judgment is scarcely ever rendered justly unless it is rendered in dependence on, and in agreement with, an existent law. This holds true even for private property. "[N]either the law of the gospel apportions possessions, nor reason by itself alone prescribes the ways of distinguishing one's property, unless agreement [*consensus*] is added to reason." The theoretical basis for this statement, of course, is the Scholastic doctrine, with Scotistic rather than Thomistic overtones. According to Scotus, possessions are justly labeled as private, not according to the adjudication of the natural law, but according to the dictates of reason: not reason by itself, but reason as supplemented — or implemented, to use contemporary terminology — by human law. Typically Scotistic, too, is the concept of agreement (*consensus*). For just as individuals and families agree to surrender some of their powers to a king or democratic government, so reason persuades them to a partition of lands and goods for the preservation of peace and order. This agreement or arrangement finds expression in human positive law. Divine positive law, of course, does not assign property to individuals or particular groups (except in the case of the apportionment of the Holy Land to the Hebrews), since there is no trace of such divine legislation by God in the Old Testament or by Christ in the New. This is the meaning of More's clause that "the law of the gospel does not apportion possessions." [16]

To sum up briefly, More's position is that neither the natural law nor the divine positive law (say, the gospel of Christ) is the basis of private property. But human reason sees readily that private property, and not common possession, is the system best adapted to man's nature. Men therefore divide up the goods of the world according to an agreement. But what is this agreement? Nothing but a human law. More writes: "This agreement [*consensus*] is, in the common form of mutual negotiation, a public one: and this agreement, whether reached by custom or expressed in words, is a public law." If Luther does away with laws and gives the magistrates a free rein, one of two things will happen: (1) they will issue no command or prohibition, and then magistrates will be useless, or (2) they will rule according to their own natural impulses and carry out every arbitrary whim, and then the populace will not enjoy greater freedom but suffer even worse slavery. This is what will happen if "one must obey, not certain and stated laws, but wills which are uncertain and changing from day to day." [17]

Luther congratulates himself, says More, on having modified this foolish opinion in which he wishes to abolish all human laws. At the Diet of Worms (1521), the reformer answered that the law of the gospel will be alone sufficient and human laws useless at last (1) if magistrates were good and (2) if the genuine faith were preached. More continues: Luther maintains this view "as if even the best magistrates could bring about that the whole Christian people would wish to live in common, or that the wicked would refuse to steal, or [as if] any preaching of the faith could effect that no persons would ever be bad." To prove that the human law which alone is the basis for the right of property is just and obligatory upon Christians, More argues as follows:

The law of the gospel which forbids theft is just and obliges Christians.
But the human laws which punish theft and safeguard private prop-
    erty merely carry out the law of the gospel in regard to theft.
Therefore these human laws are just and oblige Christians.

In fact, the basic assumption of the argument is that the human laws which define just possession and unjust theft are the implementation of the law of the gospel, so that if they were abolished, the law of the gospel would mean nothing since no one would know what was possessed justly or taken unjustly. All this is contained in More's few words: "If the law of the gospel does not permit theft, certainly the human law which punishes theft is not useless, and the human law which alone distinguishes private possessions [*lex humana quae sola rerum proprietatem diuidit*] is obligatory upon Christians, since with the abolition of the latter law theft could not even exist." Telltale is the modifier "alone" (*sola*), for it betrays the Scotistic cast of More's mind in regard to private property. Not the natural law, but positive human enactments, are the only source of private property.

More then declares that it will do Luther no good to take refuge in the advocacy of communism in order to establish the uselessness of human laws: "[I]f he [Luther] maintains that it would be more advantageous for us to lack the law from which the private possession of goods is born and to live in a certain community of nature [*in communitate quadam naturali*], thus eliminating the object of theft, it would in no way help his cause, even if one conceded him that point; for even if people could live in common with fewer laws by far, nevertheless they could not live without any laws at all."

As examples of necessary laws in a communistic commonwealth, More instances the laws regulating labor and the laws punishing crimes, which, after all, would be rife even in that kind of life. He concludes: "Now if, in spite of the most genuine preaching of the faith (even according to the way in which the apostles kept preaching it most authentically) and in spite of the elevation of the very best magistrates everywhere to positions of authority over the Christian people, private property could stay and many people remain unjust, it is undeniable that human law is obligatory for Christians lest one man should snatch what the law has apportioned to another, and that it is not useless insofar as it punishes the offender if anyone should commit theft." The meaning of this rather obscurely phrased sentence is clear: human laws, say, on property and theft, are useful and obligatory on Christians as long as one or both of the following conditions are present: as long as the right of private property is just or/and as long as some people are wicked. The latter, of course, will exist whether communism or private property prevails in a commonwealth.

This single page from his work against Luther gives the admirers of More's *Utopia* a much clearer picture of his real views on communism. The passage from *A Dialogue of Comfort against Tribulation* which is usually cited as presenting More's opinion is far less informative. It begins as follows: "[M]en of substance must there needs be; for else shall you have more beggars, pardie, than there be, and no man left able to relieve another." It is immediately evident from this sentence that More is dealing, not with the broad philosophical foundations of communism and property as he did in *Utopia* and in his answer to Luther, but with a particular scheme of some Protestants to "share the wealth." The plan plainly envisaged a general census of the money and land in the nation and then a fair and equal division of both among all the citizens. Practical More, of course, considers such a scheme absurd: "For this think I in my mind a very sure conclusion, that if all the money that is in this country, were to-morrow next brought together out of every man's hand, and laid all upon one heap, and then divided out unto every man alike, it would be on the morrow after worse than it was the day before. For I suppose when it were all equally thus divided among all, the best should be left little better than a beggar almost is now; and yet he that was a beggar before, all that he shall be the richer for that he should thereby receive, shall not make him much above a beggar still. . . ." [18]

In these sentences More points out the manifest unreasonableness and infeasibility of this particular plan, not of communism in general. The words prove, not that More is in favor of individual proprietary dominion, but that under these special circumstances it constitutes for him the lesser evil. What follows in the *Dialogue* is as true in communistic Utopia as in private-propertied England, because it merely advocates a division of labor. In Utopia, the one who provides a livelihood for the many is the government or the community as a whole.

Men cannot, you wot well, live here in the world, but if some one man provide a mean of living for some other many. Every man cannot have a ship of his own, nor every man be a merchant without a stock: and these things, you wot well, must needs be had; nor every man cannot have a plough by himself. And who might live by a tailor's craft, if no man were able to put a gown to make? Who by masonry? Or, who could live a carpenter, if no man were able to build neither church, nor house? Who should be makers of any manner of cloth, if there lacked men of substance to set sundry sorts a work?

All these trades have been more than adequately organized and provided for in Utopia. Consequently, what More is here disclaiming and repudiating is not the vision of a perfect commonwealth which can always exist as an ideal to be contemplated, but petty schemes for sharing the wealth. Rather than adopt any of these harebrained reforms, it is far better to continue the present system in which "surely the rich man's substance is the wellspring of the poor man's living." As long as this latter remains true, "[s]ome man that hath but two ducats in his house, were better forbear them both and leave himself not a farthing, but utterly lose all his own, than that some rich man, by whom he is weekly set a work should of his money lose the one half: for then were himself like to lack work."

It is not fair to argue, as some have done, from these sentences in the *Dialogue of Comfort* that More had no concept of anything like the communistic state of today, in which the government owns the agents of production and distributes the products of industry with a certain attempt at equality. He may have had specifically no idea of the dictatorship of the proletariat in a totalitarian state, but the very existence of the *Utopia* refutes the view that he had no picture of a communistic state in which democratic forms of election and deliberation play the major role. In the *Dialogue of Comfort*, More is writing as a statesman who is scanning closely the contemporary economic setup. His final decision is that for the present a continuation of the existing economic and social organization is best. Consequently he advises strongly against the equal distribution of all the wealth among all the citizens as absolutely ruinous. As for the Utopian system of government, men are so far from being willing or perfect enough even to discuss it that More does not hint at it even as a possibility. He has no intention of casting pearls before swine. The most that can be gathered from the *Dialogue* is that More as a statesman finds the retention of private property and private enterprise the best and the most reasonable policy under contemporary circumstances. But he would undoubtedly agree that, if human nature has remained the same through the ages, Utopian communism will always remain mainly an ideal, and private property the most practical system for the preservation of peace and order.

In his heart, More realizes that his Utopian commonwealth, like the republic of Plato, will never exist in the Christian West, unless the perfect sons of the perfect God are born to dwell therein. The ideal Christian Utopia must wait until men become ideal Christians, perhaps only in "the holy city, New Jerusalem, coming down out of heaven from God" (Apoc. xxi. 2).

By way of afterthought and conclusion, it might be useful to add that Hythloday's description and defense of the Utopian common life, although not a declamation in the strict sense of the term, partakes of the nature and properties of the genre.[19] More viewed the *Utopia* as a literary achievement, not primarily as a serious document which outlined impartially the arguments for and against communism. Here are found the exaggeration of the advantages and the minimization of the disadvantages of communism which are essentially characteristic of the declamation. Here are discovered the artful tricks which aim to provide the reader with manifold and rich pleasure. A serious purpose, as has been seen, is far from absent, but it is directed much more to the denunciation of contemporary abuses and to the depiction of a reasonable and just commonwealth than to the aggressive advocation of communism as a practical solution and plan. If More, like Erasmus, had been attacked for heterodox and radical opinions, he would have answered as his friend had done, namely, that it was not the truth of the matter (that is, the rightness and justice of communism) which was to be regarded, but the literary powers of the author. He would be little more prepared to defend seriously the adoption of a communism of property than that of a communism of women, although just as he had espoused the one in an idealistic way in his *Utopia*, so he had upheld the other in a youthful dialogue.[20] Ideas which one treated idealistically in a literary piece could be retracted and damned in practical life. The important thing was the lesson to be learned, since every true work in the Renaissance was to combine the useful with the delightful, the profitable with the pleasurable. The lesson for Christians to take from the Utopian common life was twofold: poverty in spirit, namely, the blessedness of the first beatitude (Matt. v. 3), and brotherly love, which was to be like that of the primitive Church, especially readiness to share one's goods with the poor (Acts ii. 44–45).

UNITY OF CONCEPTION

An epitome of the principal philosophical and educational ideas in More's *Utopia* must be necessarily bald, since it can contain only the high lights and must dispense with the rich illustrative and probative material. Such a summary, however, must almost inevitably lead to greater simplification of expression and clarification of thought, and thus help to reveal the present study as a unified and self-explanatory whole.

Before the task of summary is begun, it would be well to point out two qualities of the *Utopia* — (1) indirection and (2) irony — which have not been sufficiently stressed in the course of the discussion. This lack of emphasis is due to the fact that ideas, rather than style and form, have constituted the immediate subject matter. Indirection, for example, is evident in the eager welcome extended by the Utopians to the Greek classics, although not a word of exhortation is addressed directly to Europeans to have them drop their subtle Scholastic disputations in exchange for living and useful studies. Irony is patent, for instance, in the marked inferiority of the Utopians to contemporary Schoolmen in dialectic on account of their ignorance of suppositions, amplifications, and second intentions, in spite of the fact that the Utopians are almost the equal of Aristotle and Porphyry in logic. Both these traits of More's masterpiece must be kept in mind if, not only the effectiveness of his expression, but also the subtlety of his thought, is to be appreciated. Utopia, it seems almost futile to say, is a complex and enigmatic book.

Manifest through the all-pervasive irony, More's general intention is to have England and Europe remedy contemporary evils by great open-mindedness and freedom in adopting the best institutions ever conceived by the intellect of man. To this end he has fashioned a city founded solely on reason and philosophy, independently of faith and revelation. Unfortunately, for purposes of satire or irony he has introduced into his "philosophical city"[1] institutions which impart an air of realism but which he himself terms silly or even absurd. Correct interpretation becomes troublesome and elusive. *Utopia,* however, is not a mere *jeu d'esprit* of a callow humanist, nor is it a serious proposal and defense of imperialism or communism on the part of an astute modern statesman. It is essentially a document of the English Renaissance of the Pre-Reformation, in which a reference to a prevalent abuse or a suggestion of practical reform lies behind every passage, whether serious or playful in tone. More's strategy of attack is the employment of arguments *a fortiori.* If the pagan Utopians who are guided solely by reason have such excellent institutions and moral characters, the Christians of Europe who possess both the light of reason and the treasures of revelation ought all the more to surpass them in high morality, intellectual culture, and benevolent government.

As for the laws and practices of the Utopian state, More wishes European nations to adopt — or to adapt to special conditions — only those which are sane and prudent, just and virtuous, not merely according to the criteria of human reason and philosophy, but also according to the light of Christian revelation and faith. It is more important to absorb the spirit than the institution, to imitate the virtue than the external custom, of the Utopians. Europeans, above all else, must change or improve their ethical attitudes and moral principles. The blessedness of the isle of Utopia merely shows what *could* be done by following the dictates of reason alone. The dream that *could* be realized if genuine

Christianity, as well as right philosophy, permeated the whole structure of society is too bright to portray in words.

To discover More's real intent and thought, the best policy seems to be to study each problem by itself in the light of all his letters and writings and against the background of antecedent and contemporary literature and philosophy. The chief works consulted and employed have been Plato, Aristotle, and Cicero among the ancients; Aquinas, Scotus, and Antoninus among the Schoolmen; and Pico, Ficino, Vives, Colet, and Erasmus among the humanists. Of these great figures, Erasmus is the most important in view of the closeness of his friendship with More and of the striking similarity of his ideas to More's, especially at the time of the publication of *Utopia*.

Erasmus' *Praise of Folly* is an elaborate example of a *declamatio*. In the *Utopia*, too, the section on pleasure as the ultimate end of human life is essentially a brief *declamatio*. The purpose of the praise of pleasure is to incite and provoke to serious thought careless Christians who are behaving as if the pleasure found in wealth or glory, and not the contemplation and love of God, were the end of life. More cunningly prejudices the whole question by using the word *pleasure* in its most loose and generic significance, not in its proper meaning which Cicero gives as "the enjoyment of a delightful stimulation of one of the senses." More does not give the Utopian definition of pleasure ("every motion and state of the body or mind wherein man hath naturally delectation"[2]) until late in the discourse after his reader has been laboring for some time under the impression that the Utopians are upholding *bodily* gratification. In the same tenor he astonishingly appeals to religion and virtue as two sources of arguments for the Utopian position. Religion holds forth the promise of a future life of intense pleasure. Virtue is life lived according to nature and therefore according to reason, which leads all men, including oneself, to strive for an existence free from care and full of joy.

Utopians distinguish between true and false pleasures. False

pleasures — such as the abuses of hunting, gambling, extravagant
apparel, thirst for honor, lust for gems and money, etc., prevalent in Europe — take their rise in sickness, inordinate desire,
erroneous judgment, or evil custom. To satisfy the Utopians, a
true pleasure must be natural (and this is the prime requisite),
noninjurious to society, nonoriginative of pain, and nonproduc-
tive of the loss of a greater pleasure. As far as bodily pleasures
are concerned, the Utopians maintain against certain ancient
philosophers that health, although there is no perception and
enjoyment of motion, is the greatest of them all. Pleasures
which involve motion, such as eating and drinking, are definitely
inferior, and cannot constitute the principal object of happiness,
since they are always accompanied by their corresponding pains.
Necessary functions and activities are not to be despised, nevertheless, since nature itself has surrounded them with pleasure.
Food and drink, for example, are preventive and remedial medicine for the defense and maintenance of health. But the supreme
pleasures are those of the soul. The Utopians take a moralistic,
rather than intellectualistic, view of mental pleasures, for they
seem to place the practice of virtue and a good conscience above
the contemplation of truth. In the main, the Utopian philosophy
of pleasure is that of Epicurus. But More, like Valla and Erasmus,
silently and surreptitiously removes those features of the teachings
of Epicurus which are objectionable to the theistic or Christian
philosopher, especially his denial of the immortality of the soul,
the providence of God, and future retribution.

The Utopians derive their knowledge and love of true pleasure
from their education and learning. They independently have discovered almost all the truths unearthed by the ancient scientists
and philosophers, but have not surpassed them in the knowledge
of the *causes* of natural phenomena. In particular, they have
mastered the equivalent of the logical treatises of Aristotle and
his classical commentators, but not of medieval texts like the
Small Logicals; in fact, they have no patience or capacity for
second intentions and universals. Thomas More, as is also clear

from his letter to Dorp and his approbation of Vives' *Against the Pseudo-Dialecticians,* is calling here for the use of the logical tracts of Aristotle unencumbered by medieval commentaries and accretions and uncontaminated by subtle disputation over realism and nominalism. Europeans should center their attention on the really vital problems of the day: poverty and wealth, peace and war, superstition and religion.

The path to sanity lies in an intensive and extensive study of the Greek language and literature. According to More's letters to Dorp and to the University of Oxford, Greek leads to an enlightened virtue, the acquisition of prudence in practical affairs, the knowledge of philosophy in its undefiled sources, the consummation of theology by recourse to the Greek New Testament and Fathers, and, finally, the perfecting of all arts and sciences; for, in brief, without Greek "all erudition is blind." [3] As examples, More offers the complete and true understanding of Aristotle himself, the idol of the Schoolmen, and the advancement of the art and science of medicine through the study of Hippocrates and Galen. The books which Hythloday and Tricius Apinatus carry with them may constitute More's basic list of the most valuable and essential Greek works. This list of "Great Books in Greek" may be complemented and completed by Erasmus' catalogues of recommended authors, especially in his *Plan of Study* (1511), which contains a number of remarkable, if coincidental, resemblances to *Utopia.* Both Utopia and Europe have Greek origins: let Europe welcome back the Greek pagan and Christian classics, not in a mood of resentment and reaction, but in the fine spirit of tolerance and progressiveness manifested by Utopia.

Greek originals had proved to be a disturbing element in Western thought. The rediscovery and revaluation of Plato, for example, helped to resurrect the question of communism. Discontented with the Aristotelian critique, many humanists reexamined communism more carefully in the light of the teaching of Christ and the practice of the primitive Church. The subject was often touched lightly in humanistic writings, but the most significant humanistic work on the matter in the early sixteenth century was More's *Utopia*.

Communism has an intimate connection with the Utopian philosophy of pleasure. The man who takes pleasure in the accumulation of wealth at the price of the impoverishment of good citizens is violating the primary command of nature: Thou shalt "not so seek for thine own commodities that thou procure others' incommodities." For the Utopians, commodities (food, clothing, shelter, work, land, etc.) constitute "the matter of pleasure" (*materia uoluptatis*),[4] a very important phrase philosophically. They have deliberately and freely chosen communism, not private ownership, as the best system for the equitable participation of all the citizens in the matter of pleasure. Utopia is a *commonwealth* worthy of the name because through the common life all its citizens can attain a maximum of pleasure and a minimum of pain during their life on earth.

More's own attitude toward communism can be determined only after a rapid review of the history of communism: Plato's communistic republic, Aristotle's searching criticism, the New Testament featuring the common poverty of Christ and His apostles and the apparent common life of the church in Jerusalem, the Greek Fathers with their emphasis on voluntary communism and their concept of private property as stewardship, and Gratian's *Decretum* with the Pseudo-Clementine epistle and its glosses. Among the Schoolmen there was agreement that if Adam had not sinned and fallen, things would have remained common. There was disagreement about the present state of man. Aquinas and his followers maintained that the right of private property is a natural right determined in the concrete by human positive law. Scotus and his disciples traced the right, not immediately to the natural law, but to human positive enactment, for the natural precept of common ownership was revoked after the fall in the interests of peace, order, and justice.

As for the humanists, a study of the English Colet, the Italian

Ficino, the French Budé, and the Dutch Erasmus reveals that
they share a more or less common attitude. God originally intended communism to be the social system best suited for
human beings. Once fallen, man divided up the common possessions and introduced the right of private property. Christ
tried to recall men to the original arrangement made by God,
as is clear from His own practice and that of the church in
Jerusalem. Except for the triumph of the common life in religious communities, Christ's program of reform was a failure,
according to the humanists, on account of the avarice and pride
of man, the authority of Aristotle, and the ingenuity of preachers who trimmed Christ's doctrine to suit evil men in evil times.
Communism is the ideal system, but since it is unrealizable
except among ideal men, the *spirit* of the common life must domi-
nate human thought and policy and manifest itself especially in
a sense of stewardship and common use of the earth's goods.

More's position is very much the same as that of the humanists
as a group. Provided the citizens possess the spirit of the primitive
Christians, a common life is best in the ideal order for a Christian
nation. If Christians, however, are taken as they actually exist,
the Aristotelian objections are valid, and private property is the
most practical solution. A few years after *Utopia*, in refutation
of Luther's arguments for the Christian's freedom from all human
laws, More indirectly clarifies his views on private property and
communism. His attitude is revealed to be fairly Scotistic. Not
the natural law, not the divine positive law (as expressed in the
gospel), but man's reason, working through an agreement on
the part of the community and through the agency of human positive law, is the basis for private possession. This human law is
obligatory even on Christians because it merely implements the
gospel's prohibition of theft. Judging from his book against
Luther as well as his *Dialogue of Comfort*, one is led to conclude that More believes the retention of private property and
private enterprise to be the most practical policy under contemporary social and economic conditions. The ideal Christian

Utopia, as has been stressed previously, must wait until men become ideal Christians.

Utopian philosophy, Utopian education, and Utopian communism are thus seen to hang together as a coherent and systematic unit. With reason and philosophy alone to guide them and without revelation and faith to light their path, the Utopians have chosen good and upright pleasure as the end of human existence and activity. As a practical result, their life is one of physical health, intellectual enjoyment, and moral rectitude. To secure a minimum of pain and a maximum of pleasure for their citizens, they have adopted communism as the most practical and equitable means for the distribution of the matter of pleasure, namely, the commodities of life. As for learning and education among the Utopians, it is not merely the source of real pleasure, as in the discovery and absorption of Greek literature: it is also the means for the transmission and preservation of their hedonistic philosophy, theistic religion, and democratic communism. It is not extravagant to say that the whole Utopian state is waiting breathlessly, as it were, for fulfillment in the reception of Christ's faith and morals. Christ would not come to destroy the Utopian law and the Utopian prophets but to fulfill (Matt. v. 17). Little would have to be discarded: nearly all could be retained. If by reason and philosophy pagans could devise and maintain a natural commonwealth of such perfection, ought not Christians to be ashamed that, although aided also by the incomparably superior gifts of revelation and grace, they have failed to provide a life of greater happiness for the individual and to establish a system of greater prosperity and justice for their people as a whole? *Utopia*, in the last analysis, is a cry of distress over the exploited poor and a call to reform in every department of human endeavor in England and in Europe.

NOTES

As announced in the Preface, the sources and references in each paragraph have been gathered into a single note.

I

PREMISES FOR INTERPRETATION

1. *The "Utopia" of Sir Thomas More, in Latin from the Edition of March 1518, and in English from the First Edition of Ralph Robynson's Translation in 1551*, ed. J. H. Lupton (Oxford, 1895), pp. 297–298, 309; Ep. 288, *Opus Epistolarum Des. Erasmi Roterodami*, eds. P. S. Allen *et al.* (Oxford, 1906–1947), I, 554. Lupton's edition will hereafter be referred to as *Utopia*; the spelling and punctuation are modernized in this present work. Allen's edition of Erasmus' letters will be designated as *Eras. Ep.*

2. John Greenleaf Whittier, *Maud Muller*, stanza 53.

3. See the author's "Interpretations of *Utopia*," *The Catholic Historical Review*, XXXVIII (1952), 156–174. This article summarily covers the principal views, including Russell Ames, *Citizen Thomas More and His Utopia* (Princeton, 1949), who finds "the core of the book . . . republican, bourgeois, and democratic" (p. 6). Since the publication of the article the most significant and vital work has been *More's "Utopia": The Biography of an Idea* (Princeton, 1952), in which J. H. Hexter gives an acute analysis of the structure of *Utopia* and an interesting history of its composition.

4. *Utopia*, p. 118; Philip Sidney, *The Defense of Poesy*, ed. Albert S. Cook (Boston, 1890), pp. 9, 11; Richard Pace, *De Fructu Qui ex Doctrina Percipitur Liber* (Basileae, 1517), p. 86. The term *Abraxas* is deciphered from the numerical values of Greek letters: $a = 1$, $\beta = 2$, $\rho = 100$, $a = 1$, $\xi = 60$, $a = 1$, $\sigma = 200$, total = 365. For references to Basilides and Abraxas during this decade, see Erasmus, "Moria," *Opera Omnia* (Lugduni Batavorum, 1703–1706), IV, 474;

"Ad Theodoram Epitaphium Lucini Betici: Scholia," in Hieronymus, *Opera Omnia* (Basileae, 1516), I, 88v; "Commentariorum Hieronymi in Amos Prophetam Liber Primus," *ibid.*, VI, 36v; Erasmus to Nicholas of Hertogenbosch, *Eras. Ep.*, IV, 574. For an explanation, see Gerardus Joannes Vossius, *Opera*, IV (Amstelodami, 1699), 340–341. Joseph Hall later mentions "*Abraxia*, the *Basilidians* state; wherein there were iust 365. houses, the townes-men being forbidden by an ancient law, either to increase their number, or diminish it" (*The Discovery of a New World*, ed. Huntington Brown [Cambridge, Mass., 1937], pp. 120–121).

    5. *Utopia*, pp. 307, 309; *Defense of Poesy*, p. 7.

    6. *Utopia*, pp. xciii–xciv.

    7. *Utopia*, pp. 210–211, 297–298.

    8. William Blake, "Milton," Preface, in *The Prophetic Writings*, eds. D. J. Sloss and J. P. R. Wallis (Oxford, 1926), I, 355–356.

    9. *Defense of Poesy*, pp. 10–11, 17.

II

THE PRAISE OF PLEASURE

    1. *Utopia*, pp. 187–188.

    2. "Moria," *Opera*, IV, 405, note by Gerard Lister; "Apologia pro Declamatione de Laude Matrimonii," *Opera*, IX, 108; "Dilutio Eorum quae Iod. Clithoveus Scripsit Adversus Declamationem Suasoriam Matrimonii," *ibid.*, IX, 812–813; "Apologia Adversus Monachos Quosdam Hispanos," *ibid.*, IX, 1089; *Liber Utilissimus de Conscribendis Epistolis* (Amstelodami, 1670), p. 267. Erasmus was forced to explain the nature and purpose of the declamation especially in the defense of his views on matrimony (vs. celibacy) expressed in his *Institutio Christiani Matrimonii* and in his *De Conscribendis Epistolis*, pp. 236–266, as "Exemplum Epistolae Suasoriae" (which is his *Encomium Matrimonii*, first printed in 1518 [*Eras. Ep.*, IV, 17, n.]).

    3. *Utopia*, p. 194.

    4. Cicero, *De Finibus Bonorum et Malorum*, tr. H. Rackham (London, 1921), p. 93; Ficino, "De Voluptate," *Opera Omnia* (Basileae, 1575), I, 987. See the discussion of the terms *delectatio* and *felicitas*, with many quotations from Mantuan, in Jacques Lefèvre d'Étaples, *Artificialis Introductio . . . in Decem Libros Ethicorum Aristotelis, Adiectis Elucidata Commentariis* [*Jodoci Clichtovei*] (Paris, 1506), foll. 53v–58r.

    5. *Utopia*, pp. 188–194. The statement about the emphasis on bodily pleasure depends upon the view that the discussion of pleasure embraces only pages 187 to 212. It is evident that the disquisition on pleasure is a long digression in the section on learning and education and is introduced as "the chief and principal question" of the ethics

or moral philosophy of the Utopians. Non-Greek subjects (pp. 184–187) are treated before the defense of pleasure; Greek studies (pp. 212–219), after it.

6. *Utopia*, pp. 190–193, 199, 201–202, 206–208. For a more detailed account, see the present writer's "The Defense of Pleasure in More's *Utopia*," *SP*, XLVI (1949), 102–103.

7. *Utopia*, p. 214; Erasmus, "Antibarbari," *Opera*, X, 1732; Vergil, *De Rerum Inventoribus* (Argentorati, 1606), p. 47.

8. *Supplementum Ficinianum*, ed. P. Kristeller (Florentiae, 1937), II, 8–10. See also the letter to Lorenzo de' Medici, *Opera*, I, 660–663.

9. *Utopia*, p. 187; Erasmus, "In Ps. I," *Opera*, V, 174; "Moria," *ibid.*, IV, 501; *Eras. Ep.*, II, 60, 389; *Bibliotheca Erasmiana*, Series I (Gand, 1893), p. 161. On happiness in Aristotle's thought, see *Nicomachean Ethics*, Books I and X, of which the essential passages are reprinted in James B. Schuster, *De Eudaimonia sive de Beatitudine* (Romae, 1933).

10. Aquinas, *Summa contra Gentiles*, lib. III, cc. 25–40; Antoninus, *Summa Sacrae Theologiae, Iuris Pontificii et Caesarei* (Venetiis, 1581–1582), IV, 115r–117v; Ficino, "Argumentum de Summo Bono," *Supplementum*, II, 97; Erasmus, "De Amabili Ecclesiae Concordia," *Opera*, V, 484 (cf. also "De Praeparatione ad Mortem," *Opera*, V, 1296). See Pecock, *Reule of Crysten Religioun*, ed. W. C. Greet (London: E.E.T.S., 1927), pp. 40–46, on God as the object of man's happiness, and pp. 103–109, for a discussion of "natural" reward in the future life if man had not been appointed to a "supernatural" end.

11. *Utopia*, pp. 277, 298.

12. *Utopia*, p. 194. On the existence of a natural beatitude in Limbo, see S. Harent, "Infidèles: Cinquième Système," *Dictionnaire de Théologie Catholique*, VII, 1894–1912, and A. Gaudel, "Limbes," *ibid.*, IX, 760–772.

13. Heliseo Heivodo, *Il Moro* (Fiorenza, 1556), pp. 173–174.

III

THE DEFENSE OF PLEASURE

1. *Utopia*, pp. 187–188, 190. One of the principles borrowed from religion is the proposition: "That the soul is . . . by the bountiful goodness of God ordained to felicity." One must be careful not to confuse *happiness* (*felicitas*) with *pleasure* (*uoluptas*), as Christopher Hollis seems to do in *Thomas More* (Milwaukee, 1934), p. 66: "Most of that [hedonistic] philosophy is mere common sense — merely a working out of the platitude that . . . no man can aim at anything other than good for himself. My happiness must be my end, whether my conception of happiness be a lofty or a low one. . . ." The Utopians take for granted that man's final end is *happiness*, but stoutly

maintain that the object of that happiness is *pleasure*, not virtue or anything else. At its historical origin Epicureanism was opposed to Platonism rather than to Stoicism which arose later, according to Norman Wentworth DeWitt, *Epicurus and His Philosophy* (Minneapolis, 1954), pp. 6–7, 10–11. This book came to the author's attention only after the completion of his research and writing, and thereby served to corroborate several of his own findings and conclusions.

2. *Utopia*, pp. 187sqq. The same tone of mild disapproval is found earlier: "For they be much inclined [*aliquanto procliuiores* really means *somewhat too much inclined*] to this opinion: to think no kind of pleasure forbidden whereof cometh no harm" (*Utopia*, p. 166).

3. *Utopia*, pp. 188–190, 192, 194, 274. On Pomponazzi, see F. Ueberweg, *History of Philosophy*, tr. G. S. Morris (London, 1880), II, 13. Here the letter of Hegius to Agricola, December 17, 1484, on Valla's *De Vero Bono*, "in which Vegius defends the position of pleasure, Cato that of virtue," is of particular interest. Hegius declares: "Vegius has made me an Epicurean." See the long quotation in Paul Mestwerdt, *Die Anfänge des Erasmus* (Leipzig, 1917), pp. 155–156. For a contemporary view of the close connection between public morality and religion, see Joannes Antonius Campanus, "De regendo magistratu," *Omnia Opera* (Venetiis, 1502), I, xxxxiiii.

4. *Utopia*, pp. 192, 194, 207; *Laws*, tr. R. G. Bury (Cambridge, Mass., 1926), I, 123 (here the whole context, 119–127, is important).

5. The Epicurean is Torquatus in Cicero, *De Finibus*, p. 47. Seneca's answer is found in "On the Happy Life," *Moral Essays*, tr. J. W. Basore (Cambridge, Mass., 1932), II, 121, 123. On the *distinction* and the *separation* between pleasure and virtue, see II, 115, 117.

6. *Utopia*, p. 190. "Virtue alone is sufficient for the good and happy life, as say Zeno, and Chrysippus, . . . and Hecato" (Diogenes Laertius, VII, 127, Arnim, *Frag. Stoic.*, III, n. 49), quoted in Schuster, *De Eudaimonia*, p. 32.

7. *Utopia*, pp. 190, 192; Diogenes Laertius, VII, 87, Arnim, *Frag. Stoic.*, I, n. 179, quoted in Schuster, *De Eudaimonia*, p. 32; Seneca, "On the Happy Life," *Moral Essays*, II, 131; Cicero, *De Finibus*, p. 251.

8. *Utopia*, pp. 191–192. The argument is based on a refinement of the Stoic concept that man is born for the sake of helping man and of the Aristotelian doctrine that the individual is not self-sufficient to procure food, clothing, shelter, justice, etc., and hence civil society is natural to man. The refinement, of course, consists in directing the principle toward pleasure. Another basic assumption is that nature is concerned, less with the individual, than with the species and its preservation, and hence treats all the members of the species impartially.

9. *Utopia*, pp. 191–192; *A Dialogue of Comfort against Tribulation* (London, n.d.), pp. 49, 59–60.

IV

FORTUNES OF EPICURUS IN UTOPIA

1. *Mundus Novus*, tr. G. T. Northup (Princeton, 1916), p. 6;
The Four Voyages of Amerigo Vespucci, tr. M. E. Cosenza (New
York, 1907), p. 97, Latin text, p. liii.
2. Erasmus, *The Whole Familiar Colloquies*, tr. N. Bailey (London, 1877), p. 401; Barclay, *Eclogues*, ed. B. White (London, 1928),
p. 53; *Ship of Fools*, ed. T. H. Jamieson (Edinburgh, 1874), II, 293.
Aeneas Sylvius' Latin original for the *Eclogues* reads in translation as
follows: "The moment now warns us that we should discuss PLEAS-
URES, in which many mortals have placed the essence of happiness,
especially Epicurus, a man once great, whom the philosophers of
our own time condemn with words more than actions" (*Éclogues*,
p. 53). The latter clause finds an echo in Erasmus' "Profane Banquet"
where Austin admits: "I recommend Zeno's rules; but I follow Epicurus' practice" (*Colloquies*, p. 66). Note also the following: "The
philosophers of our time are wiser who are content to dispute like
Stoics, but in living outdo even Epicurus himself" (*Colloquies*, p. 69).
For Barclay's *Ship of Fools*, see also Brant, *Stultifera Navis*, Latin tr.
J. Locher (Basileae, 1497), fol. cxxxiiv, where the term *Epicurei*
appears in the margin opposite the portion which begins:

Nostra sophi veteres coluerunt numina: quorum
Scripta manent positae me defendentia sectae, *etc.*

3. Antoninus, *Summa*, I, 158v.
4. Vives, *Opera Omnia* (Valentiae Edetanorum, 1782), III, 17;
Beroaldus, *Varia Opuscula* (Basileae, 1513), foll. cxiiv–cxiiiir. In his
Proverbiorum Libellus (Venetiis, 1498), sig. c viiv–viiir, Polydore
Vergil explains the proverb, "Hic Epicurus subans est" ("This fellow
is an Epicurus in heat") by reference to Book II of Jerome's attack on
Jovinian.
5. Pace, *De Fructu*, pp. 9–10; Landino, *Disputationes Camaldu-
lenses* (Argentorati, 1508), sig. C vr; Edmond Vansteenberghe, *Le
Cardinal Nicolas de Cues* (Lille, 1920), p. 439. See Richard Hope,
The Book of Diogenes Laertius (New York, 1930), pp. 11–12, 21–23,
for early Latin translations and early printed Greek texts. For favorable comment on Epicurus, or at least a fairminded defense of his
doctrine against false charges, in Boccaccio, Petrarch, Valla, Filelfo,
Landino, Ficino, and Erasmus, see Don Cameron Allen, "The Rehabilitation of Epicurus and His Theory of Pleasure in the Early
Renaissance," *SP*, XLI (1944), 1–15. Consequently the statement of
DeWitt that "scholars of the Renaissance were not interested in Epicurus" (*Epicurus*, p. 355) needs modification.

6. *Utopia*, pp. 176–212; letter to Agricola from Hegius, Deventer, December 17, [1484], quoted in P. S. Allen, *The Age of Erasmus* (Oxford, 1914), p. 28; Erasmus, *Colloquies*, p. 401. For Valla's great influence on Erasmus, see Paul Mestwerdt, *Anfänge des Erasmus*, pp. 20–78, 155–157, 234–237, and Albert Hyma, *The Youth of Erasmus* (Ann Arbor, 1930), pp. 41–45, 157–160, 186–189, 196–199. "The Epicurean" first appeared in the March 1533 edition of the *Colloquies* (see P. Smith, *A Key to the Colloquies of Erasmus* [Cambridge, Mass., 1927], p. 55). On the date of "De Contemptu Mundi," see Erasmus, *Opera*, VI, 1239–1240. Erasmus mentions or uses Diogenes Laertius sixty-four times in the *Chiliades* of 1526 (see T. C. Appelt, *Studies in the Contents and Sources of Erasmus' Adagia* [Chicago, 1942], p. 144). *Epicurus Christianus* is mentioned as one of the designations which closely approach the nature of an adage in Ep. 126, Erasmus to Mountjoy (Preface to first edition of *Adagiorum Collectanea*, 1500), *Eras. Ep.*, I, 293. As for More, there are an epigram and its answer in *Omnia Latina Opera* (Lovanii, 1565), fol. 23:

DILEMMA EPICVRI

Deijciat miseram tibi nulla molestia mentem.
Si longa est, leuis est. si grauis est, breuis est.

CONTRA

Deijcit heu miseram, prosternit & utraque mentem.
Longa nec vlla leuis, nec grauis vlla breuis.

THE DILEMMA OF EPICURUS

Let no trouble drive you to misery. If the trouble is lasting, it is easy to bear; if it is hard to bear, it cannot last long.

THE OPPOSITE OPINION

Alas, both kinds of trouble drive me to misery and break my heart, long-lasting trouble which is not trivial and serious trouble which is not short-lived.

See *The Latin Epigrams of Thomas More*, eds. Leicester Bradner and Charles A. Lynch (Chicago, 1953), p. 161.

7. *Utopia*, pp. 188, 274–275; Augustine, *Confessions*, tr. F. J. Sheed (New York, 1943), p. 127; *Confessiones*, ed. J. Capello (Taurini, 1948), pp. 195–196. See Lucian's reference to the Epicurean doctrine on the gods in Erasmus' translation of "Icaromenippus," *Opera*, I, 213. Erasmus calls this view blasphemous in "Explanatio Symboli," *Opera*, V, 1148. In "De Quatuor Sectis Philosophorum," *Supplementum*, II, 9, Ficino expounds Epicurus' teaching on the

happiness and the indifference of the gods, and then quotes Lucretius (II. 646sqq.):

> omnis enim per se divom natura necessest
> inmortali ævo summa cum pace fruatur,
> semota a nostris rebus seiunctaque longe.

8. "Alexander," Latin tr. Erasmus, *Opera*, I, 237, 240–241 (see other references to Epicurus and Epicureans in the rest of the dialogue). The Utopians, too, "be delighted with Lucian's merry conceits and jests" (*Utopia*, p. 216).

9. Diogenes Laertius, "Epicurus," *Lives of Eminent Philosophers*, tr. R. D. Hicks (London, 1925), II, 653, 655; Cicero, *De Finibus*, p. 33. According to DeWitt, *Epicurus*, pp. 217–222, the *summum bonum* for Epicurus is life, but the end or *telos* is pleasure.

10. *Colloquies*, p. 401; "De Contemptu Mundi," *Opera*, V, 1257. For other references of Erasmus to Epicurus' doctrine of pleasure as the highest good, see *Adagia*, No. 3734 (*Rumor publicus non omnino frustra est*), col. 1257, and *Adagia*, No. 3790 (*Verbis coquariis*), col. 1268. *Adagia* is used here as the abbreviation for *Adagiorum Opus* (Lugduni, 1541).

11. Diog. Laert., "Epicurus," *Lives*, II, 655; Erasmus, "The Epicurean," *Colloquies*, p. 402; "De Contemptu Mundi," *Opera*, V, 1257. Cf. also the following: "[*Hedonius*]. Is it not a notable way of merchandising, to purchase a pleasure, neither real, solid, nor of long continuance, with so many evils, greater and longer-lasting? *Sp[udaeus]*. If there were nothing of pain in the matter, I should think him a foolish trader who should barter jewels for bits of glass" (*Colloquies*, p. 405).

12. *Utopia*, pp. 189, 193–194, 209.

13. *Utopia*, p. 208; Diog. Laert., "Epicurus," *Lives*, II, 657, 661. In their defense of health as a true pleasure (*Utopia*, pp. 204–206), the Utopians tacitly uphold the opinion of Epicurus against that of Aristippus and the Cyrenaics. Erasmus describes picturesquely the evils of drunkenness as follows: "When hard drinking throws a man into a fever, the headache, the gripes, dizziness, a bad name, decay of memory, vomiting, loss of appetite, and the palsy, would Epicurus himself think this was a pleasure worth seeking after?" ("The Epicurean," *Colloquies*, pp. 404–405).

14. Cicero, *De Finibus*, p. 43. Epicurus' principle is implicit in the argument for health as a pleasure in *Utopia*, pp. 205–206. Socrates, on the other hand, maintains that there is "such a thing as a neutral state, . . . intermediate between them [pleasure and pain], and in the mean, being a quietude of the soul in these respects." Such is health to sick men and freedom from pain to men afflicted with severe pain. Hence, it is not "right to think the absence of pain

pleasure, or the absence of joy painful." See Plato's *Republic*, tr. P.
Shorey (London, 1930–1935), II, 381, 383.

15. *Utopia*, pp. 206–207; Diog. Laert., *Lives*, II, 661, 663; Erasmus, "The Epicurean," *Colloquies*, p. 405; "De Contemptu Mundi,"
Opera, V, 1257–1258, 1260. For Epicurus, however, bodily pleasure
is indissolubly connected with mental pleasure either as source, or
concomitant, etc. This he taught in opposition to the Cyrenaics, who
held that the pleasures like friendship or honor are independent of
sensation. To abandon this opinion of Epicurus is to abandon true
Epicureanism. Hence, Cicero attempts to silence Torquatus the Epicurean by this dilemma: "Do you, Torquatus, . . . do you personally
never experience delight in some thing for its own sake? I pass over
moral worth and goodness, and the intrinsic beauty of the virtues. . . .
I will suggest less serious matters, reading or writing a poem or a
speech, the study of history or geography, statues, pictures, beautiful scenery. . . . Is there nothing which of itself affords you delight? Persist in tracing back the pleasures I have instanced to the
body — and you show yourself impervious to argument; recant — and
you abandon Epicurus's conception of pleasure altogether" (*De
Finibus*, pp. 199, 201).

16. *Utopia*, pp. 193–194, 207; Diog. Laert., *Lives*, II, 657, 663;
Plutarch, "Cum Principibus Maxime Philosophum Debere Disputare,"
tr. Erasmus, *Opera*, IV, 48.

17. *Colloquies*, pp. 402–404, 409. On Epicureanism as "a prepara-
tion for Christianity in the Graeco-Roman world," see DeWitt, *Epicurus*, pp. 31–32, 336–339.

18. "Paraclesis," *Novum Instrumentum*, ed. 1516, sig. aaa 5v
(*Opera*, VI, 4r); "De Contemptu Mundi," *Opera*, V, 1257; *Colloquies*, p. 404. "The common people seek for a pleasant life from
external things, when nothing will produce that but a good conscience;
for a heavier stone hangs over the heads of those that have a guilty
conscience than hangs over the head of Tantalus himself; nay, it does
not only hang over their heads, but vexes and presses their minds;
nor is their mind tormented with a vain fear, but expects every hour
when they shall be cast into hell" (*Colloquies*, p. 410).

19. Seneca, "On the Happy Life," *Moral Essays*, II, 129, 131. Note
that Seneca and Cicero are the only two Latin authors who are recommended by name in the *Utopia* (p. 27). In Erasmus' "Soldier and
Carthusian," the Carthusian explains that the body "is satisfied with
very little, if we live according to Nature" (*Colloquies*, p. 138).

20. Erasmus, *Opera*, V, 1257; Telle, *Érasme de Rotterdam et le
septième sacrement* (Genève, 1954), p. 11.

21. See *Utopia*, pp. 188–192. If the statement of Diocles as given
by Diogenes Laertius is correct, More and Epicurus differ on a policy
basic to *Utopia*, namely, communism. "He [Diocles] further says that

Epicurus did not think it right that their property [that of Epicurus and his friends] should be held in common, as required by the maxim of Pythagoras about the goods of friends; such a practice in his opinion implied mistrust and without confidence there is no friendship" (*Lives*, II, 539, 541).

V

CRITERIA OF TRUE AND FALSE PLEASURE

1. *Utopia*, pp. 188–189; *Republic*, II, 301. As his criteria for determining which life is "not merely . . . the more honourable or the more base, or the worse or the better, but which is actually the more pleasurable or free from pain," Socrates chooses "experience, intelligence, and discussion." Since the philosopher has all three, he is the best judge. See *Republic*, II, 377, 379.

2. *Utopia*, pp. 194–196, 201–202. Cp. page 207: "For such things of their own proper nature [*per se*] be not pleasant." Cp. also page 147, where Hythloday observes that if all the citizens worked, "little time would be enough . . . to store us with all things that may be requisite other for necessity or for commodity; yea, or for pleasure, so that the same pleasure be true and natural" (*quae quidem uera sit ac naturalis*).

3. *Utopia*, pp. 166, 209. Robinson's translation does not bring out the true sense and force of this important passage: "natura iucundum est, ad quod neque per iniuriam tenditur, nec iucundius aliud amittitur, nec labor succedit. . ." (p. 194). R. P. Adams properly emphasizes the fact that "any pleasure which is not known to have injurious social effects may be presumed to be good and honest." See his "Philosophic Unity of More's *Utopia*," *SP*, XXXVIII (1941), 64. But the Utopians stress as the negative norm of true pleasure the avoidance, not merely of social harm, but also of individual harm (whether by loss of greater pleasure or by the incurrence of unnecessary pain).

4. *Utopia*, pp. 189, 209; "Dialogue Concerning Heresies," *Works* (London, 1557), p. 157; Cicero, *De Finibus*, p. 37. See also *Utopia*, p. 194: "so that it [pleasure] may be gotten without . . . letting or debarring a greater pleasure, nor causing painful labor." The English *labor*, like the Latin *labor*, can mean *hardship, distress, pain*, or even *sickness*. Erasmus applies the proverb, "Seek not softness, lest hardship come upon thee," to those men who, while they catch at pleasure without moderation, fall into trouble (*Adagia*, No. 1548 [*Ne quaere mollia, ne tibi contingant dura*], col. 670).

5. *Utopia*, pp. 190, 192–194, 303. In *Il Moro* of Heywood, More is fittingly made to speak of "our common mother nature, who has created man of such great excellence in himself that he has merited that grand title of the μικρόκοσμος" (p. 171).

6. *Utopia*, pp. 57, 193, 303–304; *Statutes of the Realm*, II (London, 1816), 542, and III (London, 1818), 127, 176–177.

7. *Utopia*, pp. 193–194; Plutarch, "Cum Principibus Maxime Philosophum Debere Disputare," Lat. tr. Erasmus, *Opera*, IV, 48. Robinson has made almost an expanded comment of his translation of the latter half of the simple Latin sentence, "Hiis inoffensis legibus tuum curare commodum, prudentia[e] est; publicum praeterea, pietatis": "These laws not offended, it is wisdom that thou look to thine own wealth. And to do the same for the commonwealth is no less than thy duty, if thou bearest any love or any natural zeal and affection to thy native country" (*Utopia*, p. 193).

8. *Utopia*, pp. 195–196, 202. According to Epicurus, desires which are "neither natural nor necessary . . . are due to illusory opinion." Examples are "desires for crowns and the erection of statues in one's honour" (Diog. Laert., "Epicurus," *Lives*, II, 673). The author of the fourteenth-century *Cloud of Unknowing*, ed. P. Hodgson (London, 1944), pp. 116–117, traces the erroneous judgment of pleasures and goods to original sin (*text modernized*): "Will is a might through the which we chese [choose] good, after that it be determined with reason. . . . Before ere man sinned, might not will be deceived in his chesing, in his loving, ne in none of his works, forwhy [because] it had then by kind [nature] to savor each thing as it was. But now it may do so but gif [if] it be anointed with grace. For ofttimes, because of infection of the original sin, it savoreth a thing for good that is full evil and that hath but the likeness of good."

9. "Four Last Things," *Works*, pp. 73–74, 98; Erasmus, *Adagia*, No. 3794 (*Scarabaeo citius persuaseris*), col. 1269. By way of example, Erasmus pictures graphically the beetle which conducts all its vital activities in dung, especially goat dung. In a later proverb, he writes as follows: "In the first book of his *Rhetoric*, Aristotle in his discussion of pleasure teaches that those things are pleasurable which are according to nature or, what is closest to this, which are habitual. For he thinks that there is no difference between nature and habit, except the difference between 'always' and 'frequently.' For that is permanent which is implanted by nature, and that is frequent which is imprinted by habit. Therefore, that man gave a most wise and holy counsel who bade that we choose, immediately from our most tender years, the best and highest things, which, later on, become from habit pleasurable as well" (*Adagia*, No. 3825 [*Usus est altera natura*], col. 1276). Many years before, he had written in his "Enchiridion": "Your desires were corrupted. You loved what was worthy of hate: you hated what should have been loved. Sweet was bitter to you, and bitter sweet" (*Opera*, V, 38). Pico had asked earlier why a pregnant woman prefers to eat earth or charcoal more willingly than all the most exquisite kinds of edibles, and found his

answer in her constitution rather than in the stars ("In Astrologiam,"
Opera Omnia [Basileae, 1601], I, 350).
10. *Utopia*, pp. 195–201.
11. *Utopia*, pp. 194–195, 201–202.

VI

FALSE PLEASURES IN EUROPE

1. *Utopia*, pp. 151, 181; "Treatise on Passion," *Works*, p. 1272.
2. *Utopia*, pp. 56–57; *Latin Epigrams*, pp. 43–45, 166–167; "De-
bellation of Salem and Bizance," *Works*, pp. 952–953, 993; Barclay,
Ship of Fools, I, 36–37, II, 97; Skelton, *Complete Poems*, rev. ed. P.
Henderson (London, 1948), pp. 133–139, 148; Fitzherbert, *The
Book of Husbandry*, ed. W. W. Skeat (London, 1882), p. 102; 1°
Hen. VIII, c. 14, 6° Hen. VIII, c. 1, *Statutes of Realm*, III, 8, 121sqq.
On spiritual harm, e.g., sins of vanity, arising from extravagant dress,
see "Supplication of Souls," *Works*, p. 337. On the bad example set
by princes, see Erasmus, *The Education of a Christian Prince*, tr. L.
K. Born (New York, 1936), p. 151.
3. *Utopia*, pp. 140, 151, 195–196; "The Soldier and the Carthusian," *Colloquies*, p. 137. For a description of the Carthusian habit,
see Dom Lawrence Hendriks, *The London Charterhouse* (London,
1889), p. 80.
4. *Utopia*, pp. 150–151; Erasmus, *Adagia*, No. 2615 (*Baeta tum
hyeme, tum aestate bona*), col. 989; "Apophthegmata," *Opera*, IV, 127.
5. *Utopia*, p. 151; Ep. 999, Erasmus to Hutten, *Eras. Ep.*, IV, 15;
Ioannes Iovianus Pontanus, "De Splendore," *Opera Omnia Soluta
Oratione Composita* (Venetiis, 1518–1519), I, 139v–140r.
6. *Utopia*, p. 196; Ep. 999, Erasmus to Hutten, *Eras. Ep.*, IV, 15;
Silvester, *Summa Summarum* (Bononiae, 1514–1515), fol. 313r. In
the same place, Silvester gives the twofold meaning of *honestas*:
(1) as excellence or virtue worthy of honor and (2) as an aspect of
temperance and justice.
7. *Utopia*, p. 233.
8. "Picus," *Works*, pp. 1–2; *Eras. Ep.*, X, 137; Pace, *De Fructu*,
pp. 98–99; Geiler, *Nauicula siue Speculum Fatuorum* (Argentorati,
1511), sig. t iijv; Lily, in Paolo Giovio, *Descriptio Britanniae, Etc.*
(Venetiis, 1548), fol. 53r. For other references by Erasmus to honor
as the proper reward of virtue, see "Ratio Verae Theologiae," *Opera*,
V, 102; "Institutio Christiani Matrimonii," *ibid.*, V, 669–670; "Ecclesiastes," *ibid.*, V, 939; *Adagia*, No. 792 (*Honos alit artes*), col.
369. At this time, Budé lamented the host of obscure commoners in
France who were elevated to the highest civic offices and to the
nobility, some worthily and others unworthily (*Annotationes . . .
in . . . Pandectarum Libros* [Parisiis, 1542], p. 72).

9. *Utopia*, p. 233; "Picus," *Works*, p. 2; Fisher, *English Works*, ed. J. E. B. Mayor (London, 1876), I, 290; *Eras. Ep.*, V, 364; *Colloquies*, p. 364. See also Erasmus, "Ad Philippum Panegyricus," *Opera*, IV, 541.

10. *Utopia*, pp. 53, 196–197, 308; Erasmus, *The Praise of Folly*, tr. H. H. Hudson (Princeton, 1941), p. 59. For another reference to tracing one's ancestry back to Brutus, the legendary founder of Britain, see Erasmus, *Adagia*, No. 2201 (*Sileni Alcibiadis*), col. 815. In the scholia to a letter of Jerome's, Erasmus laments the Christians' love of money even to the point that it is a licit reason for war — although that love is contrary to the clear teaching of Christ on the hatred of wealth ("Hieronymus Algasiae: Scholia," *Hieronymi Opera*, IV, 79*v*).

11. *Il Moro*, pp. 19, 25–52, 86–95, 168–170.

12. *Utopia*, pp. 178, 197.

13. *Utopia*, pp. 181, 197–198; "Four Last Things," *Works*, p. 73; "Treatise on Passion," *ibid.*, p. 1272; Erasmus, "Moria," *Opera*, IV, 451, tr. Hudson, *Praise of Folly*, p. 64.

14. *Utopia*, pp. 198–199. In his "Enchiridion," *Opera*, V, 59, Erasmus insists that God had created all things for man's *use*.

15. *Utopia*, pp. 174, 181, 196. Here, again, the Utopians follow Epicurus who declares: "Gratitude is due to blessed Nature because she has made life's necessities easy of acquisition and those things that are difficult of acquisition unnecessary" (H. Usener, *Epicurea* [Leipzig, 1887], 469, quoted in DeWitt, *Epicurus*, p. 324 [cf. p. 128]). When it serves his rhetorical purposes, Erasmus, of course, can argue that the more excellent a thing is, the more hidden it is — for example, gold and gems! See *Adagia*, No. 2201 (*Sileni Alcibiadis*), col. 863.

16. More, *Dialogue of Comfort*, p. 212 (italics added); "Treatise on Passion," *Works*, p. 1272 (italics added); Erasmus, "Enchiridion," *Opera*, V, 59–60.

17. *Utopia*, p. 175; Erasmus, *Adagia*, No. 468 (*In matellam immeiere*), col. 234; Martial, *Epigrams*, tr. W. C. A. Ker (London, 1930), I, 53; Plutarch, *Lives*, tr. B. Perrin (London, 1914), I, 231; Plato, *Republic*, I, 313, and *Laws*, I, 371; D'Anghiera, *De Orbe Novo*, tr. F. A. MacNutt (New York, 1912), I, 49–50, 108, 221–222, 333; Vespucci, *Four Voyages*, p. 98, and *Mundus Novus*, p. 8.

18. *Utopia*, p. 178; *Lucian*, tr. A. M. Harmon (London, 1913–), I, 113, 115; Plutarch, *Lives*, I, 481; Erasmus, "Moria," *Opera*, IV, 481, tr. Hudson, *Praise of Folly*, p. 96; Georg Ellinger, "Thomas Morus und Machiavelli," *Vierteljahrschrift für Kultur und Literatur der Renaissance*, II (1887), 20.

19. *Utopia*, pp. 144, 199; Erasmus, "Moria," *Opera*, IV, 441–442, tr. Hudson, *Praise of Folly*, p. 55; *Eras. Ep.*, IV, 16.

20. Skelton, *Complete Poems*, p. 137; Barclay, *Ship of Fools*, II, 69, 72–73; Fitzherbert, *Book of Husbandry*, p. 104; Silvester, *Summa Summarum*, foll. 38*v*, 418*r*–419*r*. For other contemporary attacks on dicing and other forms of gambling see Geiler, *Nauicula Fatuorum*, sig. 1 i*v*–1 ij*v*, and Beroaldus, "Declamatio Ebriosi, Scortatoris, et Aleatoris," *Varia Opuscula*, foll. cxl*v*–cxliv.

21. *Utopia*, pp. 144–145; Elyot, *The Boke Named the Gouernour*, ed. H. H. S. Croft (London, 1880), I, 272–285; Lefèvre, *Arithmetica*, etc. (Parisiis, 1514), *ad finem*.

22. *Utopia*, pp. 196, 199–201.

23. "Moria," *Opera*, IV, 441–442, tr. Hudson, *Praise of Folly*, pp. 53–54; Elyot, *Gouernour*, I, 186–202. On the necessary safeguards for hunting and shooting, see Geiler, *Nauicula Fatuorum*, sig. b i*v*–iiij*v*.

24. *Utopia*, p. 200; Plato, *Laws*, II, 119–123; Jacobus Wimpheling, *Adolescentia*, etc. (Argentinae, 1515), fol. ii; "Jagd," Pauly-Wissowa, *Real-Encyclopädie*, IX, 558–604.

25. *Eras. Ep.*, IV, 16, 546.

VII

TRUE PLEASURES IN UTOPIA

1. *Utopia*, pp. 202–212.

2. *Utopia*, pp. 152, 193–194, 202, 206–207; Erasmus, *Colloquies*, pp. 405–406; Plato, *Republic*, II, 375.

3. *Utopia*, pp. 152, 207; "Twelve Weapons," *Works*, p. 27; Erasmus, "Enchiridion," *Opera*, V, 42.

4. *Utopia*, pp. 202–204; Erasmus, "Similia," *Opera*, I, 569.

5. *Utopia*, p. 204; Erasmus, "Similia," *Opera*, I, 568.

6. *Republic*, I, 111, 143; *Laws*, I, 25, 117; Erasmus, *Adagia*, No. 2090 (*Primum recte valere, proxima forma, tertio loco divitiae*), col. 830; cf. *Adagia*, No. 2201 (*Sileni Alcibiadis*), col. 865.

7. *Utopia*, p. 205; Diog. Laert., *Lives*, II, 661; Plato, *Republic*, II, 383. On Robinson's "outward motion," see J. Churton Collins, ed., *Sir Thomas More's Utopia* (Oxford, 1904), p. 213. Antoninus, *Summa*, I, 158*v*, maintains that every pleasure cannot be motion because man will finally *rest* in God as his final end.

8. *Utopia*, pp. 205–206.

9. *Utopia*, p. 206.

10. *Utopia*, pp. 204–205; Cicero, *De Finibus*, p. 43; Plato, *Republic*, II, 381, 383. Aristotelian Schoolmen often used the example of fire and heat in this connection: cf. Antoninus: "since perfect happiness [*beatitudo*] is nothing else than the attainment of the highest good, it cannot exist without pleasure [*sine delectatione*] as its concomitant, just as fire cannot without heat" (*Summa*, IV, 127*r*).

11. *Utopia*, p. 205.

12. *Utopia*, pp. 202–203, 209. Since Epicurus' "Supreme Good, or blessedness, is composed . . . of a body free from pain and a soul free from disturbance," Seneca observes: "Whatever delights [*blandimenta*] fall to his lot over and above these two things do not increase his Supreme Good; they merely season, so to speak, and add spice to it [*condiunt et oblectant*]" (*Epistulae Morales*, tr. R. M. Gummere [Cambridge, Mass., 1917–1920], II, 29–31).

13. *Utopia*, p. 208; "Four Last Things," *Works*, col. 99.

14. *Utopia*, pp. 203, 207–208; "Answer to *Supper*," *Works*, p. 1047. On the date of this "Answer," see *Correspondence*, p. 468.

15. *Utopia*, pp. 205–207, 209; "Four Last Things," *Works*, pp. 80–81; "Confutation of Tyndale," *ibid.*, p. 356.

16. *Utopia*, pp. 161, 166, 208–209.

17. *Utopia*, pp. 281–282; Augustine, "De Civ. Dei," *PL*, XLI, 622; Ficino, "De Voluptate," *Opera*, I, 990. On the necessity of pleasure even in studies, see *Eras. Ep.*, I, 172.

18. *Utopia*, pp. 166, 209.

19. More, "Ps. XV," *Works*, p. 19; *Eras. Ep.*, IV, 15.

20. *Utopia*, p. 209.

21. *Utopia*, pp. 189, 202, 209–210.

22. *Utopia*, pp. 210, 232; *Omnia Latina Opera*, fol. 32v; *Lucian*, tr. Harmon, Introd., I, ix.

23. *Utopia*, pp. 187–188, 210–211.

24. *Utopia*, pp. 190, 210–211, 282. Epicurus himself would consider unmarried ascetics also "the wiser" (*prudentiores*), for he says: "Nor . . . will the wise man marry and rear a family" (Diog. Laert., "Epicurus," *Lives*, II, 645).

25. *Utopia*, pp. 110–111, 211.

26. *Utopia*, p. 212.

VIII

EDUCATION AND LEARNING IN GENERAL

1. *Utopia*, p. 183.

2. *Utopia*, pp. 181–182, 285; Letter to Gonell, Stapleton, *The Life . . . of Sir Thomas More*, tr. P. E. Hallett (London, 1928), p. 102 (Latin original, *The Correspondence of Sir Thomas More*, ed., E. F. Rogers [Princeton, 1947], p. 122); Plato, *Republic*, I, 328–329; Erasmus, "De Pueris Statim ac Liberaliter Instituendis," *Opera*, I, 491; Wimpheling, *Adolescentia*, fol. vir. On modeling a human being, see Erasmus, "Institutio Christiani Matrimonii," *Opera*, V, 710; on forming good morals early, see *Adagia*, No. 161 (*Senis mutare linguam*), col. 108.

3. *Utopia*, pp. 143, 183, 202, 212.

4. More, *Correspondence*, pp. 404–405; Elyot, *Gouernour*, I, 99; Pace, *De Fructu*, p. 15.

5. Dudley, *The Tree of Commonwealth*, ed. D. M. Brodie (Cambridge, Eng., 1948), p. 45; C. A. Sneyd, tr., *A Relation . . . of the Island of England . . . about the Year 1500* (London, 1847), p. 22; Castiglione, *The Courtier*, tr. T. Hoby (New York, 1907), p. 66; J. D. Mansi, *Sacrorum Conciliorum Collectio*, XXXII (Paris, 1902), 699. See Beroaldus, "Oratio Dicta apud Rectorem Scholastici Conuentus Ineuntem Scholasticam Praefecturam," *Varia Opuscula*, fol. xvr, for the influence of temperate climate on the brilliance and power of English minds in the pursuit of learning. The ingoing rector is called *Thomas Anglicus uel Britannicus.*

6. *Utopia*, pp. 184, 187; *Republic*, I, 257, 259, II, 163, 171, 173, 187, 189; *Laws*, I, 93sqq., II, 101. See Aquinas, *The Division and Methods of the Sciences: Questions V and VI of His Commentary on the "De Trinitate" of Boethius*, tr. Armand Mauer (Toronto, 1953), esp. Introd., pp. vii–xv, xxvii–xxxv.

7. Villoslada, *La Universidad de Paris durante los estudios de Francisco de Vitoria O.P.: 1507–1522* (Romae, 1938), pp. 75–76.

8. *Utopia*, pp. 186, 279; Diog. Laert., "Epicurus," *Lives*, II, 661; Cicero, *De Natura Deorum*, tr. H. Rackham (Cambridge, Mass., 1951), p. 279; Alexander Anglus, *Destructorium Viciorum* (Norimbergae, 1496), pars VI, cap. lv (no pagination); Angelus Carletus de Clavasio, *Summa Angelica de Casibus Conscientiae* (Lugduni, 1512), fol. xvir. See Vergil, "De Duobus Divinandi Generibus, & de Origine Aruspicinae Artis, et Sortium Praenestinarum, & Quis Somniorum Interpretationem Docuerit," *De Rerum Inventoribus*, pp. 68–71. For a capable and comprehensive survey, consult Don Cameron Allen's *The Star-Crossed Renaissance: The Quarrel about Astrology and Its Influence on England* (Durham, N.C., 1941).

9. *Utopia*, pp. 186–187; Letter to Dorp, *Correspondence*, p. 65; Fisher, "Sermon on the Passion," *English Works*, I, 388–389. For Pico's views, see "In Astrologiam," *Opera*, I, 325, 329–332. Pace's attack on astrology and other vain superstition occurs in *De Fructu*, pp. 37–44.

10. *Utopia*, pp. 27, 184, 213.

11. *Utopia*, p. 184; *Republic*, II, xxxviii, 197, 209.

IX

LOGIC IN UTOPIA

1. *Utopia*, p. 184; *Correspondence*, pp. 37, 145.

2. "De Ratione Studii," *Opera*, I, 522; "Apologia ad Iacobum Latomum," *ibid.*, IX, 102; *Adagia*, No. 855 (*Illotis manibus*), col. 396; *Epistolae Obscurorum Virorum*, tr. F. G. Stokes (London, 1909), pp. 265, 519; Pius II, "De Liberorum Educatione," *Opera Omnia*

(Basileae, 1571), p. 989; Reuchlin, *Defensio contra Calumniatores Suos Colonienses* (Tubingae, 1514), sig. C iiv.

3. *Correspondence*, pp. 36–38; R. W. Chambers, *Thomas More* (London, 1935), p. 98; Villoslada, *Universidad de Paris: 1507–1522*, p. 73. In the last-mentioned book, see pages 45–53 for a list of works published at Paris from 1469 to 1500; pages 90–92 on the triumph of nominalism in Paris at the end of the fifteenth century; and pages 220–229, 252–253, 339–341, on Jacques Lefèvre d'Étaples.

4. *Utopia*, pp. 184–186. In a prefatory letter, Dorp praises Agricola's *Dialectica* for avoiding the "garrulous ravings" of sophists who in their confusion of the sciences attribute dialectical elements to rhetoric and supply what is wanting in the works of Aristotle and Cicero, to which the present book is in no way inferior (*Dialectica* [Lovanii, 1515], title page).

5. Barclay, *Ship of Fools*, I, 147. For books objectionable to the humanists, see the brief survey in P. S. Allen, *Age of Erasmus*, pp. 33–65. For a reference by More to the *Doctrinale* of Alexander of Ville-Dieu, see *Correspondence*, p. 38.

6. *Utopia*, pp. 184–185; *Correspondence*, pp. 38sqq.; *Eras. Ep.*, IV, 268; Vives, *Opera*, III, 37–68. For the aftermath of the humanistic attack on medieval logic, see Wilbur Samuel Howell, *Logic and Rhetoric in England, 1500–1700* (Princeton, 1956).

7. *Correspondence*, p. 38; *The "Summulae Logicales" of Peter of Spain*, ed. J. P. Mullally (Notre Dame, Indiana, 1945), Introd., p. xxxviii. There is an extensive bibliography of editions and commentaries, pp. 132–158. Mullally's edition was chosen because it is based upon two versions (1500 and *ca.* 1494) printed in More's own day. The excellent version of the complete *Summulae Logicales* edited in Latin by I. M. Bocheński, O.P. (Torino, 1947) follows a thirteenth-century manuscript and thus gives an original uncorrupted by countless later "corrections." The Bocheński edition divides Tract VII into distinct tracts with numbers of their own, changes the order of Tracts VI and VII, and excludes the tract on "exponibles" as not belonging to the *Summulae* (pp. xiv–xvi).

8. *Summulae*, pp. 3–5. See Introd., pp. xxxviii–lviii, for the historical connections of "suppositions" with previous and subsequent philosophy. The harsh criticism of supposition, etc., by the humanists is hardly to be approved. Supposition happens to be a truly important question, useful in many philosophical and theological studies.

9. *Summulae*, pp. 5–11.

10. *Summulae*, pp. 39–43, 47–61. See the elucidating remarks on amplifications and restrictions, Introd., pp. li sqq.

11. *Epist. Obscur. Vir.*, pp. 484–485 (Aloys Bömer's edition [Heidelberg, 1924], II, 166, has "XXXVI" instead of thirty years); *Summulae*, Introd., pp. lxxvii–ci; Gerson, *Opera Omnia*, ed. du Pin

(Antwerp, 1706), I, 21. In April 1515, Beatus Rhenanus wrote to Erasmus (Ep. 328, *Eras. Epist.*, II, 64) to tell him of the escapade of "our Glareanus." Seated on a horse, Glareanus burst into the hall where the usefulness of the *Small Logicals* was being argued. This would seem to indicate that even the Schoolmen of the universities were calling into question the merits of the work. About 1517 at Paris, a program still recommended that the *Small Logicals* be learned as fundamental: see *Heptadogma seu Septem pro Erigendo Gymnasio Documenta*, published at the end of *Compendium de Multiplici Parisiensis Universitatis Magnificentia* by R. Goulet, quoted in Villoslada, *Universidad de Paris: 1507–1522*, p. 72.

12. *Utopia*, p. 185; "Confutation of Tyndale," *Works*, pp. 431–432, 503–504, 562; "Answer to *Supper*," *ibid.*, p. 1115. For an explanation of the figures and modes of syllogisms, see E. Hugon, *Logica*, Cursus Philosophiae Thomisticae, I (Paris, 1904), pp. 181–199, or P. Coffey, *The Science of Logic* (London, 1912), I, 318–355.

13. See Robert W. Schmidt, S.J., *The Domain of Logic according to St. Thomas Aquinas*, Unpublished Doctoral Dissertation, University of Toronto, 1947. For the Scotistic position, which holds much in common with the Thomistic explanation given here, see C. R. S. Harris, *Duns Scotus* (Oxford, 1927), II, 4–5, and the various entries under "Intentio" in M. F. Garcia, O.F.M., *Lexicon Scholasticum Philosophico-Theologicum, in quo Termini . . . a B. Ioanne Duns Scoto Exponuntur* (Ad Claras Aquas, 1910), pp. 360–361.

14. *Works*, p. 748.

15. *Utopia*, pp. 185–186. "The universal is sometimes understood to be the second intention, which follows the first operation of the intellect by which the nature is known absolutely. The universal is understood thus when the intellect viewing that nature as predicable of many inferiors attributes to it the aspect of species or genus. . . ." (Scotus, *Quaest. de Anima*, q. xvii, n. 14; Latin quoted in Harris, *Duns Scotus*, II, 5, n.1). "Man in common" is practically the same as "man as a universal." Thus Scotus writes in his *Quaest. super Elench.*, q. i: "Logic deals with being in common. . . . Logic deals with that kind of intentions which are applicable to all things [i.e., genus, species, cause, etc.]" (Latin quoted in Harris, *Duns Scotus*, II, 4, n. 2).

16. "Moria," *Opera*, IV, 462–463; *Eras. Ep.*, II, 407, Introd.; IX, 449–450. *Ecceities*, as is evident from the context, should certainly be *haecceities* (thisnesses). Medievalists who were consulted agreed that *ecceitates* is another form of *haecceitates*. See also André Lalande, *Vocabulaire Technique et Critique* (Paris: Presses Universitaires de France, 1947), p. 248, where *ecceitas* and *haecceitas* are equated and where the *Lexicon Philosophicum* of Goclenius (1547–1628) is quoted as follows: "Barbari *Haecceitas* dicunt ab *Haec* pro differentia

individuante . . . Scotus *Ecceitatem* appellavit eam essentiam, quae est individuorum propria, cujus merito *Ecce ipsum* de omnibus dici potest."

Among the *nugae* mentioned in Erasmus and Lister, *instantia, formalitates,* and *haecceitates* in particular belong to Scotistic terminology and were the subject of much debate.

17. "Moria," *Opera,* IV, 465; "Novum Testamentum," *ibid.,* VI, 927.

18. Gilson, *The Unity of Philosophical Experience* (New York, 1937), p. 3. The charge of exaggerated realism has been brought against Scotus, but can be refuted by appeal to many passages in his indisputably genuine writings. See Parthenius Minges, *Der angebliche exzessive Realismus des Duns Scotus* (Münster, 1908), esp. pp. 81–102, and also the same author's *Scoti Doctrina Philosophica et Theologica* (Ad Claras Aquas, 1930), I, 67–106.

19. *Utopia,* p. 187.

20. Wimpheling, "Ad puerorum preceptores vt doceant eos vtilia," *Adolescentia,* prelim. leaf 4. One Latinist consulted on the point suggested the following translation for the opening words (*volunt parentes & amici liberos nepotesque suos institui, etc.*): "Forsooth, parents want the children even of a friend and their own descendants to be trained," *etc.* Villoslada assigns the moralistic tendency of the times, not only to humanism with its emphasis on individualistic and psychological values, but also to nominalism with "its critical, analytical, positive, and individualistic tendencies" (*Universidad de Paris: 1507–1522,* p. 123). He claims that the moralistic bent prevailed in the universities from the middle of the fourteenth century. He appends a list of classical and Scholastic works of an ethical nature published from 1489 to 1516 (*ibid.,* pp. 124–126).

21. Latomus, *De Trium Linguarum et Studij Theologici Ratione Dialogus* (Parisiis, 1519), sig. B vr.

22. John of Salisbury, "Metalogicus," *PL,* CXCIX, 866; Peter of Blois, Letter CI, *PL,* CCVII, 312–313; Maurice De Wulf, *History of Mediaeval Philosophy,* tr. E. C. Messenger (London, 1926), I, 206.

23. Seneca the Elder, *Suasoriae, Controversiae, Declamationumque Excerpta* (Parisiis, 1619), p. 60; Seneca the Philosopher, *Epistulae Morales,* II, 374–375 (cp. II, 258–259); John of Salisbury, *Metalogicon,* ed. C. C. I. Webb (Oxonii, 1939), p. 74.

X

THE CRITICISM OF SCHOLASTICISM

1. *Opera Omnia,* Ep. CV, p. 604.

2. Huizinga, *Erasmus,* tr. F. Hopman (New York, 1924), p. 37; More, *Correspondence,* pp. 6–9.

3. *Eras. Ep.*, IV, 520, 523, tr. J. H. Lupton, *The Lives of Jehan Vitrier and John Colet* (London, 1883), pp. 32–33, 39. For information on this bishop of London, see *Eras. Ep.*, IV, 518, note.

4. *Eras. Ep.*, II, 101sqq.; III, 519, Introd.; "Apologia ad Iacobum Latomum," *Opera*, IX, 103.

5. *Eras. Ep.*, IV, 523, tr. Lupton, *Vitrier and Colet*, pp. 39–40; "Paraclesis," *Opera*, V, 140.

6. *Eras. Ep.*, IV, 520, tr. Lupton, *Vitrier and Colet*, p. 33; *Opera*, VI, 554; *Adagia*, No. 870 (*Elephantus capit murem*), col. 400; "Erasmus Roterodamus divinarum litterarum studiosis omnibus S. D.," *Hieronymi Opera*, II, 3v.

7. More, "Picus," *Works*, p. 5; Erasmus, "Dialogus Ciceronianus," *Opera*, I, 1009; Pico, "De Hominis Dignitate," *Opera*, I, 214; Pace, *De Fructu*, p. 82.

8. More, "Confutation of Tyndale," *Works*, pp. 676, 679; *Omnia Latina Opera*, fol. 87v; Stapleton, *More*, p. 10.

9. "Confutation of Tyndale," *Works*, pp. 679, 693; Lee, *Annotationū Libri Duo* (Parisiis, 1519–20?), foll. xxviv–xxviir.

10. "Confutation of Tyndale," *Works*, p. 368; "Answer to *Supper*," *ibid.*, p. 1111.

11. *Assertionis Lutheranae Confutatio* (Coloniae, 1528), pp. xxxiiii, xxxvi, xxxviii, dxxxii–dxxxiii; *Defēsio Regie Assertiōis cōtra Babylonicā Captiuitatē* (Coloniae, 1525), foll. 24v–26r, 40v–41r. In his controversy with Jacques Lefèbre d'Étaples, Fisher appeals to Albert "who is surnamed the Great on account of the breadth of his doctrine" and Thomas "who is called the Flower of Theology" as the most representative of the Schoolmen (*De Unica Magdalena* [Parisiis, 1519], fol. xlr).

12. *De Veritate Corporis et Sanguinis Christi in Eucharistia* (Coloniae, 1527), foll. 148v–149r.

13. *De Veritate Corporis Christi*, fol. 5r.

14. *De Veritate Corporis Christi*, fol. 72.

15. *Eras. Ep.*, I, 463. See also I, 464–465.

16. "Novum Testamentum," *Opera*, VI, 928. It is interesting to note that, to say nothing of Pico and others, Colet and Fisher, Erasmus' own friends, entertained favorable views of the Cabala: see Fisher's "Sermon against Luther," *Works*, I, 335–336, and Colet's *Super Opera Dionysii: Two Treatises on the Hierarchies of Dionysius* (London, 1869), pp. 110–113. Lists of subtle theological questions are given by Erasmus in "Ratio Verae Theologiae," *Opera*, V, 134, and "Novum Testamentum," *ibid.*, VI, 927–928. For a careful and illuminating study of the relations of Erasmus to the Schoolmen living both before and after the Reformation, see Christian Dolfen, *Die Stellung des Erasmus von Rotterdam zur scholastischen Methode* (Osnabrück, 1936). For a summary of the great influence of the

Devotio Moderna on Erasmus, see Albert Hyma, *The Christian Renaissance* (New York, 1925), pp. 226–235.

17. *Eras. Ep.*, IV, 33–34; "Ratio Verae Theologiae," *Opera*, V, 83; "Paraclesis," *ibid.*, VI, *4r;* "Methodus," *Novum Instrumentum Omne* (Basileae, 1516), sig. bbb 3r, reprinted in *Ausgewählte Werke*, eds. A. and H. Holborn (München, 1933), p. 155.

18. "Lectori Pio S.D.," at end of "Catalogus Scriptorum Ecclesiasticorum," *Hieronymi Opera*, I, 138r; "Divinarum Litterarum Studiosis Omnibus S.D.," *ibid.*, II, 2r; "In Librum II Apologiae adversus Ruffinum Scholia," *ibid.*, III, 104v; "In Epistolam ad Ctesiphontem adversus Pelagianos Scholia," *ibid.*, III, 117v; "Hieronymus Fabiolae: Scholia," *ibid.*, IV, 23v. In 1520, Beatus Rhenanus attacked Edward Lee as a *theologaster*, one of those "who, since they attribute everything to Scotus and Thomas, have nothing to do with the ancient Doctors of the Church or, if they do glance at them, they do so only under compulsion and then do not understand them" (*Epistolae Aliquot Eruditorum Virorum* [Basileae, 1520], p. 164).

19. *Dialectice . . . Libri Tres* (Parisiis, 1509), fol. 1r.

20. Latomus, *De Trium Linguarum et Studij Theologici Ratione*, sig. C iv–iir.

21. "Ratio Verae Theologiae," *Opera*, V, 136; "Paraclesis," *ibid.*, VI, C*4r;* "Apologia adversus Monachos Quosdam Hispanos," *ibid.*, IX, 1090.

22. "Actas originales," cited in Villoslada, *Universidad de Paris: 1507–1522*, p. 349.

23. *Utopia*, pp. 271–272.

24. *Colloquies*, p. 96; "Ratio Verae Theologiae," *Opera*, V, 80–81; Pace, *De Fructu*, pp. 20, 26.

25. *Letters and Papers . . . of the Reign of Henry VIII*, Vol. I, Part 1, No. 935, p. 47, a letter in which Warham tells him that he is sending him twenty gold angels to cure him "inter quos Raphaelem salutis medicum reperies." Flemish merchants had a ship called *Raphael* on an Indian voyage of Albericus Vespuccius: see *The Voyage from Lisbon to India, 1505–6, Being an Account and Journal by Albericus Vespuccius*, tr. and ed. C. H. Coote (London, 1894), p. 30.

XI

INTELLECTUAL SALVATION

1. *Utopia*, pp. 183–220. See above, page 82.

2. *Utopia*, pp. 40, 112–113, 218–220. In basic political matters, such as the retention of communism, the Utopians are prudently conservative. On political conservatism, see Aristotle, *Politics*, tr. B. Jowett (New York, 1943), pp. 105–107, and Erasmus, *Education of Christian Prince*, p. 211, and "Similia," *Opera*, I, 621.

3. More, *Correspondence*, pp. 174sqq.; *Eras. Ep.*, II, 167; "Apologia," *Opera*, VI, ** 2v; *Adagia*, No. 3401 (*Ne bos quidem pereat*), col. 1171; Budé, *De Studio Literarum Recte & Comode Instituedo* (Parisiis, 1536), fol. ivv. In another adage, No. 664 (*Jucunda vicissitudo rerum*), col. 321, Erasmus makes the observation that love of variety has such great power in everything that sometimes even the worst is more pleasing than the best for no other reason than its novelty.

4. *Complete Poems*, pp. 293–294; William Nelson, *John Skelton: Laureate* (New York, 1939), pp. 161sqq.; Ian A. Gordon, *John Skelton: Poet Laureate* (Melbourne, 1943), p. 205. On Skelton's somewhat conservative attitude toward Greek, see Nelson, pp. 148–157, and Gordon, pp. 157–158.

5. Antoninus, *Summa*, III, 74; Gerson, *Opera*, I, 108–109. For a most interesting summary of the arguments used by the Italian humanists of the late fourteenth century, see Johannes Dominici, *Lucula Noctis*, ed. E. Hunt (Notre Dame, Indiana, 1940), pp. 6–118. The rest of the work is a refutation of the humanistic arguments.

6. Colet, *An Exposition of St. Paul's First Epistle to the Corinthians*, tr. J. H. Lupton (London, 1874), pp. 109–110; "Statuta Paulinae Scholae," in J. H. Lupton, *A Life of John Colet* (London, 1887), p. 279; "Statutes of St. Paul's School," in Samuel Knight, *The Life of Dr. John Colet* (London, 1724), p. 364.

7. Colet, *Corinthians*, Introd., pp. xxxii–xl.

8. *Correspondence*, pp. 114–115.

9. Erasmus, "Enchiridion," *Opera*, V, 9; *Colloquies*, p. 96. For the Erasmian program of learning, see Rudolf Pfeiffer, *Humanitas Erasmiana*, Studien der Bibliothek Warburg, XXII (Berlin, 1931).

10. "Dialogus Ciceronianus," *Opera*, I, 998, 1004–1005; "Hyperaspistes," *ibid.*, X, 1249. In his work *In Calumniatore Platonis* (Venetiis, 1516), foll. 33r–59v, Bessarion contends that Aristotle does not hold certain doctrines usually credited to him, such as creation "immediate . . . ex nihilo . . . libera voluntate . . . omnimoda omnipotentia," nor a rudimentary Trinity, nor the immortality of the soul.

11. *Adagia*, No. 3001 (*Dulce bellum inexpertis*), col. 1071.

12. *Lucubrationes, etc.* (Basle, 1563), p. 365.

13. *Utopia*, p. 213; *Correspondence*, pp. 115–116.

14. *Correspondence*, p. 63.

15. *Utopia*, p. 27; *Correspondence*, pp. 117–118.

16. Erasmus, "Ecclesiastes," *Opera*, V, 1026; "Apologia ad Iacobum Latomum," *ibid.*, IX, 85; Fisher, *De Unica Magdalena*, fol. xiiiir.

17. More, *Correspondence*, p. 66; *Eras. Ep.*, II, 106–107, 135–136.

222 NOTES TO CHAPTER XI

18. *Eras. Ep.*, I, 352, 406, VI, 403; "De Ratione Studii," *Opera*, I, 522; "Ecclesiastes," *ibid.*, V, 855; "Apologia ad Iacobum Latomum," *ibid.*, IX, 83.

19. Pace, *De Fructu*, pp. 100–107; Budé, *Annotationes*, p. 286; *De Asse & Partibus Eius* (Venetiis, 1522), fol. 10r. Pace probably means John Stokesley (1475?–1539), later bishop, whom Erasmus in 1518 describes as expert in Scholastic theology and in Latin, Greek, and Hebrew (*Eras. Ep.*, III, 357) and whom in 1519 he ranks with the greatest English humanists at court (*Eras. Ep.*, IV, 22).

20. *Utopia*, p. 184.

21. "For I think that this nation took their beginning of the Greeks because their speech . . . keepeth divers signs and tokens of the Greek language . . ." (*Utopia*, p. 214). The identification of Utopia with Britain would receive additional confirmation from an investigation of the claim of Greek origins for the British. John Noble Johnson in his *Life of Thomas Linacre* (London, 1835), writes: "I cannot avoid urging a few objections to the supposed existence of the Greek language in Britain during the earliest ages of its history, intimately connected, as it is, with the name of *Linacre*, and with his claims, if not to the introduction of it into this country, at least to the title of its chief reviver and earliest cultivator" (p. 27, note). Among the arguments urged by the supporters of the theory was the "fancied mixture of Greek with British words, or the additions of Greek terminations to British roots" (*ibid.*, p. 31, note). Extremely interesting is the following passage in an adage of Erasmus: "*Lindus* is a city in Rhodes, as Stephanus witnesses, from which London [*Londinum*] in Britain could seem to have been derived. Stephanus calls this city *Lindonium* and cites Martian as his authority. Indeed, both Rhodes and Britain are islands, and the old language of the people of the latter, which is now called Welsh, is sufficient indication that it either had originated from the Greek or had certainly been mixed with it. Not even their customs are altogether at variance with Greek customs" (*Adagia*, 1543 [*Rhodii sacrificium*], col. 668). Stephanus was a Byzantine geographer who seems to have lived in the early sixth century. Polydore Vergil also has a reference to the Greek origin of Welsh: "Whereas the Welsh speech differeth from the English, they which derive their race and stem from the Trojan stock affirm that their tongue is compounded and intermeddled partly with Greek, partly with the Trojan antiquity" (*English History*, Early Translation, ed. H. Ellis [London, 1846], I, 13); *Anglica Historia* (Gandavi, 1556–1557), p. 15.

At a later date, Holinshed in the "Description of Britanny" in his *Chronicles* writes in regard to the British, i.e., Welsh language: "I deny not but that the Celtish and British speeches might have great affinity one with another, and the British above all with the Greek, for both do appear by certain words, as first in *tri* for three, *march*

for a horse, and *trimarchia*, whereof Pausanias speaketh, for both."
Holinshed cites Giraldus to the effect that "there is not one word in
all their language [the Britons'] that is not either Greek or Latin."
This affirmation, "being rightly understood and conferred with the
likeness that was in old time between the Celts' and the British tongue
will not a little help those that think the old Celtish to have some
savor of the Greek." The Druids, besides, committed their religious
beliefs to "the Greek tongue insomuch that Wolf. Lazius (upon the
word of Marcellinus) declareth how the Greek letters were first
brought to Athens by Timagenes from the Druids. And hereupon it
cometh also to pass that the British tongue hath in it remaining to
this day some smack of the Greek" (*The Chronicles of England, Scot-
land, and Ireland* [London, 1587], I, 12–13, II, 2–3).

XII

THE GREAT BOOKS IN UTOPIA

1. *Utopia*, pp. 184–186; *Correspondence*, p. 37.
2. *Utopia*, pp. 27, 215. For the dates of publication of Erasmus'
works, see *Eras. Ep.*, I, 121, and *Bibliotheca Erasmiana*, Series I, pp.
11, 78, 167, 169.
3. "Similia," *Opera*, I, 615; Pius II, *Opera Omnia*, p. 983.
4. *Utopia*, p. 215; "De Ratione Studii," *Opera*, I, 523. In the latter
work, Plotinus, considered "the combination" of Aristotle and Plato,
is included among the philosophers (*loc. cit.*). The comparison and
reconciliation of Plato and Aristotle to the mutual advantage of both,
as is well known, was the goal set for the genius and effort of Pico
della Mirandola (Letter to Marsilio Ficino, *Opera*, I, 253).
5. Elyot, *Gouernour*, I, 93; Erasmus, *Adagia*, Introduction, cols.
9–10, where Aristotle, Theophrastus, and Plutarch also are mentioned
as outstanding in their use of adages.
6. Quoted in Montagu Burrows, "Linacre's Catalogue of Books
Belonging to William Grocyn . . . Followed by a Memoir of William
Grocyn," Oxford Historical Society, *Collectanea*, Series II (Oxford,
1890), pp. 351–352.
7. More, *Correspondence*, pp. 63–64; Erasmus, "Ratio Verae
Theologiae," *Opera*, V, 80.
8. *Utopia*, pp. 186–187; *Correspondence*, pp. 65–66; Lefèvre, "In
Quatuor Libros Meteororum Aristotelis Paraphrases," *Totius Philosophie Naturalis Paraphrases* (Paris, 1504), foll. 152r–194v; *Meteorologica Aristotelis Eleganti Jacobi Fabri Stapulensis Paraphrasi Ex-
planata Commentarioque Joannis Coclaei Norici Declarata* (Norin-
bergae, 1512), fol. iiv. See briefly *Meteorologica*, tr. E. W. Webster,
in *Works of Aristotle*, ed. W. D. Ross, III (Oxford, 1931), pp. v–vi,
for a summary of contents. For Gaetano's commentaries on Aristotle's

Meteorology, published in 1491 and 1496 at Venice, see *Gesamtkatalog der Wiegendrucke,* Band II (Leipzig, 1926), Nos. 2421–2422, cols. 626–628. E. F. Rogers (*Correspondence,* p. 66, note) identifies More's *Gaitanus* with Cardinal Cajetan (1469–1534), but this is less likely. On Gaetano Tiene, see Ernest Renan, *Averroès et l'Averroïsme* (Paris, 1866), pp. 347–352; M. De Wulf, *Histoire de la philosophie médiévale,* 16 ed. (Paris, 1947), III, 180–181; F. Überweg, *Grund-riss der Geschichte der Philosophie,* Zweiter Teil: *Die patristische und scholastische Philosophie,* herausgegeben von Bernhard Geyer (Basel, 1951), p. 619; and Silvestro da Vansanzibio, *Vita e Dottrina di Gaetano di Thiene, Filosofo dello Studio di Padova (1387–1465),* 2nd ed. (Padova, 1949).

9. *Eras. Ep.,* I, 9; I, 442, n.; II, 125–126, and note; II, 264–265; "De Ratione Studii," *Opera,* I, 522; "Ratio Verae Theologiae," *ibid.,* V, 80. Hythloday carries with him only Lascaris whom Erasmus had mentioned as early as 1501 (*Eras. Ep.,* I, 367). The translation of Gaza's second book appeared in February 1518 (*Eras. Ep.,* II, 264, Introd.).

10. *Utopia,* p. 216; *Colloquies,* p. 105; *Adagia,* Introd., col. 10, No. 2901 (*Quo transgressus, &c.*), col. 1043; "Ecclesiastes," *Opera,* V, 856; "Apologia ad Iacobum Latomum," *ibid.,* IX, 83.

11. *Correspondence,* p. 11 (also in *Opera,* fol. 31v); *Eras. Ep.,* I, 425–426; IV, 16; "De Ratione Studii," *Opera,* I, 521. See C. R. Thompson, *The Translations of Lucian by Erasmus and More* (Ithaca, N.Y., 1940). See *Eras. Ep.,* I, 425–426, according to which the title of "atheist" applied to Lucian is really a compliment insofar as it comes from the impious and the superstitious. For the view of Lucian as an enemy to all sham and hypocrisy, especially of philosophers, see Goclenius' preface to his translation of Lucian's *Hermotimus,* dedicated to More, *Correspondence,* pp. 267–272.

12. Erasmus, "De Ratione Studii," *Opera,* I, 521; Elyot, *Gouernour,* I, 57–58.

13. *Utopia,* p. 216; "Dialogue Concerning Heresies," *Works,* p. 153; Elyot, *Gouernour,* I, 58–59; Erasmus, "De Ratione Studii," *Opera,* I, 521, 526; Plato, *Republic,* II, 459sqq. Erasmus refers to Plato's attitude toward Homer in "Hieronymi Vita," *Opuscula,* ed. W. K. Ferguson (The Hague, 1933), p. 136, and "De Amabili Ecclesiae Concordia," *Opera,* V, 501. On the nature of true poetry, consult "Ecclesiastes," *Opera,* V, 853. See Sophocles also on the list of authors in "Apologia ad Iacobum Latomum," *Opera,* IX, 83, where the names of Pindar, Theocritus, and Hesiod too occur. The genealogy of the gods is to be learned from Hesiod supplemented by Boccaccio.

14. *Eras. Ep.,* I, 130–131; "De Ratione Studii," *Opera,* I, 521; "Apologia ad Iacobum Latomum," *ibid.,* IX, 83.

15. "Apologia ad Iacobum Latomum," *Opera,* IX, 83.

16. See "De Ratione Studii," *Opera*, I, 521–526; "Ecclesiastes," *ibid.*, V, 856; "Apologia ad Iacobum Latomum," *ibid.*, IX, 83.

17. *Utopia*, pp. 27, 213.

18. *Eras. Ep.*, I, 184–185; "De Ratione Studii," *Opera*, I, 521–523, 529; "Ratio Verae Theologiae," *ibid.*, V, 80; "Ecclesiastes," *ibid.*, V, 856.

19. "De Ratione Studii," *Opera*, I, 521; "Ecclesiastes," *ibid.*, V, 856; *Eras. Ep.*, II, 358. For high praise of Cicero's *De Officiis*, see *Eras. Ep.*, I, 357. For a good study of the relation of Erasmus to Cicero, see Walter Rüegg, *Cicero und der Humanismus* (Zurich, 1946), pp. 65–125.

20. See *Gouernour*, I, 53–98.

21. *Utopia*, pp. 216–217; "Apologia ad Iacobum Latomum," *Opera*, IX, 84–85; *Adagia*, No. 3401 (*Ne bos quidem pereat*), col. 1172; Pace, *De Fructu*, pp. 27, 85.

22. Johnson, *Linacre*, p. 270; Budé to Lupset, *Utopia*, pp. lxxxi–lxxxii, xci (Budé had read *De Sanitate Tuenda* in manuscript). Erasmus also refers to Linacre's labors of translation of Galen at this time (September 1515): see *Eras. Ep.*, II, 139, in which he mentions the compliment to be paid to Linacre in the scholia to his edition of St. Jerome (1516).

23. *Utopia*, pp. 217–218; *Eras. Ep.*, I, 233 n.; "Encomium Medicinae," *Opera*, I, 537–544; Plato, *Republic*, I, 269sqq. On the attention lavished on the sick and on "the continual presence of cunning physicians" in the excellent Utopian hospitals, see *Utopia*, pp. 159–160, 222–223. Elyot, it is surmised from his own words, was a pupil of Linacre: see *The Castel of Helth* (1541), Introd. S. A. Tannenbaum (New York, 1937), sig. A ivr, and *Galeni de Temperamentis et Inaequali Intemperie Libri Tres*, Thoma Linacro Anglo Interprete, Introd. J. F. Payne (Cambridge, 1881), p. 44. For a simple study of Erasmus' relations with medicine and physicians, see Maria Hermanns, *Erasmus von Rotterdam und seine ärztlichen Freunde* (Würzburg, 1937). For Erasmus' views on natural science, see "De Pronuntiatione," *Opera*, I, 923, and "Ratio Verae Theologiae," *Opera*, V, 79–80.

24. *Utopia*, pp. 209, 217–218, 279–280.

25. *Utopia*, p. 27; Pace, *De Fructu*, p. 82.

26. In the scholia to Jerome's letters, Erasmus berates the theologians who scorn the classics and call a man "poetical and not at all religious because he does not write questions in the Scotistic style"; but, on the other hand, he approves the decree of Leo X and the Lateran Council that no more than five years be spent on poetry and rhetoric to the neglect of other disciplines (*Hieronymi Opera*, I, 61v).

27. *Utopia*, p. 27.

28. Villoslada, *Universidad de Paris: 1507–1522*, pp. 274–275; Renaudet, *Érasme et l'Italie* (Genève, 1954), p. 243.

XIII

GREEK, PLEASURE, AND COMMUNISM: THE LINK

1. *Utopia*, p. 183. See above, Chap. VIII *ad init.*
2. *Utopia*, pp. 147, 189–190, 192, 194, 306.
3. *Utopia*, p. 193.
4. *Utopia*, pp. 118, 137, 190–191, 193, 297.
5. *Utopia*, pp. 159, 161, 166, 193, 302–303.
6. Diog. Laert., *Lives*, II, 539, 541.
7. *Utopia*, pp. 105, 169, 299.
8. *Utopia*, pp. 104–105, 107, 300–302.
9. More, *Utopia*, p. 303; Plato, *Laws*, I, 375; Plutarch, *Lives*, I, 409; Lucian, "Cronosolon," tr. Erasmus, *Opera*, I, 188; Erasmus, *Adagia*, No. 422 (*Paupertas sapientiam sortita est*), col. 212; No. 847 (*Dives aut iniquus aut haeres iniqui*), col. 391; No. 1507 (*Pro beneficentia Agamemnonem ulti sunt*), col. 654; No. 1664 (*Boni viri lachrymabiles*), col. 704; No. 2001 (*Herculei labores*), col. 795.
10. *Adagia*, No. 812 (*A mortuo tributum exigere*), col. 376; "In Ps. XXXIII," *Opera*, V, 400.
11. *Utopia*, pp. xcvii, 303.
12. *Utopia*, pp. 57–58, 107–109.

XIV

HUMANISM AND COMMUNISM: THE BACKGROUND

1. *Utopia*, p. 299; "Apophthegmata," *Opera*, IV, 124–129, 144. See Plutarch, "Lycurgus," *Lives*, I, 227–229, on the methods by which Lycurgus divided equally territory and movable property in order "to banish insolence and envy and crime and luxury, and those yet more deep-seated and afflictive diseases of the state, poverty and wealth."

2. Plato, *Republic*, I, 311, 471; *Laws*, I, 365; W. L. Newman, *Aristotle's Politics* (Oxford, 1887), I, 158–168. Shorey's comment is pertinent: "Plato's communism is primarily a device to secure disinterestedness in the ruling class, though he sometimes treats it as a counsel of perfection for all men and states" (*Republic*, I, 310, note a).

3. M.-B. Schwalm, "Communisme," *Dict. de théol. cath.*, III, 578. The distinction between a counsel and a commandment was taken for granted among Christians in the Middle Ages and the Renaissance. Even the Wife of Bath says of St. Paul's advice on virginity: "conseillyng is no comandement" (*Prol.*, line 67).

4. R. B. Taylor, "Communism," *Encycl. of Rel. and Ethics*, III, 777: "The assumption is that the Jerusalem Church was communistic. Of this there is no proof." Consult the exhaustive note in C. Lattey, *The Acts of the Apostles* (London, 1936), pp. 141–142. For numerous

and representative quotations from the Fathers, see Schwalm, *art. cit.*, III, 579–586, and for the legitimacy of the right of property in the Fathers, see E. Dublanchy, "Morale," *Dict. de théol. cath.*, X, 2440. Consult also John A. Ryan, *Alleged Socialism of the Church Fathers* (St. Louis, 1913).

5. *Decretum Gratiani cum Glossis Joannis Theutonici, etc.* (Venetiis, 1514), foll. ii, viii, cccxii (preface by Erasmus' friend, Beatus Rhenanus); W. J. McDonald, "Communism in Eden?" *The New Scholasticism*, XX (1946), 124. See Bede Jarrett, *Mediaeval Socialism* (London, 1935), pp. 41–55, and *Social Theories of the Middle Ages, 1200–1500* (Boston, 1926), pp. 122–149.

6. *Utopia*, pp. 105–106, 304; Budé's and Busleyden's letters, *ibid.*, pp. lxxxvii, 317; Aquinas, *Summa Theologica*, I–II, q. 94, a. 5; II–II, q. 66, a. 2; *Com. in Arist. Polit.*, lib. 2, lect. 2 & 4; Drostan Maclaren, *Private Property and the Natural Law* (Oxford, 1948), pp. 12–13. See William J. McDonald, *The Social Value of Property According to St. Thomas Aquinas* (Washington, 1939), *passim*, and B. W. Dempsey, "Property Rights," in *Summa Theologica*, tr. Fathers of the English Dominican Province (New York, 1948), III, 3357–3365.

7. Scotus, *In Lib. IV Sent.*, dist. 15, q. 2, *Opera* (Paris, 1891–1895), XVIII, 255–270, translated in Jarrett, *Social Theories*, p. 124; *Ox.* 1. 3, dist. 37, q. un., quoted in Minges, *Scoti Doctrina*, I, 409 (cf. 433–434); Antoninus, *Summa*, III, 55 (cf. Bede Jarrett, *S. Antonino and Medieval Economics* [London, 1914], p. 76); Richard Schlatter, *Private Property: The History of an Idea* (New Brunswick, N. J., 1951), p. 55, n. 1. For Suarez's criticism of Scotus' "precept," see *Opera* (Paris, 1856–1878), V, 140.

8. See McDonald, *Social Value*, pp. 73–79; Jarrett, *Social Theories*, pp. 145–146; and esp. Jarrett, *Mediaeval Socialism*, pp. 29–41.

9. "De Modo Vivendi," quoted in Latin in Hyma, *Christian Renaissance*, p. 372, n. 150 (cf. excellent summary of whole treatise on pp. 67–79); "Consuetudines Domus Nostrae," quoted in Latin in Jacobus Traiecti, alias de Voecht, *Narratio de Inchoatione Domus Clericorum in Zwollis, met Akten en Bescheiden betreffende dit Fraterhuis*, ed. M. Schoengen (Amsterdam, 1908), pp. 266–267; Josse Bade, "Vita Thomae Malleoli," tr. in Thomas à Kempis, *Meditation on the Incarnation of Christ*, ed. D. V. Scully, pp. xxvii–xxviii, quoted in Hyma, *Christian Renaissance*, pp. 61–62.

10. *The Vision of William Concerning Piers the Plowman*, ed. W. W. Skeat (Oxford, 1886), I, 595 (cf. II, 283 n.); Pecock, *The Repressor of Over Much Blaming of the Clergy*, ed. C. Babington (London, 1860), II, 316–317; Barclay, *Ship of Fools*, II, 103; Brant-Locher, *Stultifera Navis*, fol. xciir; *A Supplication of the Poore Commons*, ed. J. M. Cooper (London, 1871), pp. 71–72. See also Locher's "Epiodion: De Morte Plutonis & Reliquorū Demonum," *Poematia* (Augustae,

228 NOTES TO CHAPTER XIV

1513), sig. a ivr, which describes the golden age of communism ensuing on the death of Pluto, e.g., "En natura parens rerum cõmunia fecit/Omnia constituit omnibus atque modum."

11. Colet, "Exposition of Epistle to Romans," *Opuscula Quaedam Theologica*, tr. J. H. Lupton (London, 1876), p. 134.

12. Lupton, *Colet*, pp. 74–75.

13. *Gouernour*, I, 2–11, II, 27.

14. *Opera*, I, 642, II, 1402.

15. *Utopia*, pp. lxxxvii–lxxxviii.

16. *Utopia*, pp. lxxxvi–lxxxviii; Taylor, "Communism," *Encycl. of Rel. and Ethics*, III, 777.

17. *Adagia*, Introd., p. 11.

18. *Adagia*, No. 1 (*Amicorum communia omnia*), col. 20; No. 2 (*Amicitia aequalitas, amicus alter ipse*), col. 21.

19. "Moria," *Opera*, IV, 456, and note; tr. Hudson, *Praise of Folly*, p. 69.

20. *Adagia*, No. 3001 (*Dulce bellum inexpertis*), col. 1071.

21. "Prisca Lacedaemoniorum Instituta," in "Apophthegmata," *Opera*, IV, 146.

22. "De Amabili Ecclesiae Concordia," *Opera*, V, 505. On the conservative aspect of Erasmus' political ideas, see, e.g., Ferdinand Geldner, *Die Staatsauffassung und Fürstenlehre des Erasmus von Rotterdam*, Historische Studien, Heft 191 (Berlin, 1930), pp. 115, 155, n. 3.

23. "Confutation of Tyndale," *Works*, p. 656.

XV

THOMAS MORE AND COMMUNISM: THE SOLUTION

1. *Utopia*, pp. 269, 305–306.

2. *Correspondence*, pp. 195–196.

3. Alexander Anglus, *Destructorium Viciorum*, pars VI, cap. xli (no pagination); Erasmus, "Paraclesis," *Novum Instrumentum*, sig. aaa 6r; Vives, "De Subventione Pauperum," *Opera*, IV, 450–451.

4. *Utopia*, pp. 100–102. In his letter to Dorp written at this time, More again refers to the leaden or Lesbian rule (*Correspondence*, p. 43). For a current explanation of the expression, see Erasmus, *Adagia*, No. 493 (*Lesbia regula*), col. 243 (cf. Adage 1436, col. 629). See also Budé, *Annotationes*, p. 2, for reference to, and explanation of, "Lesbia structura" with employment of "plumbea norma." Read the section "Of hym that dare not vtter the trouth for fere of displeasour or punysshement," in Barclay's *Ship of Fools*, II, 231sqq.

5. Egidio of Viterbo, "Oratio Prima Synodi Lateranensis," Mansi, *Concilia*, XXXII, 669; Erasmus, "Enchiridion," *Opera*, V, 40; *Adagia*, No. 3616 (*Quod volumus sanctum est*), col. 1226. See other pertinent observations by Erasmus, "Ratio Verae Theologiae," *Opera*, V,

114, and "Explanatio Symboli," *ibid.*, V, 1136. The cincture in honor of St. Thomas Aquinas was blessed with a prayer which asked God for the gift of chastity for the wearer (*Rituale Romanum* [Mechliniae, 1926], p. 705).

6. "Moria," *Opera*, IV, 493, note.

7. *Adagia*, No. 3001 (*Dulce bellum inexpertis*), col. 1071.

8. Budé to Lupset, *Utopia*, pp. lxxxiv–lxxxv; Erasmus, *Adagia*, No. 3001 (*Dulce bellum inexpertis*), cols. 1071–1072.

9. *Utopia*, p. 306.

10. *Utopia*, pp. 57–58, 107–109.

11. *Utopia*, pp. 97–100. For analogous views, see T. E. Bridgett, *Life and Writings of Sir Thomas More*, 2nd ed. (London, 1892), p. 103; C. Hollis, *More*, pp. 71, 73; M. Carmichael, "Utopia: Its Doctrine on the Common Life," *Dublin Review*, CXCI (1932), 186. Carmichael remarks: "If he [More] could write, as he has done, in praise [of the common life], in commendation, with convincing persuasiveness, and yet not believe — then the *Utopia* is an unprofitable and dangerous extravaganza" (*loc. cit.*). The simple position that More expresses his personal and real objections to compulsory state communism in *Utopia* is defended tenaciously by W. E. Campbell, *More's Utopia and His Social Teaching* (London, 1930), e.g., pp. 28–29, 140sqq.

12. *Utopia*, pp. 109–111.

13. *Utopia*, pp. 65, 308.

14. "Confutation of Tyndale," *Works*, p. 656.

15. *Gulielmi Rossei . . . Opus . . . quo Retegit ac Refellit Insanas Lutheri Calumnias: Quibus . . . Regem Henricum . . . Scurra Turpissime Insectatur*. The work will be noted here as *In Lutherum*.

16. "In Lutherum," *Opera*, fol. 80v. On *consensus*, see Harris, *Duns Scotus*, II, 346–349.

17. "In Lutherum," *Opera*, fol. 80v. All the following references to Luther in the text are to this work and page.

18. This and following references are to *A Dialogue of Comfort against Tribulation*, p. 184.

19. See above, Chapter II *ad init.*

20. *Eras. Ep.*, IV, 21.

XVI

UNITY OF CONCEPTION

1. *Utopia*, p. xciv.

2. *Utopia*, p. 194; Cicero, *De Finibus*, p. 93.

3. *Eras. Ep.*, VI, 403.

4. *Utopia*, pp. 192–193.

INDEX

Abraxas, explained, 4, 201–202 n4
Ad Philippum Panegyricus. See Erasmus, Works
Adages. See Erasmus, Works, Adagia
Adagia. See Erasmus, Works
Adams, Robert P., quoted, 209 n3
Aegidius, Petrus. See Gilles, Peter
Aeneas, Vergil's, 50
Aeneas Sylvius. See Pius II, Pope
Aeschylus, 149
Aesop, 141, 143, 144
Agricola, Rodolphus, 26, 100, 144, 204 n3, 206 n6, 216 n4
Alain de Lille (Alanus ab Insulis), 102
Albert of Saxony, 83
Albert the Great, St., 32, 102, 111, 112, 116, 139, 219 n11
Albigensians, 164
Aldus. See Manutius, Aldus
Alexander Anglus (or Carpentarius), 215 n8, 228 n3; on astrology, 84; on property, 176
Alexander of Aphrodisias, 84, 137, 138, 145
Alexander of Hales, 102, 111
Alexander of Ville-Dieu, 216 n5
Allen, Don Cameron, 205 n5, 215 n8
Allen, Percy Stafford, 201 n1, 206 n6, 216 n5
Ambrose, St., 118, 128
Ammonius Hermiae, 137
Ampliation, or amplification, in philosophy, 90, 91, 92–93, 98, 113, 192
Anabaptists, 173, 174, 184
Ananias, 170
Anemolian ambassadors, 52, 55
Angelus Carletus de Clavasio, 215 n8; on astrology, 84
Anghiera, Pietro Martire d', 212 n17; on gold, 54
Anselm, St., 108

Answer to "Supper of the Lord." See More, Works
Antibarbari. See Erasmus, Works
Antoninus, St., 194, 203 n10, 205 n3, 221 n5, 227 n7; on happiness, 14; on languages, 122–123; on pleasure, 24–25; 213 nn7, 10
Antony of Bergen, 1, 130
Apollonius of Perga, 149
Apologia adversus Monachos Quosdam Hispanos. See Erasmus, Works
Apologia ad Iacobum Latomum. See Erasmus, Works
Apologia pro Declamatione de Laude Matrimonii. See Erasmus, Works
Apophthegmata. See Erasmus, Works
Apostolics, 164
Apparel, as false pleasure, 44–47; of More, 47; of Utopians, 44, 46
Appelt, Theodore C., quoted, 206 n6
Apuleius, Lucius, 144
Archimedes, 149
Aristides, Aelius, 143
Aristippus of Cyrene, 65, 207 n13
Aristo of Sicyon, quoted, 64
Aristophanes, 141, 149
Aristotle, 12, 115–116, 194, 203 n9, 220 n2, 223 nn4, 5, 8, 226 n2; Barclay on, 89–90; Christianization of, 35; on civil society, 204 n8; on communism, 171, 174, 182–183, 196, 197, 198; criticism of Plato by, 161, 197; and Elyot, 144; on habit, 210 n9; influence on Christians, 105, 113, 114–116, 121, 126, 172, 177–180, 198; logic of, 87–90, 91, 98, 135, 192, 195; and Linacre, 145; on marriage, 125; Meteorology of, 138–139; on money, 157; paraphrased by Lefèvre, 223 n8; on pleasure, 65; on preservation of species, 204 n8; Rhetoric quoted